antonovs over the arctic

Trevor Henderson

antonovs
over the arctic

flying to the north pole in russian biplanes

Robert Mads Anderson

Captain's Logs by Shane Lundgren

David Bateman

First published in 1998 by
David Bateman Ltd, 30 Tarndale Grove,
Albany, Auckland, New Zealand

ISBN 1 86953 419 0

Editorial services by Michael Gifkins and Associates
Designed and typeset by Chris O'Brien
Printed in Hong Kong by Colorcraft

dedication

To Myles Mads Anderson, Alexander Gregory Sheardown, Géza Maximilian von Baumbach and all the young explorers in Alaska and around the world who followed our journey — and will one day set out on their own flights of exploration.

Ben Eielson (left) and George Wilkins in 1928, the year of their successful flight across the Arctic from Barrow, Alaska, to Spitsbergen, Norway. Shane had a copy made of the parka Eielson was wearing and wore it on our flight in 1998.
(PHOTO COURTESY ALASKAN AVIATION HERITAGE MUSEUM)

contents

Author's Note

The quotes utilized are reproduced directly, including original spellings and grammatical usages without correction. Place names, notably Spitsbergen/Spitzbergen, have changed in the intervening 70 years, but are easily recognizable in any case. The majority of the quotations are from George H. Wilkins' *Flying the Arctic*, Penguin Putnam, New York. All sources are quoted and detailed as accurately as possible and are taken from archival copies, originals of which are resident at the American Geographical Society in New York. All maps are by Miklos Pinther. Photographs are by the author using Kodak EPP 200 professional film unless otherwise noted. Lithographs are by Werner Maier.

ſOREWORD

you can smell the earth doing this kind of flying

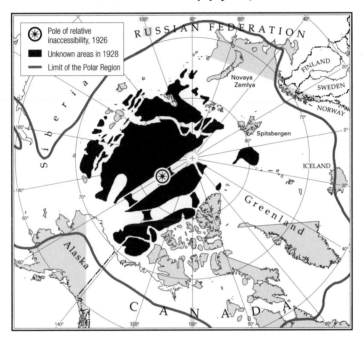

After the fall of the Communist empire, a friend of my family's was among the first Americans to establish a joint venture in the Russian Far East city of Khabarovsk. It sounded a fascinating opportunity to be involved in. I became familiar with the flight from Berlin to Moscow and across Siberia, but no matter how hard I studied our routing, I could rarely see any sign of civilization below. Imagine a nine-hour flight over land, with scant trace of human existence. I was intrigued. Who lived down there, if anyone? What went on down there?

On one flight I ended up in Ul'yanovsk, Russia, due to fog in Moscow. Out the muddy airport window were row upon row of biplanes. They had an upper wing as high as a two-story building, an immense bulging round engine and a four-bladed propeller that looked as if it had been built to power the *Titanic*. Herge might have created these cartoon machines with pen and ink for Tintin and Snowy to explore the world. After I first saw them they suddenly seemed to pop up everywhere: in Vladivostok, Khabarovsk, Sakalin Island and St Petersburg. I learned they were called Antonovs, with the designation An-2.

I began to wonder at the quantities of these single-engine, bi-wing oddities sitting parked at seemingly every airport in Northern Russia. With rapid supply-and-demand calculation, I figured that with hard currency I could probably buy one of the aircraft for the price of a used car in the States. At the time I was able to fly across Russia on Aeroflot for US$2.95.

I have grown up with airplanes. Before I could see out the windows of a plane my father taught me how to fly using instruments. When I was five years old he planned to buy a Stearman biplane in Florida and we were going to fly it across the US to California, thus planting the seed in my mind of a bi-winged adventure. The poet Shelley once wrote that 'sung melodies are sweet, yet those unsung are sweeter.' The biplane adventure was an unsung melody, as we never made the flight. From then on I wanted to fly a biplane. My favorite books when I grew up were *Pilot Small* and *Buster B-T*. My best friend and I spent our early days flying model airplanes around stump hill. That same friend and I went through training together on the Boeing 737 twenty years later and are both currently airline captains.

Meanwhile back in Russia, in their desire to 'make business', the first Russian entrepreneurs were eager to promise anything, to give anything. The Slav heart is very warm. Anyone who has been to Russia, and in particular to Siberia, eaten three enormous meals a day, and drunk copious amounts of the vodka and cognac, will attest to this. The problem is that once you have left their immediate field of vision, there is no follow-through in accomplishing whatever it was that you agreed upon. When I asked if it would be possible to go for a flight in an Antonov, everyone immediately said yes and seemed to begin shuffling priorities to make this possible. Somehow the objective was always lost en route, and by the time we hoped to fly, everyone spent a good deal of time looking at their shoes. 'You must to return to Russia my friend, druzhba da!' they would promise. 'Next time it will all be organized!'

In my naive American optimism I figured that all it would take to barnstorm across Siberia was a bit of cash and some Russian pilots to speak the language on the radio. Despite the previous setbacks, I was confident that I could talk to my acquaintances at Aeroflot in Moscow. They could come up with a plan, or at least understand what it was that I wanted to undertake. But they didn't get it at all. 'Nobody just flies around looking at things...unless...you're not a spy, are you comrade? You look very young.'

Tushna airport in Moscow offers airplane 'rides'. The airport is an open grass field in the middle of the city surrounded by concrete apartment buildings. An old, low building has a balcony which Stalin used to review his air forces from, and his bust still stands outside. The drab green Antonov that I climbed into had a red star on the tail, and a distinctly no-nonsense, military feel. I was surprised when three Russian pilots climbed in behind me. But when I witnessed the six arms and legs in action during the engine start, I realized that this Antonov was no toy. After a year of frustration, I was finally going to fly an An-2.

We had a difficult time communicating, but our good spirits were obvious to one another as we prepared for takeoff. It seemed strange as an American raised during the height of the Cold War, to be flying with Russians. I could see how the world might be a better place with a bit of 'biplane diplomacy'. Nikolai, the pilot in the left seat, let me fly once we were airborne. As we made our way out of Moscow, flying above the massive boulevards leading to the countryside, my first impression was of the noise. The huge radial engine roared and I could feel my heart beating up into my throat. It is a magnitude and pitch that you never forget. My second impression was of the weight of the controls. This was no Cessna, this was a Mack truck — a Boeing with the hydraulics turned off. I wondered if my mad pursuit was really worth all the trouble. But as we flew low over a beautiful gold-domed monastery outside Moscow with autumn light in the yellow trees, I realized that I wanted to do more of this. You can smell the earth doing this kind of flying.

The next day as I headed back to the airport, I noticed army tanks moving into the center of the city and long lines at the petrol pumps. Something was up. That afternoon Boris Yeltsin began his bombardment of the White House. It seemed like a good time to leave Russia, and forget barnstorming across Siberia.

It looked like my dream of flying across Russia in an An-2 would remain a dream, like the Stearman flight I'd been promised as a five-year-old but never happened. But circumstances and chance encounters conspired to keep the dream alive, and I could not get the flight out of my mind. The impulse to explore this strange country, to do something so different, so unheard of, still strongly beckoned. After re-reading *Michael Strogoff* by Jules Verne I could almost see myself climbing out of the biplane with a beard and tunic in Irkutsk.

At a dinner party in London in the spring of 1994 I encountered a piercing set of eyes framed by a large pair of spectacles, which drifted in and out of the smoke from an endless stream of cigarettes. Gleb Shestakov, a young raconteur of the new Russia, cool and aggressive, proposed meeting me in Moscow to see what he could do. Returning to Tushna airport in May 1994, Gleb arranged a meeting with Yevgeney Otrabannikov from the Federation of Aviation Enthusiasts (FLA), a flying club for ex-military pilots, run by ex-cosmonaut, Igor Volk. Yevgeney, dressed in fatigues, had the black beard and quick eyes of a Chechen. I liked him immediately. Over the next two hours we plotted a route across Siberia, following the Arctic Circle.

I had finally met someone who had the aircraft, the pilots and the background to get the tricky over-flight permission for a group of Westerners to see the depths of the Russian heartland. There was no time for me to organize sponsors for the flight, as it was late May and we needed to get flying by 20 June. My immediate concerns consisted of how to smuggle $100,000 in cash into Russia in my leather boots, and how to get the best journalists and photographers I could find to join me and record the expedition. For this expedition we produced the first 'on-line expedition' ever on the Web, with *Wired* magazine. We smuggled and then wheeled the biggest satellite phone in the world across Siberian military bases. 'Interesny Sputnik apparat,' they would comment, 'we should have one of those soon.'

The Explorers Club in New York awarded me with flag #7, whose history linked back to Arctic aviation. When I looked at the flag I noticed that 'George Hubert Wilkins, Detroit Arctic Expedition, 1926-1928, Barrow to Svalbard' was written on the border. I had never heard of Wilkins or his expedition, but vowed to learn more about him when I returned from my Arctic flight.

When we dropped into the 'closed' city of Nadym in Siberia in our behemoth aircraft, I met William Fitzhugh, Head of the Arctic Studies Center of the Smithsonian. He was astounded by the unlimited access I'd been allowed during the 1994 expedition, and asked if it might be possible in 1995 to fly him across the Far Eastern region of Siberia, or Chukotka, to study the indigenous people.

For the 1995 expedition, I made two more cash runs through Russian customs, praying that my $100,000 socks would work again. The An-2s were purchased in Moscow and were then flown by my Russian pilots to the starting point of Yakutsk, the capital of the Sacha Republic. From one year to the next, it seemed like Russia had changed. Perhaps our archaeologists from the Smithsonian seemed too important, or perhaps the collapse of the empire was too pressing. We bogged down almost immediately in formalities and spent the better part of a month struggling to extricate ourselves from one bad spot only to land in another. In 1995 it was not possible to visit the small native villages that were so important to Fitzhugh's mission. We were pressed to land at the major landing strips, where grim concrete blocks awaited and where we were as closely watched and guarded as prisoners.

A few almost comical encounters with local 'archaeologists' and Mafia thugs who sold artifacts as coffee table pieces were the reward for our efforts. Our crossing of Chukotka ended on the Russian side of the Bering Strait when the comrades at the Provedenya airport decided that they were going to hold onto my airplanes and I was forced to leave the planes there. An endless array of correspondence was faxed back and forth to Moscow, Provedenya and Alaska. I made two trips from Europe to Alaska and once chartered an airplane to Provedenya on the notion that everything was cleared up. I paid the fees that they demanded only to be given new invoices. It was a fool's game, but my heart was with the aircraft and I wanted to finish what was begun.

Four hundred and thirty-five days passed. I had given up hope of ever seeing my Antonovs again. But finally, in November 1996, the planes were released to fly to Alaska. The Russians realized that the fish was played out and they would be stuck with two airplanes on the airport with nobody to pay the accumulated landing, navigation, and parking fees. One day after departure, the largest storm to hit the Bering Strait in 22 years left a record of 55 foot waves and 100 knot winds off the Nome, Alaska, buoy. If the biplanes had still been parked in Russia, out in the open as they were, they would never have survived that kind of wind.

I was introduced to Ron Sheardown in Anchorage as one who had flown the Antonov. He struck me immediately as the kind of person who can get things done. Ron owns an An-2, and he likes to spend his time working on it. His mining interests had also taken him to Russia for business, and he was no stranger to the contorted ways of business and protocol there. In the end it was Ron who went over and actually rescued my biplanes and flew them across the Bering Strait. It seemed like more than outrageous fortune that had saved the airplanes from destruction in the storm. The paint was faded, the fabric worn, and the red star on the tail looked dim, but now I felt my planes were finally free. Reason dictated that I sell the planes immediately and get on with my life. They had consumed an inordinate amount of my time and money. But I was still attached to them and we had been through a few things together. I was sitting in the jacuzzi of a ski resort in Austria in the winter of 1996 when I met Ferdinand von Baumbach. He had joined a ski week that I make every year with about fifty Dutch companions. Ferdinand wanted to know where to visit in the US for his summer holiday with his wife. I invited them to my family home, a small ranch in Oregon. One evening I showed them the slides from Siberia and I could see Ferdinand's eyes glaze with enchantment. He wanted to join me for another flight. At this point I needed a break from expedition planning, and told him so. I was drained financially and emotionally on the Antonov project. I told him that if he wanted to raise the money, and buy into one of the aircraft, I might consider 'one more flight'. A few months passed, but when the aircraft landed safely in Alaska, Ferdinand made the emotional commitment, paid his money, and got to work on the phone to raise funds. Now we just had to decide where to fly.

During my time in Alaska my acquaintance with Ron Sheardown grew. We did some flying, enjoyed some skiing, and drank a few beers together. Ron is older than my father, but there was no generation gap and we shared a mutual enthusiasm for the Antonov. I told him about the Wilkins flag that I had carried and about the upcoming anniversary of their trans-Arctic flight. Ron shared an interest in the flight and had extensive background in flying the Arctic. While flying his An-2 around Anchorage he taught me many of the things about running it that the Russians couldn't explain. First and foremost was just how to start it! He also gave me advice on approach and landing, which had always seemed to terrify the Russians. Sure, the aircraft has a big tail and a propensity to ground loop, or spin around on the runway, but this was manageable.

I finally got around to reading Wilkins' book *Flying the Arctic*, the Eielson story *Polar Pilot* by Dorothy Page, and *Famous Flights that Changed History* by Lowell Thomas and Lowell Thomas, Jr. It had been seventy years since Wilkins and Eielson carried the same Explorers Club flag that I had been carrying on my own Siberian expeditions and I was beginning to believe it was my turn to fly the Arctic. I had been moving towards this goal for some time and had a desire to do something different from my friends, who all seemed so settled in their jobs, their houses, their lives. I still wanted to pursue the impossible dream, the unheard of experience, the richness of life which comes from working as a team during difficult and changing conditions. I wanted the freedom of flying that I had first dreamed of in my youth, of flying a big biplane, of cruising over unseen territory at low level. It was time to take the Antonovs to the Arctic.

Shane Lundgren
Berlin, Germany

Introduction

Wings of wood and cloth

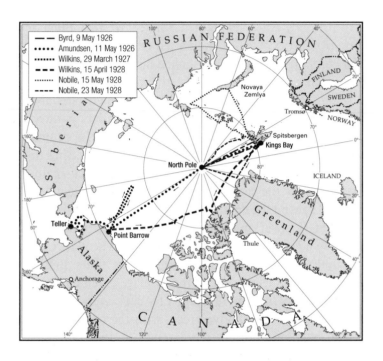

Legend:
— Byrd, 9 May 1926
•••• Amundsen, 11 May 1926
•••••• Wilkins, 29 March 1927
– – Wilkins, 15 April 1928
••••••• Nobile, 15 May 1928
– – – Nobile, 23 May 1928

To one who had been dreaming development of airplanes for eighteen years, the sight of this machine was the materialization of a vision. It gave me the thrill that another might experience if he saw his ideal woman in the flesh. Conscious of a deep satisfaction, I said to myself — if that machine checks up in aerodynamic qualities anything like it looks, I am going to have one like it for my work. I sensed unmistakably in my own mind that the transient glimpse of that machine was the beginning of the road to success.

Flying the Arctic *by George Hubert Wilkins*

Shane Lundgren and I first met in a Tibetan cafe in New York City when a group of us from The Explorers Club wandered out for a meal. Our second meeting a few weeks later occurred just over the Brooklyn Bridge at a dinner party. As the evening wound into ports and coffee, Shane produced several scruffy prints. Set against a few ramshackle buildings, dirt runways, and the starkness of Siberia, crouched the biplane.

'An Antonov An-2,' explained Shane. 'We flew them across Siberia from Moscow,' he commented casually.

The biplanes in the photos looked nothing like what I imagined a biplane to look like. They were far bigger, with a presence that filled the photographs. Tipped back on their tails, they appeared to be sitting on their haunches, propellers pointed skywards. The props spread out in four long, powerful prongs that extended far out into the air. The cowling surrounding the engine bulged out. A massive exhaust pipe flared back against the right side below the cockpit. It was burnt black, like a dragster. Above and behind the engine, the cockpit was something out of a World War II novel on great air battles. Heavy metal framing held the foot-square window plates in place. The glass extended far around to the side and up over the pilots' seats. Behind the cockpit, the cylindrical tube of the fuselage extended large and round, with only the hint of a taper, far back to the tail.

The plane was drab olive green, with the occasional scrape and dent belying a not entirely happy life. Just visible on the tops of the wings were large yellow Cyrillic characters. High on the tail, a large faded red Russian star completed the picture. The biplane had none of the elegance of the airplane that Wilkins had first seen in 1927 in San Francisco. It was obviously not quick, it looked heavy in the body, the lifting surface of the wings was immense and the bulbous tires hung off the undercarriage like overweight balloons. But it was in a strange way beautiful, well proportioned, its function dictating form with clean simple lines. This was not just an airplane, but an adventure waiting to happen.

When the dinner party wound down, Shane, my wife Margaret

and I shared a cab back to Manhattan, where an Irish pub on 35th Street lured us inside for a final cleansing ale.

'I'm trying to get the biplanes out of Siberia right now, fly them over the Bering Sea and into Alaska,' Shane said.

'I'd like to go, just for the ride,' I commented, 'take a few pictures.' My interest was in the planes, not yet in the Arctic, but it seems that was a common beginning. For as the man who would eventually inspire us to follow his airborne trail across the Arctic had begun his own book:

> It was in 1913 that I first proposed to fly over the Arctic Ocean. I had no thought then that the machines available could make a crossing from Barrow to Spitsbergen. But even in those days, it would have been possible to make a sortie with airplanes into the unknown Arctic area, seeing as much new territory in one day as could be seen on a twelve months' trip by dog team.

It was Wilkins experience down on earth with the dogs that would eventually give him the confidence to fly over the Arctic. He knew if he had to crash onto the ice he could always just walk home. Wilkins' book *Flying the Arctic* had provided Shane with the initial inspiration to begin planning our own expedition. But Wilkins, perhaps because his fame had preceded him or just because he was the master of understatement, provided little background as to his qualifications in the book. Press reports prior to his 1926 expedition to the Arctic aptly covered what had already been an illustrious career, best outlined in a special supplement to the *Evening World* newspaper in Detroit on 22 December 1925. This contained quotation from E.S. Evans, a member of his expedition's board of control.

> We believe that Capt. Wilkins is better qualified for the flight he contemplates than any other man alive. He has had more experience in aviation than any other explorer. He has had a wider experience in both Arctic and Antarctic exploration than any other aviator.
>
> He was with Stefansson on the Canadian Arctic expedition. He was with Shackleton on the Quest expedition to the Antarctic. He was second in command of the British Imperial Antarctic ex-

pedition in 1921. He has recently returned from Australia, where he commanded an exploring expedition for the British Museum of Natural History.

In 1910 Wilkins began taking photographs from airplanes and free balloons. In 1911 he flew the first monoplane ever fitted with a 100 horsepower motor. He served with the Australian Army Corps during the World War as commander of a squadron of six planes and was described by Sir John Monash, commander-in-chief of the Australian Army, as one of the bravest men in that army.

Following the war, Capt. Wilkins participated in the attempt to fly from London to Australia. He is an expert air pilot, air navigator and gasoline engine mechanic. He has commanded ships at sea and large bodies of men on the Western front.

More importantly, Wilkins extensive time in the Arctic gave him a supreme self-confidence, as he related in the opening chapter of his book:

Early in our efforts, and soon after rounding Point Barrow, the main expedition ship, the Karluk, *became fast in the ice. Six of us, including Stefansson, became separated from the ship, which drifted to its doom. Some of the crew were saved, but many of them perished, either on the way to Wrangel Island, or before they reached there.*

Those of us marooned on the ice had to travel many miles by dog team. We followed the coast first to Barrow for assistance, and later went eastward to join two other boats of the expedition. Early in my Arctic experience, I learned what is meant by 'living off the country' — which is simply living on the proceeds of hunting. And from Stefansson, I found out how to take care of myself under Arctic conditions. For many miles we traveled along the Arctic Coast and across the Arctic Pack, crossing leads of open water, hauling on the sleds, running in front of the dogs and living as did the dogs on food we procured with the aid of our guns. It was a romantic, hard, yet not unpleasant life.

Speaking so simply of living through conditions that killed other men so efficiently, of traveling over the ice with a gun and a dog, of summing it all up as 'romantic, hard, but not unpleasant', indicates a man who was so confident on the ground that only the challenge of the sky was left for him. And like great explorers everywhere, Wilkins was certainly not without his dreams:

> *I did not enjoy following the dogs or running ahead of them over the soft, spring-thawed snow or wandering along the ice-strewn beaches during the long winter darkness. My feet were unused to the soft, flatsoled skin boots, my ankles ached and muscles swelled. My eyes ached from eye strain and it was not a rare thing, in going ahead of the dogs picking the trail, as was usually my job, to suffer the excruciating pains of snow blindness. I like to imagine I was up in the air, sailing along in an airship or an airplane with the broad panorama of ice beneath me. Is it any wonder that I should often say to Stefansson, 'We should give up this old-fashioned mode of travel, go back and get airplanes with which we could cover in one season all the work you have planned to do.'*

Underneath all the knowledge he was storing up on Arctic travel, the weather, and life on the ice, Wilkins still saw the sky as where the great adventure was. In 1926, as he prepared for his first flight over the Arctic, the Far North was an infinitely more remote area. A headline in *The World* newspaper in Detroit read 'Air conquest of Arctic for undiscovered land is arranged for spring,' and the article stated:

> *The polar ice pack between Barrow and the Ice Pole is an unknown region. No explorer has ventured toward its centre, although several have touched its edge. Peary, on his sledge trip to the geographical pole, was on the opposite side of the sphere. So were Amundsen and Ellsworth on their recent polar flight. Nansen skirted the ice pack in the Fram. Stefansson skirted it with his dog teams and sledges. It is the purpose of the Detroit expedition to explore the ice pack and reach its center. It is not Capt. Wilkins' primary purpose to search for land. But if land is found the expedition will take possession of it for the United States.*

For years, there had been rumors of land north of Alaska. And a little over 60 years ago, there were many who felt that just as there was a great continent surrounding the South Pole, there must be land in the high northern latitudes. While today it seems unthinkable that so short a time ago, people were still discovering new lands, as declared in the papers of the time, the theories, carefully laid out, would have interested even the non-believer.

> *Although it is not Capt. Wilkins' purpose to hunt for land, many believe he will find land. They believe a polar continent exists between Point Barrow and the Ice Pole. Roughly, their reasons are concerned with the following facts.*
>
> *First, the prevailing Arctic winds, as observed and recorded by many explorers, indicate the possibility that a high land point exists in the neighborhood of the Ice Pole.*
>
> *Second, the Arctic tides as charted by Harris, the American oceanographer, indicate the presence of a mass of land between Point Barrow and the geographical pole.*
>
> *Third, the formation of the earth's surface in other parts of the world, taken with proved geological theories, makes it seem possible that land exists in the unexplored area. … Some whalers have reported that they saw black masses which may have been land or may have been nothing but the black polar mists. 'Keenans's Land' was on the maps for many years …*

With birds, currents, winds and even a bit of space on the map for it, little wonder that there was high interest in discovering new land. It was a theory that made headlines and made Wilkins' flight far more interesting. It also didn't hurt the additional coverage that the city of Detroit and its manufacturers, who were the primary sponsors of the expedition, would enjoy. Discovering the last bit of land on earth made any adventure worthwhile. And as the papers were all quick to point out, even though Wilkins was Australian, the land would be claimed for America.

After my initial meeting with Shane in New York I departed for my home in Seoul, Korea. Shane returned to his base in Berlin where he flew jets for Air Berlin, who had picked up Pan Am's old routes, along the corridors of Europe. The Antonovs became little more than a distant vision on a faded photograph. Shane's plans for rescuing the planes from Russia, sandwiched between the bureaucratic obstacles of Russia, where the planes resided, and the FAA in America, where the planes were now being registered and paperwork cleared, proceeded slowly. But I already had a feeling that Shane Lundgren, like Wilkins, was a determined character. When he set out to do something, he would carry it through to a conclusion, whether it actually seemed to be possible or not. I'd come across many people who one of my Everest teammates Paul Teare, had simply classified as 'wannabes'. They hover at the fringes of adventure, or take on a number of adventures half-heartedly, but never fully commit, never learn to be able to live their dreams. Wilkins' book, written after his Arctic flights, is notable in its humility. But just to remind his readers that his explorations were not all charts, map reading and fuel settings, it starts with an insight into his beliefs with:

> *Faith is the substance of things hoped for, the evidence of things not seen.*
>
> Hebrews *11:1*

a clear indication that Wilkins knew exactly what was behind successful expeditions.

And in late August 1996, Shane's call came from Berlin. 'I think the Antonovs are cleared, we'll meet in Anchorage and take it from there. I'll fax information for your Russian visa.'

The invitation letter, with distinct Cyrillic letterhead and a winged Mercury logo as seal, stated:

September 3, 1996

Dear Sirs,

The Russian Federation of Aviation Enthusiasts is inviting you to participate in a flight to deliver An-2 aircraft from the Russian Far East to the United States. The route of flight is from Provedenya to Nome and will occur between the dates 15 September and 15 December 1996.

Counselor of the President
FLA Russia
E. Otrubanikov

The Russian Embassy in Seoul, an imposing red brick structure entered through a short door and a narrow passageway, is manned by one Vladimir and one Olga, both stocky characters who might have stepped from the pages of *Dr Zhivago*.

'Where is this place, Provedenya?' Vladimir asked, so I tried to explain.

'How will you get there?' Vladimir persisted, and I explained some more.

'How will you leave Russia?' A lot more explaining.

Flying a chartered plane in from Nome, Alaska, to a remote Siberian outpost, picking up a Russian biplane and flying back across the Bering Sea, as approved by the 'Federation of amateur aviators of Russia' and stated on a winged Mercury letterhead, didn't impress him. A man in the large corner office was consulted. They retreated to look at a vast wall map of Russia. Vladimir returned to the smudged window. 'Okay, tomorrow.'

One advantage of living in Seoul is the easy access to Alaska, a direct seven-hour flight on Korean Airlines. This is the same flight, in reverse, that had been shot down by the Russians in 1982 when it had strayed off course.

Anchorage in the fall was a paradise of still-longish cool days, leaves cast yellow and orange in the lingering summer sunshine and a trail of phone calls between Anchorage, Provedenya and Moscow in an attempt to achieve final clearance of the airplanes. This had to be coordinated with a charter flight from Anchorage. Then Shane needed to find three additional pilots, who had to be able to fly the two aging Antonovs, that had been sitting untended outside in Siberia for well over a year, across the Bering Sea.

One of the pilots, Ron Sheardown, had purchased a new Antonov just a year previously from the factory in Poland, where a few still remained for final assembly. It was the last of a run of 25 for Brazil, so was a cornucopia of Russian design, Portuguese lettering and Polish assembly. Nonetheless it was a new plane and with Shane's Antonovs parked in Provedenya, gave me a chance to at least go for a ride while Shane updated (or regressed) his flying skills from his day job flying 737s to the Antonov.

A short, stubby, steel ladder with two steps led up to the wide door of the Antonov. Frequently used as a freight carrier around Siberia, the design is the ultimate in utilitarian purpose, with a wide and tall body. Inside, even with a human elevation of 6' 3" it is possible to stand upright; stretching out the arms, one's fingers still just reach opposite sides of the plane. Along each side are fold-up bench seats, with small quilted pillows. The windows, five 12-inch diameter portholes to a side, look submarine-like and cast light in large circles into the passenger cabin. It is a big step up into the cockpit, one seat each side, tucked in cozily under a dome of square glass panels. On the sides, the windows open, so if the heating is too enthusiastic, it's easy to slide them back for a bit of fresh air.

When Ron started the engine up it turned over with a grunt, then fired and burst to life with a roar. With the cockpit sitting immediately behind the nine cylinders the sound was a solid, body-vibrating bassoon, soon moving up the scale to tenor as the engine warmed. Given the proximity to power, sitting atop the 1,000 horsepower engine perched ten feet in the air, looking out between the two wings was equivalent to a first-row movie seat. The engine wound up the scale as we taxied out to the runway. Then we lined up, the throttle pushed full forward, the sound became solid, full, a crescendo back over the plane, the roll forward began almost imperceptibly on the big bubble tires. Just a few moments later, the plane still only ambling down the runway, it gently lifted off. The transition was so gradual, the angle changing only so slightly, that it was more like a helicopter lifting off than an airplane. We circled the gridded street pattern of Anchorage, hovered out over the bay and circled back. The single-shell aluminum body of the plane was a thin barrier between the air rushing past outside and its passengers — in places light came through the seams. The proximity to the outside, of really flying through the air suspended by a pair of cloth wings, felt like real flying, a feeling that is now completely alien with the advent of jet travel.

Wilkins was to make three attempts to cross the Arctic, in the spring of 1926, 1927 and 1928. In 1926, in the first test flight out of Fairbanks, he provided us with his insight into pilots, planes and crashes, when he made his first flight with Ben Eielson, the Alaskan bush pilot who would accompany him on his successful journey two years hence. Their initial outing together was certainly less than ideal.

> It was my first flight with him, and I was glad to see that he was a cautious, steady, reasoning pilot — just the type for the work in hand. I have flown with many pilots, and while I am not even a third-rate pilot myself, my experience is sufficient to enable me to understand something about the requirements.
>
> I have found that pilots, broadly speaking, are in two classes. There are others of course, and there are exceptional men who are individual in their flying. But as a rule, a pilot will be either a slap dash, brilliant dare-devil whom Lady Luck has seen fit to favor in a miraculous way, or a steady discerning cool-minded man who flies steadily, meeting every condition with ready, though deliberate, action. Eielson was a ready, deliberate, reasoning pilot.

But even for a pilot with Eielson's extensive Arctic experience, this flight with Wilkins bore out the added challenges of flying in the Arctic from an established airfield with a well-groomed runway.

> We had been in the air about forty minutes, sufficiently long to get acquainted with the feel of the ship, so I asked Eielson to land. We had discussed the advisability of testing the air and flying low over the field when coming into a strange airdrome; and had also talked many times of the difference between near-surface air layers over snow-covered ground as compared with those over sun-baked earth. It is well known by all pilots, who have flown over and landed on snow, that there is not the little extra density or uplift near ground which is covered with snow that there is over earth which is warm from the influence of the sun's rays.
>
> A mile or so from the field I felt the machine to be on the point of stalling, and was pleased, knowing by this that Eielson was getting the feel of the engine and machine controls; making a landing on the air in fact. He advanced the throttle, and we sped on, coming

closer and closer to the end of the runway. I expected, of course, that he would fly along it close to the ground, then circle, and make a second approach before actually coming to rest. I was aghast when, just before reaching the end of the runway, Eielson almost closed the throttle and the machine immediately stalled.

We had less than two hundred feet altitude. There was no room to shove the nose down and pick up speed. Eielson, feeling the stall, did the only possible thing. He shoved the engine throttle open, but the engine had not time to pick up before we crashed to the ground about fifty feet from the end of the two-thousand-foot runway. The runway at that end was bordered by a fence. As we crashed the undercarriage doubled up and the machine shot forward on a keel that had been installed in case we should alight in the water and have to haul her out on the ice. Right through the fence we ploughed and slithered for about twenty yards. Eielson was as much astonished as I. 'I had the throttle full open,' he said, 'but she did not have time to pick up.'

The most interesting thing about this crash was Wilkins reaction to it.

Since the thing had been done, and as neither of us was injured in the slightest, or even unsettled from his seat, there was little for me to say. Eielson was a good pilot. I knew that, from his past experience and the way he handled the machine in the takeoff and in the air. Every man is likely to make one or more mistakes, and there was no use crying over spilt milk.

That put Wilkins' single-engine Fokker out of commission for several weeks while repairs were made. While crashing an airplane would make most men think twice, Wilkins simply moved on to test fly the larger of the two planes he had secured, a three-engine Fokker. As they came into land, Wilkins related:

Then, exactly over the spot from which we had hauled the crippled Alaskan a few hours before, to my utter astonishment, Lanphier cut the two side engines, expecting the machine to glide on the power of the center one. But, suddenly, we dropped straight to the ground. It was a bad stall, from almost a hundred feet — exactly the same mistake that Eielson had made.

One side of the landing gear crumpled. Then the other gave way. We slithered along the ground for a few feet, slewed into the snow bank and started to turn smartly. Seated as we were between an eight hundred gallon gas tank and a six hundred pound engine, I was badly scared. We could see the frame of the engine crumpling and being forced back upon us. It was an uncanny feeling. The tail of the machine was rising rapidly, but it seemed a slow movement to us; we could sense and see every move. Up and up it went until the machine was almost vertical. Parts of the engine frame stuck through its fire-wall into our cockpit. In a fraction of a second the machine would fall on its back and we would probably be as flat as pancakes. But no! It quivered in the balance for a moment, then slowly settled back with its tail high in the air. Neither Lamphier nor myself was injured in the slightest. It was my second escape in twenty-four hours.

Wilkins related: 'Failure was plainly evident.' Yet in the next few weeks, they managed to repair the single-engined Fokker, and with Eielson at the controls, make the first flight from Fairbanks to Barrow. Perseverance, in large doses, was evidently a character trait that worked well in setting flight plans across the Arctic.

Meanwhile, Shane and I whiled away the time in Anchorage, mountain biking, chasing bighorn sheep and shooting skeet over the bay. A friend whom I had first met when he was our expedition doctor on Everest, Bill Hammel, provided us accommodation. He also served as our local area guide, so we were never short of alternative entertainment — a welcome relief in the sometimes frustrating life surrounding the care and feeding of an Antonov. A week passed, but even with the paperwork cleared and myriad of forms stamped, the Russian customs agent who needed to provide final approval still lurked somewhere in Moscow, a million miles from Provedenya, where he needed to be to release the Antonovs for the escape from Russia.

Luckily, Ron Sheardown was happy to take us up for another flight in his Antonov. Ron, one of the pioneers of mining exploration in Northern Canada and the remote reaches of Greenland, had flown his Antonov from the Polish factory, across the sea to Spitsbergen. Then he'd hopped from tiny airfield to airfield across

Northern Canada to bring it back to his home in Alaska. Ron is quiet and doesn't say much, particularly at first meeting. I was later to learn that the occasional comment I heard when I first met him wouldn't even qualify as understatement. He was obviously a natural pilot of the Antonov, and when I commented on his talents, he mentioned with a shrug that he'd flown a number of different airplanes — it was simply a matter of getting used to it. What 'a number of different airplanes' actually amounted to I learned later was:

Aircraft Flown: *DC3, DC4, C46, PBY, L18, AC-500, 681, 690, DHC-2, 3, 6, Lockheed Jet Star, Westwind 1124, Lear 35, Tupolev TU-154, Ilyushin IL-62, IL-76, Antonov An-2, An-24, AN-26 and AN-28, Yak-40 and most single and multi-engine Cessnas, single and multi-engine Pipers — as well as 30 other types.*

Helicopters Flown: *Bell 47 series, Bell-204, 205, 212, 206, 206L, Brantly B-2, Enstrom 28A, 28C, 28F, 280C, Hughes 300 and 500 series, Hiller 12E, FH-1100, Robinson R22 and Russian MI-8.*

Ron had flown over 9,000 hours in the high Arctic and 16,000 total hours, logged in every state and across five continents. One of his more memorable flights was in 1967, flying over Canada's Northwest Territories. Fifty-eight days before, a lone pilot, Bob Gauchie, had disappeared. After an extensive search he was given up for dead. Nobody lasted very long in the Arctic: the temperature the day Gauchie had left from Cambridge Bay, just inside the Arctic Circle, had been –60°F. In the *Reader's Digest* of November 1967 is the story of Ron's flight that day.

> *Bush Pilot Ronald Sheardown and co-pilot Glen Stevens were to have left Yellowknife for a mining camp near Coppermine at 2.30 that afternoon, but mechanical difficulties delayed them until after 4 pm. So it was that, near sunset, they were over Samandre Lake when Stevens happened to catch a reflection of the sinking sun on what might have been glass. It was only the briefest flash, and it vanished even as he stared at it.*
> *'Did you see anything?' he asked Sheardown.*
> *Sheardown hadn't, and for another minute he held his red turbo-*

prop on course. Then something — he will never know what — made him put the plane into a steep turn and drop to 2,000 feet. And in the next moment both men saw a dark figure moving out from an aircraft that was barely visible in the snow. Two flares lighted the lowering sky beside them.

'That's Bob Gauchie!' Stevens cried out in utter astonishment. 'My God, Gauchie's alive!'

It was the sheerest chance. The low-hanging Arctic sun, which never rose high enough to reveal the downed Beaver itself, was, at 6.10 pm, at precisely the right angle to flash off its windshield just as Sheardown and Stevens flew by. Had they left Yellowknife ten minutes sooner, they would have seen nothing.

The turboprop circled the lake, landed, then taxied toward the ghostly figure. Sheardown recalls, 'He stood there with that blue suitcase, like a man waiting for a bus.'

In an inscription on a photo in a reprint of the article that he gave to Ron on the 25th anniversary of his rescue, Gauchie says: 'Thanks again for all the extra years you gave me. Gratefully, Bob Gauchie.'

Ron had heard that men who were lost for so long in the wilderness could be dangerous and crazy. He instructed Stevens to stay in the right seat, as he could not shut down the engine due to an earlier mechanical problem on their airplane that had not been rectified. Ron told Stevens that he wanted to get well away from the aircraft to figure out if Gauchie was in good condition and mentally OK. Ron was in good physical shape at that time and wanted it one on one away from the aircraft if Gauchie did anything dangerous. Gauchie proved to be in excellent mental health and Ron put him in the right seat and even let him fly the aircraft on the flight to Coppermine and back to Yellowknife.

As Shane and I prepared to depart Anchorage, Shane broached the subject of a polar flight with Ron. If Shane could get his Antonovs to Alaska, they could take a plane each and fly across Alaska, tracing Wilkins journey. Ron's experience would provide us with the confidence to launch out across the Arctic with someone who knew the Far North as well as any man. Flying with Ron, it was evident that his skills as a pilot, honed over many years and in the ever-changing Arctic conditions, were ones comparable to the qualities that Wilkins had looked for and found in Eielson when he picked him as a partner in his flights. Ron would ultimately be as committed and would spend more time working on the planes than anyone. But at the time his response wasn't one you'd pick as enthusiastic unless you knew him and his accomplishments: 'Sure, if you can get things organised, I'll go along.'

I returned to Seoul and Shane returned to Germany. Perhaps that was it, a good break from the Seoul pollution, a few flights in the Antonov and back to work. Then, three weeks later, came a note from Shane.

> Hi Robert
> It was quite a saga for Ron. He had to have the airport opened specially on the weekend with a telex from Moscow and a busload of 35 Russian bureaucrats, and they made it out just ahead of the worst wind storm in 22 years according to the National Weather Service! Winds in excess of 100 mph in Provedenya and they think that the planes would have blown away if they had not departed...this is rather good timing considering the fact that they had been rooted for 435 days.
>
> I hope you can make it on some of the outings in store, ie polar flights and sailing.
>
> Cheers,
> Shane

Working for Air Berlin, Shane had the flexibility to fly when he wished, pursuing Antonov adventures or sailing with his father who was making his way around the world. But the Antonov was burning a huge hole in his pocket. There was no denying they were an immense amount of work and expense and after Shane's most recent expedition across Siberia, it was hard for him to find the motivation to undertake another long and costly expedition.

Living in Germany, Shane had met Ferdinand von Baumbach who, like myself, was captivated by the planes. He encouraged

Shane to not sell the two Antonovs as planned, but to keep one, which he would purchase a half share in. Now the proud owner of one of the few Antonovs in the Western world, Ferdinand wanted to fly it somewhere. As it was already in Alaska, the Arctic seemed the logical place, and when Shane mentioned Wilkins' flight, Ferdinand thought that was a very good idea.

There was one small glitch in Ferdinand's plans — he had no pilot's license. Undaunted, he went down to his local aero club and started flying, surfacing two months later with his license. Partnered with Ron, Ferdinand would be able to do much of the fair-weather flying. They would pilot Ron's new Antonov.

For the front seat of Shane and Ferdinand's plane, Shane chose Donald Olson to accompany him. Dark hair, dark mustache and a powerful body could have made Donny less than approachable, but behind all this was a humble good humor, backed up by a myriad of talents that slowly came to light. Officially, Donny herded reindeer for a living, from a helicopter. But he was also a doctor, flying on Medivac flights to remote outposts to do everything from deliver babies to patch up claw marks from marauding bears. He had also stopped by Cambridge University in England somewhere along the way, and had a law degree. With more than 14,000 hours of flying in the back country, an A & P license, as well as experience landing on the ice, he'd be an ideal partner to Shane's many hours of air time.

Shane had his team together, and Ferdinand had helped on the financial front while also reviving Shane's enthusiasm for one more airborne expedition. But there was another area of talent required, one that is rarely recognized, but essential to getting any exploration off the ground. Raising the funds to cover Wilkins' budget in 1926 was a major challenge in itself. In the *Detroit News* of 15 January 1926, Wilkins outlined what he needed for his first year:

1. Fokker three-engine plane	*25,000*
2. Fokker single-engine plane	*20,000*
3. Wright Whirlwind engines	*11,400*
Instruments	*2,194*

Plane and engine spares	1,160
Transportation of equipment to Fairbanks, Alaska	8,000
Photographic supplies, guns, etc.	5,000
Transportation of personnel	5,000
Publicity, printing, etc.	2,000
Dog-sled expedition from Nome to Point Barrow	4,000
Salaries	10,000
Miscellaneous and contingent fund	10,000
	$103,754

Like many explorers before him, Wilkins found a few individuals who became emotionally attached to his plans and threw their weight and influence wholeheartedly into raising funds for him. The Detroit Aviation Society, wishing to take the city from automobile center to airplane manufacturing center, enlisted everyone from the chief engineer of Ford Motor Company to local schoolchildren to donate to the fund. Like most explorers, Wilkins was a part of this grudgingly, as he relates in his book:

> I would not have believed it possible that I could withstand the humiliation of accepting a luncheon in my honor and there and then plead for money. The greatest hardship I have ever suffered, and the most trying ordeal ever undertaken, was to address from time to time an audience of harassed business men on a subject in which they had not the slightest interest nor understanding, and then stand while some raucous voiced, high-pressure salesman sold my photograph or my autograph for a hundred, fifty, twenty, five dollars, fifty cents or what have you. I still shudder when I think of it. No one except myself seemed to mind it, and even those who were gypped a hundred dollars for my signature scribbled on a photograph, laughed it off.

All from a man who could sit through a plane crash and say simply, 'There was no use crying over spilled milk.'

Once Shane had the key team together, Ron Sheardown and Ferdinand von Baumbach piloting Ron's plane, and Donald Olson and himself in the plane in which he shared ownership with Ferdinand, the expedition moved from being an idea to something that might actually happen. We were fortunate that team members owned the planes. But Shane and Ferdinand's needed some serious work and once we made the calculations, the flight itself wasn't going to be economy class. In Anchorage and across Alaska we could fill up the planes for about two dollars a gallon for fuel. The Antonovs burned around 40 gallons an hour. Allowing ten hours to get to Barrow would cost us a total of $1,600. But beyond Barrow, the remote airstrips we would potentially visit — Eureka, Resolute, Nord and Spitsbergen — sold fuel at anywhere between 5 and 10 dollars a gallon. In a worst-case scenario, filling both the planes up completely, with their massive auxiliary tanks, could cost up to $14,000 at a single stop. And customer service didn't extend to actually filling the planes. Pumps had to be carried to connect to the fuel barrels and pump the fuel high up into the wings.

Payment in the high Arctic was cash only, no checks, no credit cards. It wasn't until we actually arrived in Anchorage that we knew we'd be able to fuel the planes across Alaska and for the long flight over the Arctic, when all fuel costs were met by local refinery Petro Star. In the laconic way of the North, Trent Carbaugh at Petro Star told Shane after he'd been to see him and asked for assistance, 'We'll be able to look after you.' Shane, searching for a real figure as to what it would cost us probed, 'Well what will the cost be per gallon?' expecting a discount of some kind. 'Oh no, no cost, you know, we'll take care of all your fuel in Alaska.' Which solved our single biggest expense for the first third of the journey. This, along with Ferdinand's purchase of shares in the plane and sponsorship from my long-term supporter, Rolex Watch, helped keep our costs to a minimum. Though as anybody knows who spends time around airplanes, nothing involved in flying is a bargain, whether it was in the 1920s or the 1990s.

While I would be shooting stills on the journey and writing the expedition story, Shane also thought it would make a good documentary film and contacted National Geographic. David Hamlin, producer for National Geographic Explorer, agreed, and after finishing a film on camel racing in the Middle East, assented to a quick move from the hottest part of the earth to the coldest. Backed by cameraman Jim Arnold and with his son Bob on sound, they rounded out our total team of eight full-time members.

Shane pointed out to me that as the writer covering the expedition, I had to be particularly careful not to trace their journey too closely, as Wilkins' journalist Hutchinson had done when an early test flight had stalled in the snow.

> *Hutchinson was one of the first to reach us and attempt to clear the way. He carefully stamped down the snow. The sign, 'all clear' was given, and Lanphier thrust the throttles open. The machine had scarcely begun to move when we heard a dull, heartsickening thud. Lanphier, sensing trouble, throttled the engines down and then shut them off. I looked over the side and saw Hutchinson lying beneath the propeller. In the excitement of the moment, when the machine began to move, he had stepped right into the propeller instead of away from it. He was killed instantly.*

By the middle of March 1996 we had the planes, we had some funding and we had the team together. None of us had met all the other members, some had never been to the Arctic before. As David Hamlin related to me later, 'Robert, I don't even like small planes, and I mean anything with less than four engines, jets. In fact, I've never been in a small plane before this. But there is something about these planes, something about this expedition, it's going to make a great film.'

So far, we'd gotten off relatively easy with our plans. But with Shane finishing up a sailing trip around Tasmania, Australia, Ferdinand completing his pilot's training in Germany, Ron supervising work on the Antonovs in Anchorage and David trading his camel-riding clothes for a down-filled anorak, our next steps were to be much closer to Wilkins' experience when he wrote:

> *For three years we have battled against a variety of conditions; against apathy, against over-enthusiasm, against tragedy, fear, superstition, derision and distrust, yet perhaps these were the goads needed to stimulate our faith.*
>
> *We begged for money, bought machines, flew them and smashed*

them, rebuilt them and smashed ourselves. My crooked arm and Eielson's missing finger are mute evidence of trials endured. But we saw the job to be done. No man drove us to it, but there is no harder taskmaster than the 'will to do it'.

As we made our respective ways towards Anchorage, filled with hopes and dreams for our flight, little were we to know our battle was just beginning and we would be truly tested in our 'will to do it'.

Wilkins left us with more than enough inspiration to begin our own adventure:

This does not mean that we have completed all the work we planned to do in the Arctic. No, not by any means. There is still much to be done in the high Northern latitudes…

CAPTAIN'S LOG
Starting an Antonov An-2

1. An external pre-flight inspection of the aircraft should cover: fabric condition on the wings and tail, tire wear, landing gear strut level and propeller condition. I found the proverbial bird's nest inside a wing prior to our 1997 North Pole Expedition, after we'd already flown more than 1,000 miles from the Bering Sea to Anchorage. It could only have been an illegal Russian immigrant's nest.

2. During the walk around the aircraft, remove the flight control locks on the ailerons on each wing, as well as the rudder and elevator lock on the tail. Climb onto the lower wing via the tire and strut to remove the leading edge slat locks on the upper wings and the pilot heat cover on the left wing strut. Climb the hidden, built-in steps on the aircraft side to access the top of the engine, where the oil quantity can be checked by unscrewing the 20" dipstick. The oil reservoir should not be below 40 liters before takeoff and can be filled to a maximum of about 90 liters. In a cold environment such as the Arctic, the engine is kept warm at night with a large blanket-like cover and electric heaters which are placed against the front cylinders.

3. The engine has specific pre-flight requirements. Draining residual oil from the exhaust manifolds keeps it from spewing oil onto the side of the aircraft during startup. Remove the oil drain bottle which resides at the low point in the system. Fuel from the low point is also drained to remove any water or sediment which may have accumulated. Check to make sure that heaters are removed and access panels on the engine are closed for flight. The engine cover should be removed at the last moment to keep the engine warm as long as possible.

4. Upon entering the aircraft, visually check the level of fuel in the auxiliary tank and also check for any leaks. Once in the cockpit there is one final control lock rod which needs to be removed from the pilot's control column and rudder pedals so the flight controls move freely. Seated in the left seat, turn the battery switch on the forward panel to 'on' which powers the fuel gauge. The fuel gauge is marked in liters and has a

special toggle switch for the pilot to check the quantities in both the left and right tanks to insure they are balanced.

5. Check the pressure in the pneumatic brake system, as this tends to drain rapidly and the airplane often rolls ahead during starting.

6. Once these initial steps are completed the aircraft is ready to start.

Starting procedure

7. The fuel valve should be placed open and the co-pilot should walk the propeller through nine rotations to get oil to the top cylinders. This small amount of physical labor is good for the co-pilot and particularly warming on cold days.

8. The co-pilot should remain outside while the pilot commences pumping the fuel primer on his left side seven times. After this has been completed the co-pilot walks the propeller through another six rotations to bring the fuel to the top cylinders. The co-pilot makes sure that the blocks of wood (chocks) are firmly positioned in front of and also behind the main wheels to keep the aircraft from rolling forward after startup.

9. The pilot turns on the start switch. To run fuel into the carburetor, move the throttle once to full open, then close to the idle position. Check to insure the engine controls are set with the mixture control at full rich, and the run-stop lever is in the run position. With the left arm reaching across the forward panel, the pilot pulls the accumulator T-handle and listens for about 30 seconds as the starter 'winds-up'. The sound is like that of an electric train pulling out of a station, starting with a low growl and finishing in a loud high whine.

10. The co-pilot begins pumping a manual fuel boost pump located on the floor by the pilot's seat. This is done to increase the amount of fuel pressure in the lines, which will hopefully facilitate the start. Sometimes this procedure is accomplished by bending down to the floor and pumping by hand. Seasoned co-pilots accomplish this with the left foot, utilizing the small toe.

11. When the whine of the accumulator (starting coil) reaches its peak, the pilot pushes in the starter T-handle with his left hand to engage the starter. While reaching over this arm with

his right hand he turns on the magnetos, which provide spark to the plugs.

12. As the initial firing of the engine takes place the pilot moves his right hand onto the T-handle to keep the starter engaged, and quickly moves his left hand back to the fuel primer on his left side and begins priming like hell.

13. The co-pilot will be busy pumping furiously with his left foot and will look like a dog whose stomach is being tickled the wrong way. It is mandatory for him to keep his hands free to run the throttle and (just in case) man the fire extinguisher.

14. On starting, a large tongue of flame often shoots out past the co-pilot's window, followed by a billow of white smoke. The mixture of air and fuel are critical and if they are not correct the engine will backfire loudly.

15. The pilot should immediately check his gauges for oil pressure, as well as opening the cylinder and oil vents to allow for air flow over the engine.

16. Once started the pilot needs to monitor the slow rise in oil and cylinder head temperature as the engine begins her gradual warm-up.

17. It is much harder to start the engine if it is cold outside. This entire procedure may need to be repeated starting at step number nine if unsuccessful.

One note of caution: after three start attempts the battery will usually need to be removed from the tail section of the aircraft and recharged, and the starter will need at least a 30-minute cooling period, before another attempt can be made.

chapter 1

the green tortoise

Halibut steaks. Alaskan amber ale. Long circular worn wooden bars and tall stools with bearded men and long-haired women in wool and fleece tops and jeans held up by clunky boots. Into this we descended, the cosmopolitan Ferdinand von Baumbach, Shane Lundgren, fresh from the ski slopes of Austria, David Hamlin, still tanned from his last assignment, and his father-and-son crew of Jim and Bob Arnold. Scott Hamilton and Jim Enterline arrived from New York to conduct radio experiments. I flew up the longitudes with four cameras and a suitcase of film from Seoul. Wilkins, being Australian, had pegged us nearly 70 years before.

Previous experience with big expeditions had warned me of the difficulties of handling large parties of specialists, each believing that his interest or those of his particular branch were the most important. I believed three, or even two men could do all that was reasonably possible. When all is said and done, the navigator and pilot would have to do the work. But they don't do things that way in America.

If an adult asked a child the time-worn question, 'What do you want to be when you grow up?' and the child answered, 'I'd like to be a pilot. And I'd like to fly a biplane. And I'd like to fly it to the North Pole!' most adults would smile and nod knowingly. Now ten of us were in Anchorage, all in the bodies of adults, ready to fly off in search of Santa Claus.

The planes bore the brunt of our enthusiasm. David Hamlin and Jim and Bob Arnold rigged wing cameras, tail cameras and intercom recording microphones. Scott Hamilton and Jim Enterline installed computers, wired antennas and strung cable. Ron Sheardown, suddenly besieged by screwdriver-wielding, electric-drill-whirring, would-be mechanics while trying to actually ready the plane for the flight, had to keep a constant eye open for a wire misconnected, a hole wrongly drilled or a tool dropped into the wires that controlled everything from the flaps to the rudder. A departure in two days time stretched into three, then four, then five.

The tool kit for an Antonov is in a three-by-five-foot roll of heavy green canvas. Inside is a massive black steel wrench it takes two hands to lift, curly Q steel bars with socket ends turned sideways, plier-shaped clasps and tiny ring chains connecting steel plugs. The 'How to fix your Antonov at home' book is a thick volume with a translation open to some interpretation. Fortunately, Donny had been to the Antonov fix-it school in Russia, and Ron had worked on enough planes so that an Antonov was just another chance to get his hands dirty. Even I was dragged away from my cameras and put in charge of painting over the Russian registration, so we could install Shane's new registration number, N61SL.

'How do you recommend I do this?' I asked Shane. Shane, I learned quickly, is not a mechanic. Nor does he want to be one. He knows the basics. He can walk around a plane and listen to the engine and do a run-up that would locate any real problems. But when it comes to the fiddly bits, he'd rather hire a mechanic and make sure the job is professionally done and on time — as one would expect from a jet pilot. So he knew as much about painting airplanes as I did. I asked a mechanic at the airport and he described a sequence of paint removal, sanding, buffing and painting of multiple coats that I knew I would still be working on at the North Pole. So, with Shane's blessing I purchased two cans of green spray paint and dispensed with our repainting job in 20 minutes. It wasn't professional, but it really didn't look too bad. To varying degrees, this was our approach to working on the Antonovs. The important maintenance on both airplanes was completed under Ron's direction. When it came to cosmetics, a roll of duct tape, a bit of wire and the can of spray paint was all we needed.

Harold's truck rental. The clapboard brown overgrown shack, staffed by friendly, if slightly Neanderthal men, rented everything from oversized transport trucks to a brown pick-up, as nondescript a vehicle as ever existed. Ferdinand took a liking to this. Everything could fit in the back, the security system was a wing mirror he reached his hand through to unlock the door, and HAROLD'S TRUCK RENTAL was stenciled proudly on the side. We drove it back to the airport and picked up the last mechanical challenge to be installed for the journey, the auxiliary gas tank. This tank is a fiberglass, pyramid-shaped pod holding 390 gallons of extra fuel. One of the Antonov's jobs in Russia is as a crop duster, so the tank is specially designed to hold anything you need to drop from the sky.

With a little ingenuity it can be adapted to link to the fuel system, more than doubling the Antonov's range and allowing it to stay airborne for up to 20 hours. Numerically, this sounds good. Realistically, who wants to spend 20 hours in a plane so thin-shelled you can hear the wind rushing past inches from your ear, the engine roaring immediately in front of your face and with a floor so cold that ice builds up on it in the rear of the cabin?

Without the auxiliary tank, the cabin had felt spacious, a wide passage opening out behind the cockpit. The minute the tank was in place, it left only a foot-wide passageway along the far right of the plane immediately behind the cockpit. The translucent pale yellow fiberglass, petrol sloshing visibly inside, is inches in front of any passenger's face. The weight of the fuel, at six pounds a gallon, adds over a ton. So keeping baggage, or passengers, as far forward as possible was essential, if we wanted to get off the ground at all.

Wilkins, ever the master of understatement, reiterated the feeling during one of his early test flights in Fairbanks when they '...slewed into a snow bank, and started to turn turtle. Seated as we were between an eight hundred gallon gas tank and a six hundred pound engine, I was badly scared.'

The Antonovs began to develop more of a personality as we worked on them. One day a man showed up with a Geiger counter. 'A number of these planes had their cockpits painted with special glow-in-the-dark paint,' he commented. 'Like very old wristwatches that utilized radium to illuminate the numbers, the dash, if painted with radium paint, would be radioactive. Let's just see if it beeps.'

The Geiger counter was gratefully silent as he poked it in and out the many crannies of the cockpit. How many other secrets did an Antonov hold?

Ferdinand, holding a German pilot's license, needed to have an American license issued. This is a simple procedure, but they stumbled more than once over the 'von Baumbach'. As we left he told me, 'The best question I had was in a New York airport. A check-in woman, after I'd spelled it out for her, asked me, "Did they make you spell your name all the time in school when you were little?"'

The airplanes had been parked at Merrill Field, a secondary Anchorage airport. To refuel before our flight, Shane and Ferdinand flew over to International. They shut the plane down and filled the wing tanks and put 50 gallons in the auxiliary tank so we could check it worked properly on the flight to Fairbanks. When they went to start the Antonov up for the short return flight, they overprimed the engine and as Ferdinand described on his return, 'It was like a rocket ship. When we started there was too much fuel. Flames shot out of the exhaust, big flames, and then it backfired. It was so loud. The rescue service came rushing over to check on us.'

It was proving very difficult to be discreet with a five-ton airplane, with a Russian star on the tail, that belched fire. The local paper had already had us on the front page and the TV crews were circling. While the recognition wasn't unwelcome, the delay in leaving town was making us wonder if we'd ever get two Antonovs in the air at the same time and anywhere near the North Pole.

In his short hop across the city, Ferdinand had his first real chance at the controls and that night said, 'We were going to sell it after this — but now I don't know.' Just a few minutes in the cockpit had made him forget the expense, the inability to get parts, the incomprehensible instruction manual and a dashboard detailed in Cyrillic characters. Just taking it out for a neighborhood flight had been an adventure — trying to fly it across the Arctic was going to be something far beyond that.

I was again staying at Bill Hammel's house. One day he came by to look over the plane and see how we were doing. Later he saw us fly over and that night when I arrived home he said, 'Robert, that isn't just a biplane, it looks more like a sky tortoise.' It was the most apt description we had yet for its lumbering airborne appearance. We altered the name slightly for Shane and Ferdinand's plane to Green Tortoise, to distinguish it from Ron's. Ron's plane was less of a tortoise, certainly the better- and faster-looking of the two planes. One tortoise was enough.

25 April, a bit of cloud, a little wind. A final pack of the duffels, a last stop at the store for champagne, a few apples for the road.

We pulled the wheel chocks, I hitched up the stairs, a one rung steel step that hung off the back door. The door was pushed shut and latch secured with a bit of elastic band that fit over the handle. This didn't actually do anything, but was curiously reassuring.

The takeoff was smooth and noncommittal: a rumble from the engine, a gentle rolling forward on the balloon tires, and then the ground slowly moved away below the plane. Anchorage faded in minutes. We were finally on our way north. The GPS's were programmed, manifold pressure and engine revolutions set. Below us the forest began, dark pine trees set thickly in the snow, reaching across to the base of the peaks far ahead under the clouds. The occasional road was marked as a curving, narrow strip of white winding round the hills. In Wilkins' day, the planes were hauled to Fairbanks and assembled there, so that was where their flights began. For us, Anchorage to Fairbanks was more of a shakedown cruise; a chance for Shane and Donny, Ron and Ferdinand to see how the planes performed, for National Geographic to see how the camera angles looked, the microphones performed, for Scott and Jim to learn whether their radio would connect with a satellite, back to earth and then onto the Internet.

An hour out of Anchorage we passed over Talkeetna, gateway to Mt McKinley. The mountain remained shrouded in cloud and only the foothills, glaciers just peaking out at their base, were visible. It was early in the season for climbers, the heights still so cold that few would have ventured to the summit yet. My three ascents of the peak were all completed in the relative warmth of June and July. We had flown into the mountain and dropped onto the glacier in tiny Cessnas, my first experience with Alaskan bush pilots. Flying from Talkeetna in the tiny confines of a Cessna to climb McKinley, sitting on our sleeping bags, ice axes and a few weeks' food in the back of the plane, we would shoot through the narrow confines of 'one-shot pass' where you only get one chance to squeeze through a narrow gap and into the glacier beyond. Then the plane would dip low over the glacier before turning a final corner, landing on skis on the glacier, unceremoniously dumping us on the snow and buzzing off again. As the Antonov headed north, I was glad I had at least some experience in the mountains and ice. As one reporter had commented in an interview with Shane before we left, 'Most pilots would consider flying to Barrow a huge adventure in itself. Your adventure won't even be starting until you get there.'

Passing McKinley, we climbed up through the Alaska range and experienced the first dose of mountain weather. The alternating up- and downdrafts over the sharp mountain ridges buffeted the Antonov, the cabin rolling from side to side. It wasn't enough to be frightening, just enough to make our stomachs roll and make me glad when we crested the range and it was a gentle coast down into Fairbanks.

The original dirt airstrip that Eielson had helped construct and Wilkins had worked so hard on was nowhere in evidence. As long as we kept our landings to airports, we'd be in luxury compared to the early aviation pioneers.

> The snow in central Alaska is dry and sugary. It cannot be rolled or packed without great difficulty. Our machines fitted with wheels would travel through it, but steered awkwardly. Once we arrived in Barrow, we would have no trouble; the snow there in late winter and early spring was hard and wind-driven.

Outlining what would take place in Fairbanks and to a lesser extent in Barrow every time they wanted to take off, Wilkins continued:

> … I felt we should clear a runway one hundred and twenty feet wide and as long as the field would allow. We hired teams and tractors, snow ploughs and snow-shovels, in fact used every means available regardless of expense to clear the field as soon as possible.

We touched down on an asphalt landing strip five times longer than we needed and taxied over to the hangar owned by Richard Wein. Richard's father, Noel Wein, had known and worked with Wilkins and Eielson while they were in Fairbanks and had gone on to found Wein Air Alaska, one of Alaska's first flying services. He welcomed us into his hangar, the walls of which were lined with old black and white photographs dating from the early days of Fairbanks flying. How simple had been our approach, compared to Wilkins first reaching Fairbanks. His planes had been sent by railway across America, come by steamer from Seattle, Washington to Seward, Alaska, and were then again loaded on railway cars for the final trip to Fairbanks! There the planes were assembled, test flown and finally fitted out for the flight.

We arrived to balmy temperatures, the snow melting along the runway, and enjoyed pizzas in lawn chairs in front of the hangars while the planes were refueled. We were at 65° North already, and thankfully wouldn't be enduring the conditions Wilkins found on the first day he worked on the planes in Fairbanks.

> *The sun shone bright and clear. Those of us with Arctic experience knew the temperature was low, but none of us thought to look at a thermometer until returning to the town to lunch. Then we noticed that it was fifty-two below zero.*

The following morning we were up early and with good weather continuing, set a course for Barrow, with a midday stop at the remote village of Anatuvik Pass. We wove our way along the same route as Wilkins had first taken: '… follow the John River and cross the Anuktovik Pass.'

At Anatuvik, I changed from Ron's plane into a small Cessna piloted by Lee Wareham, who would be accompanying us as far as Barrow, allowing us to obtain film and photographs of both the planes in the air together. With the obligatory extra gas tank behind us, we were slotted into two tiny seats. My knees were up against the dash and my feet were wedged under the rudder pedals. After lolling about in the Antonov, this was like flying in a cracker box. Lee and I waited for the Antonovs to take off, filming them as they roared off into the sky together, leaving a cloud of dust in their wake on the dirt strip. By the time we were in the air, the Antonovs were already well out of sight and we didn't see them again for nearly four hours when we finally came in sight of Barrow.

Rising slowly over the snow from Anatuvik, gaining altitude, we moved quickly out of the mountains onto Alaska's North Slope. I wasn't the only one to feel as if we were entering a different world. On Wilkins' first journey to Barrow in 1926, he wrote of being overawed as they moved out into the huge expanse, flying like I was in a tiny two-passenger, single-engine plane.

> *We seemed to be the only speck in a boundless world. There was nothing for contrast and from which to judge space or distance; nothing in front of our eyes except the tapering bonnet of our engine; nothing below us to be seen but the same gray, gray mass. I am sure that we could find no situation more weird if we were to travel through space to the moon. The monotony and uncertainty of it would drive any man crazy if endured for long.*
>
> *Our only consolation was that the sun shone dimly, about on a level with our wing. Eerie shadows were cast on our windshield and these enabled us to note that our compass course was being faithfully followed. On the opposite side to the sun there shortly appeared two complete rainbow circles and in the center a ghost-like shadow of our plane. It seemed to me that it mocked us as we sped on. The very shape of the shadow gave it a sinister appearance. I have seldom, in a variety of circumstances, been so awed.*

Lee and I hummed along, the sunspots rising over the snow as they had on Wilkins' first journey, the Antonovs somewhere ahead, tracking a GPS course for Barrow. But in all the expanse, we never actually caught sight of them until we were also in sight of the coast. Despite the efficacy of modern communications, I began to realize just how much of a challenge what we were attempting was going to be. The radios scratched and went blank at times. The GPS, as we traveled farther and farther north, would become less reliable as we had fewer satellites from which to key off. Spotting another airplane was virtually impossible until you were right next to it. If anything went wrong and we went down, assuming we actually survived the crash, finding us would not be a simple matter. A plane could disappear into the snow so quickly out here it would never be found. I didn't relish trying to beat Bob Gauchie's record of 58 days.

When we finally came up behind the Antonovs they were slow-moving specks floating over the landscape. The day had progressed into late evening. The sun had been setting in a pale haze of purple, orange and pink for the past two hours. We swung in a long arc out over the first of the Arctic ice packed up against the shoreline and dropped into Barrow airport. The last thing I remember seeing before we lined up for the final approach and I began filming, were the endless ripples of the ice extending northward into the haze, giant pressure ridges pushed up by the sea, a dark lead of water, pitch black against the ice, extending parallel to the shoreline. Somewhere, seemingly a million miles away, was the North Pole.

Wilkins' first landing wasn't quite so easy and many had predicted disaster: ' "It will be impossible to land on the Arctic snow with a machine fitted with wheels," they had prophesized, "even if the snow crust is hard. It will break, act as a block, and the machine will turn turtle." ' Wilkins had piled all their loose gear in the tail of the machine. In the end, his landing at Barrow was as gentle as ours. 'We swept low over the ice, just cleared the sandpit, touched the snow as lightly as if touching a cloud, and quickly, but smoothly, came to rest.'

Riding in any airplane in the Arctic, the first step outside you would expect to be a cold one. At 11 pm at night, the sun was just dipping below the horizon but the temperature was like hitting a wall of ice. We couldn't just run for the hangar or jump in a car and go for dinner. Our first concern was for the airplanes and Ron directed us in installing engine covers, rolling out 100 foot lengths of extension cords and plugging in small portable heaters that would be kept running both at the front and rear of the engine for as long as we were on the ground. The wheel chocks were put in place, snapped in tightly like a pair of bear claws around the bubble tires in case the wind came up. The rudder was secured with a set of cables to keep it from banging back and forth and the forward flaps on the wings were tightened down. A few locals wandered out to watch, welcoming us with the news that spring had come and it was a balmy 22° below zero, though they admitted that with a bit of a wind, it might feel a touch cooler. Donny felt right at home as he was expanding his flying business to include Barrow and often came north. Ron's first landing ever in Alaska had been in Barrow in the late 60s. Having flown in from the high Arctic where he'd been working, he described Barrow as 'almost tropical', so I assumed he was pretty much at home here too. He threw on an extra jacket and made sure us neophytes accomplished our chores before we had time to complain.

Our methods may have changed and our electric heaters saved us from draining and rewarming the oil at every stop. But in many respects, the first earthbound duties were remarkably similar to Wilkins and designed to ward off much the same problems.

> ...I was curious to know if the machines would get off the Arctic snow without preparation. We had filled the radiator of the Liberty engine with a mixture of eighty percent water, fifteen percent alcohol and five percent glycerine, so we had no occasion to empty the radiator before a starting even at the lowest temperatures experienced. We found it necessary to drain the oil from the tank after each flight and warm it before setting out on the next journey.
>
> A special canvas cover for the engine was provided, but at Barrow, we hung over the engine a tent, the walls of which came down to the snow. Inside the tent we placed an ordinary kitchen stove. An Eskimo watchman was appointed to keep the stove going slowly in order to keep the engine well above freezing point.

Our electric heaters covered the job of Wilkins' stove. If we landed on the ice, each plane was also stocked with two small gas stoves and a stove pipe, so they could be fired up on the ground and the heat carried up to the engine. Other than that, keeping the plane happy in the Arctic had barely changed in over six decades.

Barrow at dawn was very cold and fog had crept in. Visibility varied from a mile down to a few hundred yards, dependent on wind direction. At the weather office, low pressure circles surrounded Barrow, everywhere else the weather was fine. The latest story was that a small aircraft called a Caravan, with five people on board, had set out from Barrow a few days earlier for Wainwright, a village just down the coast. Lost in bad weather and the fog, it crashed into the ice over the sea, the nose breaking through and immersing the passengers in the water. 'And he was a good pilot,' the weatherman said, raising his brows, letting us know that these things happened to even the experienced in the Arctic. No one needed to ask if anyone had survived. If the crash into the ice hadn't killed them, Arctic water temperatures alone drain the body of heat so quickly that unprotected, they would have all been dead in minutes.

Barrow has wide streets that four-wheel-drive pick-ups purr slowly up and down. The houses are low, small, squat, square structures, set into the snowdrifts. Often unpainted, they appear as dark gray containers of humanity sheltering from the elements. Around the houses are littered snow machines, sleds, drifted-in cars. Miniature squat houses hold the huskies. Garage roofs are littered with caribou horns. From the back fence hangs a polar bear skin. It is a curious mixture of oversized Ford pick-ups and dog sleds, set in a half-haze of sea fog so thick it drifts through the air in the form of ice crystals.

The discovery of oil in Prudhoe Bay has effectively made all the natives millionaires — with the corresponding problems of apathy, drink, and having access to too much, too easily. Consequently the town is dry, we discovered after we had already taken our evening sip of single malt at our hotel on our second evening there. We had been directed to the 'Arctic Hotel', where for $125 we had a small room with dirt in the corners, peeling walls and tiny twin beds. At check-in the manager informed us, 'Sorry, but the phone switchboard isn't working. But, heh heh, we ain't got no phones in the rooms anyway. Heh heh.' This was a fun hotel.

Writing as a special correspondent of the World and North American Newspaper Alliance at Point Barrow, reporter Earl Rossman described Barrow in 1926.

Utekeavik, as the Eskimos call Barrow, is no metropolis. It is a typical little frontier town without a 'Main Street' — the northernmost settlement on the Arctic shore of Alaska. What it lacks in

*civilized dwellings it makes up in snow-covered igloos scattered
about a bleak, snowfilled plain running down to the icy treeless
shore. Here begins an angry frozen ocean which has tried to push
its way across the continent with such terrific pressure that mil-
lions of tons of ice are piled along its edge. In places this pressure
ridge is more than a hundred feet high. The sun, which shines almost continuously, gives no warmth. Now it swings about the sky
in an ellipse, never beaming overhead even at noon, but wheeling
far outward and back to the horizon.*

We repacked the planes, moved hotels, ate at Sam & Lee's, told
stories and snuck sips of our illicit single malt. Jim Enterline and
Scott Hamilton ran out of time and hitched rides on a cargo flight
back to Anchorage. And then there were eight. We returned to
Sam & Lee's, which we had been told was a Chinese restaurant,
but soon discovered to be Korean. I'd journeyed to the top of North
America and the cooks came from the same Asian home I now
lived in. We ate so many meals there they cooked up a gala, extra
spicy kimchi soup with double garlic and the bill was on the house.
I felt right at home, along with David, who had filmed a documentary on sea-kayaking on the Korean coast and lived for a month
on Korean food. Others may have preferred the French toast.

Walking with Ferdinand, we stopped one afternoon to take
pictures of a garage covered with caribou horns, surrounded by
other miscellaneous detritus that seemed to sprout from the snow
— dog sleds, half a snow machine, a spare car bumper. An aging
Eskimo suddenly burst from his shack. 'I don't want you taking
no pictures, I don't want them showing up in postcards, you guys
are always doing this.' There was no way this image would make
it into a postcard — maybe an environmental brochure on public policy gone wrong. It was time to get out of town.

Wilkins spent the same amount of time in Barrow in 1926 —
probably up to much the same as us. 'After five days' delay, the
weather cleared and we were ready to start on the return journey
to Fairbanks.' He would have to ferry additional fuel and equipment north. In the end, his first flight to Barrow and out over the
ice before landing ended up being his most successful journey of

1926. He had completed the longest non-stop flight so far made in the Arctic, covering nearly a thousand miles and venturing 100 miles farther north of Point Barrow than anyone had been before. He then ran into the same weather we were experiencing: 'Day after day, this foggy weather continued; sometimes it would lift for an hour or so, but always before we could get our engines going it would cloud over again.' Even though Wilkins had never planned a flight over the North Pole, it must have been particularly frustrating as he sat in the fog of Barrow to hear of his contemporaries' progress.

> We were in constant touch with the outside world by wireless, and learned that Byrd and Amundsen were ready at Spitzbergen to make a polar flight. Shortly after we learned that Byrd had flown to the Pole and back, and that Amundsen was about to start. Then came the news that the Norge was on its way. We calculated the time and on the evening of the thirteenth of May we set watches hoping to see the airship as she passed. The weather had been very dull early in the day, but toward evening the clouds broke up just a little, and in the distance we saw a small dark object threading its way between them. We recognized it at once as the airship.
>
> That was perhaps the greatest thrill of my life, because in 1919 I had planned to use an airship to make an Arctic flight. At that time it was not possible to persuade any one that an airship could be used successfully in polar regions. The manufacturers of airships in England and Germany refused to sell an airship for a polar flight although my friends were willing at that time to pay any price the manufacturers asked.
>
> Since my earliest experience in the Arctic, I had believed that it would be possible to use both airplanes and airships for polar flying, and as I stood on the coast at Point Barrow watching Amundsen, Ellsworth and Nobile pass, it was the realization of my plan. Airships had proved useful in the polar regions. It mattered little to me who was at the control or who had organized the expedition, the fact that the machine had safely crossed the Arctic was sufficient.

Neither Wilkins nor his supporters let Byrd or Amundsen's flights deter their own plans. They still had one of their biggest cards to play — and while it would have done none of them any good to doubt that there was land north of Barrow, the stories that were passed onto the press stretched the imagination at times. The second-in-command of the expedition, Major Thomas G. Lanphier, reported back to sponsors in Detroit following the expedition and was quoted in a special to the *New York Times* on 27 June 1926:

> *All of us are convinced that land lies somewhere to the northeast or northwest of Point Barrow, the northernmost settlement in the Arctic. We have seen ducks fly up there, many of them known to be indigenous to California, continue their flight into the unknown territory and return later with their young. It is known these birds do not nest on the ice. That is one almost positive indication there is land.*
>
> *Charles Brower, perhaps the most famous white man in Alaska because of his many years' residence at Point Barrow, has talked with an Eskimo woman, now dead, who with a group of other Eskimos was carried out to sea on a floating ice pack one summer. She was the only survivor of the colony when the pack drifted back a year later.*
>
> *She told Brower that virtually all of the time they were away the party lived on land that was comparatively high, but because of a disease and a lack of anything with which to procure food sufficient for the needs of the colony, all the others died. This surely is absolute proof that land is out there.*
>
> *I know it can be found and it can be found by airplane. In fact, I am extremely eager to try it again just as soon as it appears feasible to do so.*

Wilkins, his team and his supporters were thus assured of another chance to fly over the Arctic.

All our plans, however, were to make it this year. We had no contingency plan and no funding for another attempt. We might have vintage airplanes that were not that dissimilar to what Wilkins flew in. But we did have the advantages of airfields, maps, now accurately marked with no land on them and GPS's to plot our course. We were all getting restless from being stuck in Barrow, even Donny who had an apartment here and could almost call it a second home. He stood up after our dinner one night and recited a Robert Service poem:

When you're lost in the Wild, and you're scared as a child,
And Death looks you bang in the eye,
And you're sore as a boil, it's according to Hoyle
To cock your revolver and … die.
But the Code of a Man says: 'Fight all you can,'
And self-dissolution is barred.
In hunger and woe, oh, it's easy to blow …
It's the hell-served-for-breakfast that's hard.

'You're sick of the game!' Well, now, that's a shame.
You're young and you're brave and you're bright.
'You've had a raw deal!' I know — but don't squeal,
Buck up, do your damnedest, and fight.
It's the plugging away that will win you the day,
So don't be a piker, old pard!
Just draw on your grit; it's so easy to quit:
It's the keeping-your-chin-up that's hard.

It's easy to cry that you're beaten — and die;
It's easy to crawfish and crawl;
But to fight and to fight when hope's out of sight —
Why, that's the best game of them all!
And though you come out of each gruelling bout,
All broken and beaten and scarred,
Just have one more try — it's dead easy to die,
It's the keeping-on-living that's hard.

Donny's favorite line was: 'Buck up, do your damnedest, and fight,' one that was also often quoted by the Australian Antarctic explorer Mawson.

Finally, after five days in Barrow, the fog lifted marginally, we topped off the tanks with an extra few liters of fuel and oil, pulled the heaters out from under the covers and started up the engines for a flight to the Pole. It was 4 pm, the sun was invisible and the cloud ceiling was 1,000 feet, but visibility underneath of seven miles. Visibility in the Arctic is relative — everything is white and there is nothing to see in seven miles anyway — so flying is a matter of experience and confidence in one's instruments.

The Antonovs weren't feeling quite as strong as we rolled out to the runway, the fuel pressing them low on their struts, the engine pulling hard to move us over the ground. We lined up into the wind, Ron pushed the throttle full forward and we began our journey with little more than a nudge of movement as the Antonov waddled down the runway in the direction of the North Pole.

The Green Tortoise, low on fuel and with forward vision obscured by oil on our ill-fated 1997 attempt to reach the Pole, approaching Prince Patrick Island, Canada.

Mould Bay, the Antonovs at rest after a non-stop flight of just under 12 hours in 1997, on our return from 500 miles short of the Pole.

Trevor, Ferdinand and Ron (left to right) at work on the Antonov in Anchorage prior to our departure in 1998.

Polar One touching down at the North Pole with Shane and Ferdinand in the cockpit and Donny preparing for the landing, just prior to nearly dropping over the ice cliff.

Looking straight down from 4,000 feet at old, thick Arctic ice covered with pressure ridges, a lead of black Arctic ocean and the dark gray of thin, newly formed ice.

I was short of money and short of time to prepare for the expedition. Team members were to begin arriving in a week and the Green Tortoise still needed a lot of maintenance. The challenges and logistics of flying to the North Pole started to seem as daunting as they were for Commander Wilkins seventy years ago. I had to hire mechanics to pull one of the cylinders which seemed to be losing compression. Out on the cold and breezy ramp at Merrill Field we worked for a week putting in the auxiliary tank, fixing the engine, and wiring for National Geographic Television. Finally on 25 April we were off.

The first leg of our flight was from Anchorage to Fairbanks was the first time we could compare fuel consumption between the two aircraft and to run through navigation and flying routines. Everything seemed to be working well enough.

In Fairbanks, we visited the wreckage of Ben Eielson's aircraft. It had recently been returned from where he crashed and was killed in Siberia only a short time after he returned from his flight over the Arctic with Wilkins. It was a grim reminder of the danger of flying into a whiteout. A common occurrence in the rapidly changing Arctic environment, this phenomenon is responsible for most of the fatal crashes on Alaska's North Slope. Will Rogers and Wiley Post also died this way just west of Barrow. Technology has changed the way we interact with the environment, but the environment has not changed.

Over the weekend a turbine powered Cessna Caravan shot numerous approaches into fog on the north slope before crashing short of the runway into the Arctic Sea where everyone aboard met a watery end. My Antonov has none of the anti-ice equipment, nor the instrument landing system capability of the downed aircraft.

The flight to Fairbanks was a short hop, but at last the umbilical cord to Anchorage was cut. There were no more last minute items to be bought, no more errands.

According to the weather service in Fairbanks, Barrow was clear and minus twenty. It took longer than I had hoped to get everyone out to the aircraft, get things packed away and make our departure. I was reminded of Wilkins' efforts in the 1920s and how much difficulty he had managing a large team of people. The takeoff from Fairbanks went better than Wilkins' first attempt when his aircraft ran into a snowbank. On his next attempt, as the aircraft maneuvered through the snow, their journalist slipped and was killed when he fell into the spinning propeller. When David or Robert demanded that I do various poses for the camera, I reminded them of the dangers of being the journalist on a flying expedition and hinted that they go out to play around the prop.

As a flight of two, one plane taking off to the side and right behind the other, we were airborne in mid-afternoon. The first landmark was the Yukon river, a huge physical phenomenon. Next we passed over the Arctic Circle, noted only by digital readout on the GPS as N66.33. Flying through the Brooks Range was spectacular and we did a lot of winding around mountains looking for Dall sheep and taking photographs. Ben Eielson commented in 1926 that 'these mountains look so dangerous that even the birds should get out and walk.' They were indeed remote, but as we had the advantage of modern charts, it was relatively easy to navigate between the peaks. One of my favorite stories of Wilkins and Eielson occurred out here when they were lost and trying to get back to Fairbanks on minimum fuel.

I asked Eielson to fly low over the houses while I dropped a note asking the inhabitants to spell the name of the village in the snow. With my left hand I hastily wrote the request on a piece of paper, and dropped it at the feet of the people as we flew past. Remarkably comprehensive, they soon set about stamping large letters in the snow, but the letters spelled the name of a town not mentioned on my maps. This was even more confusing. I could have sworn that my interpretation of the map was correct and that we were where I believed we were, but anxious to reach Fairbanks without mishap I still did not wish to leave until I could definitely fix our position. We circled again and I dropped a second note asking the people to please stamp out an arrow pointing in the direction of Fairbanks. The people without hesitation and without troubling to stamp the snow formed themselves in the shape of an arrow, pointing in a direction which confirmed my belief that we were at the junction of the Alatna and the Koyukuk.

With a GPS and very detailed charts, our job was easier, if less interesting. Donny had told me about a small village called Anatuvik Pass where the caribou run through on their way from the mountains to the north slope in the spring. Translated, this name means 'caribou-shit pass'. I guess that a fair number of the beasts must gallop through the old settlement. I thought it would be interesting to land there, and see how it might compare with some of Wilkins' descriptions of villages. Anatuvik lies on the north side of the Brooks Range, just before one passes onto the North Slope. We were greeted warmly by some very friendly native Alaskans, both young and old. It would have been great to have spent a few days exploring with a young friend who told me about the herd of caribou that had just passed though.

After shuffling the camera team we took off and headed out across the North Slope. The landscape turned from familiar to surreal as we crossed over the tundra. I never saw the herd of caribou that they had told me about in Anatuvik as I was completely oc-cupied with trying to grasp the vastness of the environment that we had entered. Snow and ice covered everything. Not a tree, bush, or stone could be seen anywhere. Rolling mounds of ice showed some topographical relief, but otherwise we seemed to crawl across a new scale of geography.

The sun, a bright orange orb, was the only reminder of the world that I had left behind this morning. The warm light radiated pink across the whiteness as we approached the top of the United States and Point Barrow. I got my first look at the Arctic Sea, and the jumble of ice hummocks along the shore. Crossing over the lagoon that Wilkins and Eielson used as their airport, I was very happy that we would not have to stamp our own runway in the snow. We touched down at about 2300 local time and de-spite the -20° temperature, we were flushed with excitement at

having arrived at the launching point. With any luck we would
be on our way to the North Pole in the morning.

Flight Log   Date April 25 1997   N61SL
LEG 1 Anchorage–Fairbanks
Crew: Shane, Donny, David, Bob
True Course 014   Distance 227.3 NM

Position	Gnd. Spd.	Observ.
T.O. Merrill		clear
Windy Pass	95 kts	
Fairbanks		clear
Flight Time	2+21	

Flight Log   Date April 26 1997   N61SL
LEG 2 Fairbanks–Anatuvik
Crew: Shane, Donny, David, Bob
True Course 337   Distance 221 NM

Position	Gnd.Spd	Observ.
T.O. Fairbanks		clear
Yukon River	75 kts	
Arctic Circle		clear
Brooks Range		
Anatuvik		
Flight Time	3+10	

Flight Log   Date April 26 1997   N61SL
LEG 3 Anatuvik–Barrow
Crew: Shane, Donny, David, Bob
True Course 333   Distance 217 NM

Position	Gnd.Spd	Observ.
T.O. Anatuvik		clear
North Slope	80 kts	clear
Flight Time	2+22	

chapter 2

an audience of wolves

The Antonov rolled down the Barrow runway. And it rolled and rolled. With no change in pitch, it finally left the ground, so slowly that a mile later we still appeared to be little more than 50 feet up. We flew over the lagoon that Wilkins had used for his own takeoffs and landings, a small oval pool of white with snow banks built up on its perimeter. I'd gained some confidence after reading of his frequent attempts to become airborne. He would ask bystanders to push on the wings to get them started, build hills at the end of the runway to give them a little extra lift and catapult them skyward, and like us, throw every ounce of weight

61

forward to ease the takeoff. Just thinking about not getting the plane off the ground was beyond my imagination. I kept busy, shooting video, changing lenses, loading film. It was like climbing mountains — if you are thinking about falling off something is wrong and you probably will.

Just north of Barrow there was a broad open lead of black water framed by the ice. Prior to going north, Wilkins had been interviewed for an article that appeared in the *New York World* on 29 December 1925, where he gave his opinion about flying over the ice in a single-engined plane.

> *But Capt. Wilkins has repeatedly stated that the Arctic Sea is not the best place to cruise with only one engine. The sea currents harry the ice, breaking it apart here and there, heaping it in jagged ridges. Peary estimated that in the winter about 25 percent of the surface is open water. The water channels freeze rapidly, forming relatively smooth young ice. Elsewhere there are smooth stretches of old ice. But these potential landing places may be miles apart, and consequently the polar aviator finds an advantage in three engines.*

Tucked in beside the wide-open lead of black water below us was a little circle of tents and several snow machines. The whaling season was just starting, the whaling teams heading out to camp alongside the open leads and await the arrival of their prey. Each village is allowed a quota of whales, to continue in the traditional way of life they had followed for centuries. As we passed low overhead, I could clearly see the hunters popping their heads out of their tents to wave at us. We were flying in name only; our height was little more than tree-top.

Donny had commented in Barrow, 'Fifty miles out I just want to be high enough off the ice that some big old polar bear doesn't just reach up and swat us out of the sky.' Half an hour into the flight, I could still see seals lying along a thin broken lead of water below us. The engine roared solidly though, the one constant that was reassuring. Out the rear window, I could see Shane and Donny flying along behind and just below us. The clouds, which according to the weather report should have broken up further north, started coming down in front of us. An hour out of

Barrow, the clouds touched the ice — we couldn't fly any lower. 'I'm going up,' said Ron over the radio. 'You circle down here and we'll tell you when we get through.'

He touched up the power, the engine took on an extra note of bass and we nosed up into the clouds. 'Keep an eye out for ice, Ferdinand,' said Ron.

Nothing was visible. The wingtips were wreathed in cloud. We climbed at 80 knots, the plane at a constant angle, propeller clawing us into the sky. But the weight of the fuel dragged us seemingly towards earth. There was no indication of speed or elevation gain. Eyeing the gauges gave us the only reassurance we were ascending. The altimeter crept up in tiny steps.

'Ice,' said Ferdinand, and motioned out the window. Just beginning to form on the wings, the crystals were building up, one layered over the next. It wasn't dangerous yet, but once it started to increase, the aerodynamics of the plane would change rapidly. With the huge surface area on the plane, the massive double wings would load up quickly. We kept climbing, Ron and Ferdinand with one eye on the altimeter and another on the wings.

The plane seemed silent; only the steady, omnipresent engine kept us company. If we didn't make it up through the clouds, and the clouds closed up behind us, and we couldn't see the ice below, and the wings iced up, I didn't see many options. There wasn't even anything to take pictures of, to take my mind off our ice tortoise chugging invisibly through the fog. We ascended so slowly it seemed like we had been flying upwards forever and were getting nowhere. The clouds went on and on, visibility nil, the crew looking out over the engine into solid white.

'We're breaking through,' said Ron, 'It's lighter above.' I still couldn't see anything, but was happy to take his word for it. The clouds thinned finally, barely perceptible at first, a lighter shade of gray, a light in the heavens above.

We came out ever so slowly through puffs of white and were coasting along on the top of an endless ceiling of cloud, the sun bright along the far horizon. In the midst of the clouds I'd felt trapped and frightened, not knowing what we could do if we didn't make it. Ron doesn't talk much when he is flying and I didn't know him well enough to pester him with questions at the time. Later, he was happy to relate what he had been thinking as we headed up through the clouds.

'One of the reasons I flew for so long below the clouds was to make the decision to climb at the appropriate time. You try to get everything going for you before climbing when the plane is so heavy. I flew for many miles looking up through the holes to try to figure where the tops were. We also had the Alaska Airlines report. I think it was for cloud cover ending at one or two thousand feet tops.

'Next was to look for the best sun break on the ice below and then try to climb through that hole, even though I knew we would get some icing on the aircraft. I was more concerned for the green aircraft than my capability to climb through.

'Another reason I waited so long, was that if we had gotten too much ice, we still could have turned around and headed back down. We knew we had more than 300 feet of ceiling below the clouds.

'We did not know what was ahead until we broke out on top. But I was confident that it was a safe operation.'

As Shane was to state in the National Geographic film, 'Ron has more Arctic flying experience than the rest of us combined.' He made it possible to fly safely in conditions that others would have not flown in, or that they wouldn't have had the knowledge to fly in safely.

Ron radioed back and Shane and Donny started their climb. They circled up through the fog, building up ice, climbing even slower than we had done, but with the confidence of at least knowing there was light at the end of the tunnel. They soon radioed they were breaking through, the ice was melting off the wings, they were on our tail and headed straight north again.

The GPS was set for the North Pole, a headline across the top of the flickering screen. I settled back into the cabin with Ferdinand and as self-appointed cook, made a few sandwiches for dinner. As both Jim and Bob Arnold were pilots, they would often share the flying and were as happy as I was to move forward and take over the controls. For more experienced pilots, flying a smaller plane long distances is more of an exercise than a challenge. For Ron, Shane and Donny, all with thousands of hours in many different types of aircraft, their skills came into play whenever conditions became a bit more exciting.

As Ron explained, 'Very early on I learned there are three times I'm needed as a pilot. At takeoff, landing and if anything goes wrong. Other than that, I just need to make sure I'm well rested. Too many pilots tire themselves out just flying for hours on end, and then when they are needed, are too tired to make the right decision.'

The same holds true in all adventures. The ability to relax and be comfortable in the day-to-day surroundings, even though they may be quite trying and difficult, is essential. Then, when the situation changes or becomes desperate, and life-and-death decisions need to be made, one is ready to function at top capacity. We might have been flying over cloud, in a heavily loaded single-engine plane, with 'EXPERIMENTAL' printed boldly in red paint in the cabin. But that was the easy part. Being able to retire to the cabin to stretch out and sleep on the first-class reindeer skin rug while the Antonov hummed along was one of the keys to success.

In 1927, Wilkins and Eielson had returned to Barrow with a valuable year of experience behind them. This time they had three airplanes, two of them Stinson biplanes, chosen because they had a range of about 1,600 miles and could take off and land easily in a short amount of space. These would serve for the sorties out of Barrow when they looked for land. For the longer flight, from Barrow to Spitsbergen, they planned to use the larger, single-engine Fokker that they had flown in 1926. The Fokker was damaged on an attempted takeoff in Fairbanks early in the expedition, so they flew the two biplanes onto Barrow to begin their research over the Arctic Sea. The Stinson biplanes, fitted with skis, took off and landed more easily on the ice in the early season when deeper snow was prevalent.

Each of our planes carried a full set of survival equipment aboard in case we went down and had to survive on the ice. During our stopover in Barrow, Ron had taken us out on the sea ice and showed us how to drill holes with an ice auger. Then six-inch lengths of steel pipe called duckbills were dropped in the holes. Cable led up to ropes attached to the tie-downs on the wings. In the event we landed in a storm on the ice, we'd have to jump out and secure the plane while the pilot held it steady in the wind, before the engine could be turned off.

I'd put together food to last three weeks should we be stranded, everything from peanut butter to bags of pretzels for our in-flight snacks. Wilkins, as one would expect, kept his supplies to a minimum and planned to supplement their diet with the occasional seal burger if they ran out of food.

> *Our supplies included ten pounds of Norwegian biscuits, twenty pounds of Norwegian chocolate, five pounds of Powell's Army Emergency Ration, three pounds of mixed pemmican, chocolate and biscuit prepared for consumption during the flight. One large thermos bottle full of black coffee — a gift of Fred Hopson. I had prepared as an extra precaution ten pounds of pemmican and five pounds of Norwegian biscuit, but just before starting I removed this bag of supplies from the plane with the firm belief that if absolutely necessary, food could be obtained on the ice. Nevertheless, I believed it wise to carry as much food as possible without overloading the plane, and particularly because of the possibility of slight injury in landing and a forced confinement to one area as a result.*
>
> *... As a necessary precaution we carried two Mannlicher .256 rifles, 400 rounds of ammunition and a pair of five-power Mirakel binoculars. We also carried thirty feet of fish-net, some fish hooks and lines for the purpose of catching small birds near cliffs, as well as fish.*

Obviously any injury he planned to recover from well enough to get moving again. While they did have a radio, its use was limited, and the possibility of rescue from any distance was highly unlikely. More substantial injury obviously didn't need to be prepared for and wasn't something a man like Wilkins thought much about. I tried not to think about it either.

Being stranded in Barrow had one advantage. Having escaped the confines of Anchorage, we had time to get to know the other team members far better. At dinner one night, Donny, speaking with the knowledge of long experience in the Arctic, had prodded David after he'd ordered a blueberry dessert, 'David, I really want to fly in the same plane as you.'

'Thanks Donny, but why is that?'

'Well, David, if our plane goes down, and we get hungry, I know you won't eat me, because you are a vegetarian. And the second thing, with you eating all those blueberries, if I have to eat *you*, I think you will be pretty tasty.'

Ever the professional, David replied, 'I think I need that on tape. Just for the record, of course.'

The weather forecast had said the clouds would clear 100 miles out of Barrow. Five hundred miles out of Barrow we were still flying over dense cloud. It remained below us at a constant elevation and we flew on content, two little specks humming along, the occasional hello on the radio, the occasional change of pilots.

The distance we were covering was so great that the only thing that was important was our latitude and longitude. This ticked slowly away, ever so precisely, on the GPS. Every degree of latitude was 60 miles, every minute of latitude a mile. We edged towards the Pole, no fanfare, not a sound from the engine other than the same consistent roar. The taste of the cigars Ron and I had smoked just before takeoff was still floating around in my mouth, fragrant against the icy air when I moved back in the cabin to photograph from the rear window. The plane was cozy and warm in the cockpit; we all shed clothes before we moved to the front.

Just behind the cockpit, squashed in next to the auxiliary tank, a single blast of hot air came out of a tube into the passenger cabin. A foot away it was 70°F. Two feet away it dropped to 50°, then rapidly sunk to below freezing by the rear door. A thin metal sheet separated the main cabin from the tail, where the toilet sat. We didn't have to worry about anyone spending much time back there with their pants down, although it did provide some welcome, albeit very brief, relief in our projected 18 hour flight.

Once above the clouds we caught a good tail wind and were making up to 118 knots. Behind us, Shane and Donny were moving a little slower, but a slight variation makes a big difference in a flight lasting so long. The radio clicked on, Ron calling Resolute Bay, just checking in. Their forecast: clear, visibility 17 miles, 20° below zero.

Outside, the world became expansive. Ron picked up some gospel music on the radio and I made up some bagels and cream cheese, thankful to have remembered the capers. In the other plane, Donny was taking fuel readings every half hour. Not only were they flying more slowly, they were using more fuel. We had switched over to calculations in liters, because that is how the visual scale in the Russian auxiliary tank read. We had 1,800 liters. They had 1,400 liters. They were busy doing calculations for alternative ways to get to the Pole and back to land.

The North Pole-Spitsbergen, not even close. The Pole-and-anywhere-with-solid-ground? It didn't look good. The calculation wasn't that difficult to make. Hours of fuel burned, projected time to destination, hours of fuel left. Even one of the best alternatives, Eureka, Canada, didn't leave much of a window.

Shane came on the radio, 'Eureka weather looks good.' Then they did the calculation again. They were burning 220 liters an hour and shouldn't have been burning over 165 an hour. There could be a bigger problem than just the increased fuel consumption. The tank might be leaking, their fuel burn rate could be accelerating. At the current rate their plane could fly 597 miles. Eureka was 608.

There was a big island on the chart, Prince Patrick, and a very small dot, Mould Bay. Was that a real place? 'Yes,' Ron said. 'Been there, good strip.' Back on the radio, he announced, 'This is serious business. I think we are going to have to change course for Mould Bay.'

Shane and Donny made more calculations. Mould Bay it was. At 82° North, little more than 500 miles from the North Pole, we swing in a tight circle and set course for Mould Bay.

There was no drama, no discussion. The planes would stick together. We were not going to the North Pole, because if we did, we would make it, but the Green Tortoise wouldn't get more than 200 miles back. We weren't going to Eureka, because it was unlikely that Shane and Donny, David and Bob would even make it there. No, we were going to Mould Bay. Mould Bay?

Wilkins never went to Mould Bay, although he would have flown quite close to it. Nobody really goes to Mould Bay, nobody wants to go to Mould Bay. There is nothing at Mould Bay. At the end of World War II, as the Cold War really started in earnest, it was thought the Russians might well invade America by flying 'over the top', crossing the Arctic and sneaking into America across Canada. So 'weather stations' were set up, a very light cover for what was a chain of military observation points looking northward. This was called the Distant Early Warning line, referred to as the DEW line. The other invasion threat wasn't in the sky, but under the ice, as nuclear submarines increased their range and capabilities to live below the surface for ever-increasing lengths of time. So observation posts also needed scientists, cloaked in oceanography and whale specialist titles, to venture out on the ice and do soundings for submarines. At the height of the Cold War, there were many known posts, and probably as many unknown installations, staffed with hundreds of people.

In the aftermath of the Cold War and as observations were done by satellite and less by earthbound observations, the weather stations' role decreased and they began to be closed down. Mould Bay was a few weeks from being shut, but for now it was an airstrip and a place to rest and refuel, the only priorities on our list.

Once we turned and headed south, the journey seemed to become much longer. Flying towards the Pole, floating along over the clouds had been exciting. Turning back, not making it, at least for now, made our destination important, our return to earth take on a new urgency. One big advantage, so obvious when you are there but difficult to think about in advance, is it never gets dark. As reported in the *New York Times* on 3 January 1926:

> *To pursue the sun across the top of the world is one of the expectations of the Detroit Aviation Society's Arctic Airplane Expedition when it takes off from Point Barrow, Alaska, next March.*
>
> *'From the time we take off at Point Barrow we will never lose sight of the sun,' said Captain George H. Wilkins, leader of the venture, upon his arrival here today.*
>
> *'If we start in the morning from Point Barrow and keep on flying, we should reach the geographic pole at midnight. The sun at that time will just about touch the horizon and immediately begin to rise again. We well lose twelve hours in that instant when we cross the North Pole. In other words, it will be both morning and afternoon. The sun at that time of the year will never be higher than 12 degrees.'*

In our airplane, Ron, Ferdinand, Jim and I were comfortable just flying along, munching sandwiches, drinking hot coffee, with plenty of fuel in reserve. Over on the Green Tortoise, Donny's half-hour fuel readings weren't looking so good. But the tension never came across on the radio, Shane and Donny being too cool to ever let any fears creep onto the air. We knew however their tank was rapidly being drained and there would be little to spare to get the Green Tortoise into Mould Bay. Shane started thinking about landing on the ice, reviewing their survival gear, knowing they could well be camping out soon.

Below us the clouds changed to flat white with ripples like water cut by a darker shadowed river. Soon they started breaking up and we could peer through to the gray ice below, for the first time since we climbed out on top of the clouds. It was 11 pm our time, but the sun was low enough to make life above the clouds daytime, and below the clouds and out of the sun, the twilight darkness of early evening. A bank of clouds built up in front of us and we flew into scattered clouds, dodging, disappearing, tailing the Green Tortoise through the mist, weaving in and out of cloud worlds, lacing our way through the maze.

Finally we were able to climb up above the clouds again. The sun came through and shone down on the Green Tortoise, throwing it into relief on a sea of deep purple-pink. Broken shattered leads of ice split the white carpet below, clouds flooded the background with a pastel carpet and the toy Tortoise floated along overhead. It was very early in the morning and the all-night flight had dulled the mind but sharpened our perceptions. Looking out the window at the changing colors of the sky, the ice below, cloud shadows falling across it, it was easy to see why so many explorers had claimed land sightings in their early explorations. In an article from a Philadelphia newspaper on 2 January 1926 titled 'Wilkins to solve Polar mysteries', the descriptions alone were poetic enough to make one question their validity:

> *Dr. Cook's own report of what he called the discovery of Bradley Land reads:*
> *'Soon the western heavens, ever a blank mystery, cleared. Under them, to my surprise, lay a new land.*
> *'As well as I could see, the land seemed an interrupted coast extending parallel to the line of march for about fifty miles, far to the West. It was sun-covered, ice-sheathed, and desolate. But it was real land with all the sense of security solid earth could offer.'*
> *After protesting that he was too eager to reach the North Pole to make a westward detour so that he might explore the land, Dr. Cook went on to say;*
> *'This land was never clearly seen. A low mist seemingly from open water hid the shoreline. We saw the upper slopes only occasionally from our point of observation.'*

Dr Cook was notorious for his claims, including first climbing McKinley as well as reaching the North Pole in 1908. But his writing of the way the land supposedly looked couldn't have been more accurate when we finally came closer to the shores of Prince Patrick Island. The sea ice faded flatly into white rolls of land that were barely indistinguishable from the sea we left behind. The rolls of earth extended like unbaked bread spread flat, the gentle rise and fall of hill and valley flowing to the horizon. The airstrip was a clear dark line in the landscape, with a few low buildings set like square black dots on a hill above. After nearly twelve hours in the air, Ron flew in a lazy circle and dropped the Antonov gently down, the Green Tortoise sneaking back to earth behind us.

I popped the door on our plane open and a wave of cold ran inside like it was looking for somewhere to warm up. There was no one around, it was Arctic silent, sound frozen as soon as he propellers kicked round the final turn and the engines steamed quiet. I shook Shane's hand as he stepped from the Green Tortoise. 'It's the best looking runway I've ever seen,' he said with a big smile.

The heavy insulated covers were tossed out and stretched over the engines. An electrical plug was was located behind a shed, the cords run out to the planes and heaters snuggled up next to the engine. I'd thought to kiss the ground on arrival, but the idea quickly faded. My feet, like having been at sea, still felt the motion of the plane and skittered for balance on the runway.

A short hike up the hill was a low-slung building. The door handle was an elongated steel lever, the same as on a freezer door. Pulling it back, heavy, thick and slow swinging on the hinges, I realized it *was* a freezer door. It opened into a big cloakroom stuffed with oversized down coats and thick moon boots. There was no one around, it was 4 am local time and the place was a ghost town. An expansive kitchen, a few dishes around the sink and an oversized Formica dining table with an empty whiskey bottle adorning one corner greeted us, like a party had just finished and the occupants vanished. We were groggy in the sudden heat, uncertain, the drone of the plane still playing in our ears. We had been in the air 11 hours and 40 minutes from Barrow, flying through the night with little sleep.

A large man with a beard surfaced, welcoming us. There had been a party, a closing-down party, as they were set to pack up and leave in the coming weeks, decommissioning the base. Another man with a strong French accent, the boss, wandered in. It was an Arctic Fawlty Towers, half-conversations with our hungover hosts suddenly roused from their beds a few thousand miles beyond nowhere by eight keyed-up flyers. We were not necessarily welcome, but not unwelcome once they heard our story. We drank coffee and ate ten pieces of toast. A bed was offered and we took it. Going on, either north or south, suddenly became too much to contemplate.

In 1927 Wilkins had headed out of Barrow over the ice in a reconnaissance to make soundings and look for land. They had landed successfully on the ice, and Eielson had worked on their engine while Wilkins drilled a hole, made a sounding and determined the sea was about 5,000 meters deep — a good indication there wouldn't be land anywhere in their vicinity. On the way back, they ran low on fuel and Wilkins passed a note forward to Eielson.

> 'What do you think; let her go as long as she can then drop straight down ahead?' Eielson slowly nodded his head. No word was spoken.
>
> My watch was before me beside the compass. At 9:02 the engine cut out suddenly, as if the switch had been snapped. There was no splutter or gasp because of a starved carburetor, but a sudden silence, except for the hum of the wind in the wires.
>
> Eielson snapped the switch right and left; there was no response from the engine. We could feel the sag of the falling plane.
>
> ... Near the ground the air was rough. The plane swerved and pitched, but Eielson — still calm and cool — corrected with the controls each unsteady move. In a moment we were in the snowdrift. We could not see beyond the windows of the plane. I felt Eielson brace himself against the empty gas tank; I leaned with my back against the partition wall of the cabin and waited. We bounced and alighted as smoothly as if on the best prepared landing field. I gripped Eielson's shoulder and slipped through the door of the machine to the ice.

With their plane unflyable and out of fuel, Wilkins and Eielson now faced what Wilkins had always said he'd do if they went down on the ice — a walk back. Wilkins radioed their position in the hope someone might learn of their plight and then 'Eielson stretched out in a sleeping bag on top of the empty gas tank and I huddled in a corner of the cabin and we slept.'

Awaking the next morning, Wilkins admitted, 'With the uncertainty of wireless communication, we had resigned ourselves to the fate of walking to some coast.' He also knew that despite his claims that if they were stuck somewhere, they would just walk back, the area they were in wasn't a particularly safe place to be.

> The district in which we had landed was one in which many ships and men had been caught in the ice and none except those strongly built and well provisioned had escaped. All previous parties had been lost in the autumn and drifting west had either disappeared or come ashore on the islands off the Siberian coast.

Fortunately at that time of year an eastward drift carried them closer to land and once the storm cleared and they set off, Wilkins calculated they were about 80 miles from land. For us, sitting in Mould Bay may have felt remote, but in reality it was nothing compared to the walk Wilkins and Eielson had in front of them. They would tramp over the broken ice for 13 days. Crossing a newly frozen lead, Wilkins

> … reached within three yards of the other side and turned to say 'Come on,' when the ice beneath my feet gave way. I went into the water up to my waist. Eielson was transfixed with horror. Fortunately, the ice was thicker where he stood. By throwing my weight largely on my arms and the extended icepick, the ice about held me. My feet were quickly drawn out of the water and I rolled over and over to the thicker ice.

By the end of their journey, they were reduced to an animal-like existence. Wilkins however still wrote after the fact in a manner that left little doubt that they were going to make it.

> We struggled slowly on, ten steps or one step, then a tumble. Often our feet were pinched between narrowing cracks hidden in the snow; many times we had a ten minutes' crawl on hands and knees over ridges too steep for even a dog to follow; then a cautious slithering

dash across young ice that sagged as would a stretched blanket, if you stepped on it.

These sound less like the antics of grown men and more a group of kids at play, rolling through the snow. Eielson was to lose two joints from the small finger on his right hand to frost-bite; Wilkins came out unscathed and undoubtedly with renewed confidence that if his plane went down, all they had to do was pack up and walk home. I was left wondering how far we would have lasted had the same thing happened to us. Maybe Donny hadn't been entirely joking when he said he wanted to ride with David?

I woke up a few hours later. The eternal light of the Arctic seems to lessen the need for sleep and the island called out for at least a small amount of exploration. I set out up the nearest hill after checking to see if there had been any polar bears spotted recently. The hulking station mechanic said with a laugh, 'Haven't seen no bears lately. But they are out there, mostly on the ice. When they get you, you mostly don't see them anyway, heh heh. Or you can't say whether you saw them afterwards.'

This didn't sound too serious and the little I knew about bears, I figured they would stay close to the ice and the seals. The hike up the hill, the snow crisp below, the sky an envelope of blue, was a welcome relief from the confines of the plane. A pile of rocks eight feet tall rose from the top of the hill, a landmark the Eskimos used for navigation.

Suddenly as I approached within a few feet of the rock pile, I detected a flash of movement, of fur, from behind it. I leapt back. I was going to be eaten. The rocks were right in front of me, only a few feet away. There was no reason to run; I'd be caught immediately. There was still no roar, no furry paw snaking around the rocks to snap my neck. No big teeth appeared. It couldn't be too big a polar bear. The pile of rocks wasn't that huge.

It was silent; the Arctic is so silent the air hums.

There was a little scuffle. It was moving. All my hair stood up on end. A very large curved ear appeared, then another, then a black twitching nose and some big buck teeth. It was a large, complacent Arctic hare. It was so tame I could have petted it. The hare stepped forward into the sun and after a cursory glance in my direction proceeded to go back to its nap.

On the way back down the hill I passed the cemetery, home to two graves, one that of a five-year-old girl. A white painted cross with the paint flaking off, a name, a date, stuck in the frozen ground. Whatever had she been doing here?

Ferdinand was up when I returned. 'Hey you should of woke me up, I would have gone with you.' Ferdinand was always up for anything. Chasing Arctic hares, looking for polar bears, working on his aeroplane. He had a knack for fixing things, looking through the nooks and crannies on the Antonov and figuring out what was wrong. He was invariably up on top of the wings every time we stopped to refuel, a freezing cold job that was guaranteed to produce misery — yet I never once heard him complain. He had a Harley Davidson and worked on it as well — probably good training for becoming an Antonov mechanic.

In the kitchen, the big polar chart was out on the table. The Green Tortoise was not well — and it was impossible to know exactly what was wrong with it. It used far more fuel than it should, and oil sprayed out over the windscreen to the point where it was impossible to see. Losing the oil was bad enough. Not being able to see forward made landing pretty tricky. It was fairly easy for Shane to make the first decision: going any further in the Green Tortoise would be foolish.

This still left us with the option of putting all eight of us in Ron's plane, flying across Northern Canada and on to Eureka. We could refuel there, then fly to the North Pole and onto Spitsbergen. To complete the journey would be far more rewarding. But four people in one Antonov had been just bearable on the long flights. Eight would have made economy class on United Airlines seem palatial. With the combination of the Geographic film team's requirement to move around inside the plane to get footage, the below-freezing temperatures in the rear of the cabin and putting everyone's luggage and survival equipment aboard, any joy we would have had in the flight would have been nonexistent. If we did actually have an emergency and had to put on our survival suits and jump out into the raft, there would be a long line to get out the door.

Also, if anything went wrong with Ron's airplane, we wouldn't have the back-up of a second airplane. There would be no immediate assistance, which in the Arctic, can make the difference between turning into an iceberg and getting home safely.

Ron and Donny, with their Arctic experience, were happy to try it. The rest of us weren't so comfortable with the stripped-down option. Even with all the pros and cons worked out, it wasn't a clear-cut decision. We even asked ourselves what Wilkins would have done: we agreed he probably would have gone on in the same circumstances. However, some of the characteristics that Wilkins admired most in Eielson and kept mentioning indicated he respected cool-headed decision-making over any rash bravado. As he wrote following their first two flights together to Barrow in 1926:

> *It was during those days of flying that I came to appreciate the sturdy courage and fine qualities of Eielson. He was always willing to take a reasonable chance, always recognized danger and with great care avoided as far as possible all trying circumstances. He was not a daredevil who would dash into anything. He summed up every situation and looked at it from all angles and then whenever there was a possible chance he went ahead.*

The final decision was up to Shane, and after weighing our chances he decided it was best we all returned to Anchorage. Still fresh from the flight over the ice with a near-empty fuel tank and the oil-covered windscreen, there was also a feeling that at least for the crew of the Green Tortoise, they had pushed their limits about as far as they wanted to on this journey. Shane is a pilot who flies passengers for a living and would have been feeling the added responsibility of having a film crew aboard. They were part of our team, but also doing a job and being paid to fly along with us. A year later, faced with decisions that were to put us in as much danger and with as many unknown factors as we faced in 1997 and decided to retreat from, we would take off and fly for the North Pole with hardly a second thought.

Now came the inevitable let-down, but we were still two long days of flying, if we had good weather, from Anchorage. Mould Bay may not have much of a social life, but it still held a few surprises. As we packed up and were driving back down to the runway, the weather man said, 'The wolves may be out now, they are often around the runway, let's just go and see them.'

Just above the rise of snow next to the runway they appeared. We got out and walked towards them, two big lanky Arctic wolves, pure white. 'I'll get them to come a little closer. They like frozen pork chops.'

The wolf walked with a curious effortless lope and had very big teeth that grew the closer it came to us. I wondered if baiting a wolf with a pork chop while armed with only a camera was a good idea. Our host seemed to be completely calm, so I stood innocently by. In the midst of the white snow, the land completely devoid of anything that appeared to be alive, the wolves still managed to look completely at home. They were completely un-like dogs. Their movements, their shape and their eyes marked them as very wild animals. As with any carnivore you see in the wild, without a big barricade between you, the emotional sensa-tion is completely different. You know you are on their territory and playing by their rules. It makes your hair prickle and sends shivers right down through your toes. It makes you forget you were supposed to be flying to the North Pole and weren't going to make it.

The wolves would spend the next few hours watching us as we loaded the planes, wandering back and forth in the snowy background. I'd hopped planes again and was back in the Green Tortoise for the return journey. Shane and Donny were happy to fly, but some of the crew weren't so comfortable with an aging Russian airplane that sucked fuel at mysteriously high levels and sprayed oil in all directions. As Shane had stated bluntly to me earlier, 'I'm more worried about my ass than anyone else's. I'm not flying if I don't think it's safe.' I'd always admired people who were willing to undertake adventures but had a strong dose of self-preservation built in, and jumped in Shane's plane without a second thought.

We took off that afternoon, happy to escape Mould Bay and not be stranded in bad weather — the very thought seeming like a prison sentence. The island was remote and magnificent, but being stuck for days we didn't even want to contemplate. We crossed Prince Patrick Island and were soon back over the sea ice headed south. The black leads were intersected by pressure ridges and concentric lines of ice pushed up by the sea. Patterns and light were a jigsaw below us, until the fog covered the ice and we floated on over the clouds.

These had been the same conditions we'd flown in on the way to the Pole, with no way to know what was below — ice, or leads of water. If the clouds extended all the way down to the ice, making an emergency landing would be very difficult. But the Antonov chugged along, as reliable as ever. One could almost get complacent.

It seemed though that no one got too complacent in the Antonov, even Ron. 'I swear it's watching me. The minute I start to think I can relax, can let my guard down, she'll start to drift away, something will happen. You can't be resting when you are flying this airplane.'

I didn't need to be told this because my flying lessons from Shane that afternoon hadn't gone too well and I'd been doing just about everything but loops. I'd take the controls with everything all set. Shane would drift off for a nap. Then pretty soon I'd hear him, almost in the back of my mind, 'Robert, where is the sun, where is the sun?' I'd suddenly realize I'd let the Antonov drift around and while we were still heading south, we were only marginally pointed in the right direction. Maybe Shane should leave me in charge for a while longer and I'd get us to the North Pole? I complained to Shane that the Russian dials confused me. Shane pointed out the sun, which was all I really needed, was not in Russian so I concentrated on that.

Five hours later we were over the straggly forests of Northern Canada, feeling like we had actually returned to real land, dropping down into the village of Inuvik. The houses were gingerbread cookie shaped and curious pastel colors, victim of an urban planner from far away designing a government outpost for a few thousand inhabitants. We dropped into the airport and caught a taxi to a small hotel. The low dusk and being on the ground was invigorating after the flight. We walked the length of the main and just about the only street to find a tiny restaurant filled with high school students up late on a Friday night. They stared at us. We ordered large chocolate milk shakes and cheeseburgers.

At 10 the following morning we were again in the air, trying to climb above the clouds, the Green Tortoise laboring, ice forming on the wings before we broke through into the sunshine. All day we would be crossing mountains, dodging cumulus cloud towers, climbing to 11,000 feet to clear some storms, diving down to 6,000 to dodge others. The Alaska weather would never allow anything approaching a relaxed journey. An hour outside Anchorage we flew low over two bighorn sheep as we traversed a line of cliffs. They glanced up and went back to their lunch. By the time we set up for the landing at Anchorage, the windshield was so oil-spattered that both Shane and Donny had opened their side windows to see out. Fresh warm air washed into the cockpit.

I filed our last entry to The Explorers Club website with a cliché often used by failed expeditions:

> We'd returned from just 500 miles south of the Pole, but with both our planes and all of our team intact. Having set out initially to trace the voyage of the polar explorers Wilkins and Eielson, we'd returned with an increased respect for their accomplishments over 70 years ago. Taking the Antonovs on the journey had turned what could have been an easy flight into a real adventure. And like the early explorers, our flight hadn't quite taken us to our destination, but the journey had been rewarding in itself. Wilkins and Eielson had taken three attempts to complete their plans. We are optimistic we'll do it in two.

Echoing our sentiments, the Mayor of Barrow sent a note:

From: 'City of Barrow'

Sorry to hear of your problems but we were certainly glad to hear that you are all okay. This just underscores the magnitude of Wilkins' and Eielson's accomplishments! We will be looking forward to seeing you again here in Barrow for another try.

Sincerely

Jim Vorderstrasse
Barrow City Mayor

Shane wrapped up his feelings for the National Geographic film that screened later in the year with 'While the world can only be discovered once, it can be explored forever.'

Wilkins had returned from his 1927 expedition with many successes. But the one that counted, the flight from Barrow to Spitsbergen over the top of the Arctic, he had been unable to complete. As he recounted, 'No one seemed to consider it possible for me to continue, but I was determined to complete the program and surprised that others did not realize this.'

On the last day of April, after four tedious days of fog-bound delay, the weather lifted a bit. We had a five hundred foot cloud ceiling, seven miles of visibility. The satellite pictures of the route north looked clear. It was not ideal but I thought we should take our chances. As the pack ice offshore breaks up with the spring thaw, the fog would only get more persistent. If we could just get north of Barrow and out of the shore fog, I felt that it would clear up.

With the auxiliary tank full of fuel for the first time, I was concerned about the takeoff and the plane's ability to carry the extra load. Fortunately we had lightened our load in Barrow as Scott Hamilton and Jim Enterline left the expedition to return to work while we were delayed by the fog. Ron took the runway first and I was amazed when his aircraft climbed into the air with no visible struggle. The steady old Antonov has so much wing area and power that she seems unfazed by load. We were airborne at 1630 local time and crossed the shoreline of the Arctic coast headed 360 degrees true along the W 157 degree meridian. The GPS said that the Pole was 1132 nautical miles ahead.

We began to fly a zig-zag pattern shortly after leaving Barrow to find the best visibility. The plane was still very low over the sea ice and I could see seals lying along the open water leads. I wanted to look for polar bears and whales but was preoccupied with maneuvering around the weather. An engine failure was my worst fear, as we would have little time to try to dump fuel from the aux. tank and land on the ice. I figured there was a reasonable chance that the aircraft could be landed, but I had misgivings about the aux. tank. It seemed that there was a good chance that if fuel was still in it, it could explode. I was between the choices of fire and ice, and I tried not to think about them too much.

The clouds began to lower around us, and we decided that our best option was to climb up through the overcast. It wasn't very thick, and we found a small blue hole to look up through, but loaded as heavily as we were it was tricky to climb. Pulling up into the clouds was unnerving, and as we started to pick up ice the airspeed dropped. This was concerning, but Donny did an excellent job of keeping the plane steady and climbing and finally we emerged on top of the overcast at about 2,500 feet. It took a bit of time to find Ron's aircraft as we had intentionally split up during the climb to be sure we did not collide in mid-air. It is amazing how difficult it is to see another aircraft in such a vast area. Finally we spotted them and could relax into a routine of navigation, flying, fuel management, and radio reports. Transferring from the main fuel tanks to the auxiliary tank calls for moving a red knobbed push rod, which opens the tank valve, and then actually turning the normal fuel selector to the off position...and waiting to see if the engine keeps running. I was ready to switch back to the main tanks immediately if the aux. tank transfer did not work. I had tested the system previously, but there is nothing like the real thing.

Donny and I began taking fuel readings from the gauges and the aux. tank indicator every thirty minutes, and made a position report to Resolute Bay radio every hour. I was amazed that we were still flying on top of an overcast as I had expected clear skies north of Barrow. This is what the satellite images showed. If forced to make an emergency landing now we would have to glide through the clouds in zero visibility and just hope that I liked what I saw for a landing site when I met it.

I regularly checked and compared power settings, ground speed, and fuel readings with Ron. After seven hours it became apparent that something was amiss. I was having to use higher power settings, and had burned about 400 liters, or 100 gallons, more fuel than Ron's aircraft. It looked like my plane's fuel burn was actually increasing with time and not decreasing as the load was lightened.

The alarm bell rang in my head — we were not going to make it! An immediate diversion looked like my best chance. I could have continued on to the Pole, but at the rate of fuel consumption, I would only make it two hours past the Pole before running out of gas. I was at N 81 47, W 155 51, a mere 492 miles from the Pole and about as far away from land as is geographically possible.

In the Arctic survival manual written by Vilhjalmur Stefansson for the US military in 1940, he refers to the 'Pole of Inaccessibility' or 'Ice Pole' as 'that spot or region of the Polar Sea which is most difficult to reach.' According to those calculations this Pole is located at N 82 50, W 160 00, only 120 miles from where we currently were.

Ron and I discussed alternative airports and began to check distances. Resolute Bay radio advised us that the weather was good in Eureka. When I put the coordinates into the GPS I found that it was six and a half hours away and that I only had six hours of fuel. Barrow was too far back, and even if we had the fuel, they were now completely fogged in again. Mould Bay, the Canadian High Arctic weather station on Prince Patrick Island, was my best shot. It was still solid overcast below us and I needed good weather to find the airstrip. The automatic weather report from Mould Bay indicated that the visibility was nine miles and the wind light. We tried to make a phone patch through to the station, but as it was the middle of the night, nobody answered.

Throughout the flight my aircraft had developed an annoying oil leak which began to obscure my windscreen. It didn't seem substantial enough to effect the engine just yet, but it made it difficult to see out, and was one additionally concerning factor. Luckily, the right hand windows were still fairly clear, so Donny could see clearly.

It was another four hours over the clouds towards a place I had never heard of before, Mould Bay. Fifty miles north of Prince Patrick Island we finally got a break in the clouds and could see the pack ice below us. I was greatly relieved that it would be possible to see a suitable landing place should the engine run out of fuel and quit. Eleven hours had passed with only clouds and as we neared the island, the sun shone brightly on the ice and the unworldly beauty of the Arctic was ours to behold again. One minute it is your beautiful friend, and the next a cold, deadly adversary. It all changes so quickly in the Arctic. Finding the runway in Mould Bay was a huge relief and after landing I noted that we had less than one hour of fuel remaining. I was reminded of Edmund Snow Carpenter's comment to me in Siberia in 1995 about traveling in the Arctic. 'The key to survival and success in the Arctic is to adapt quickly to changing situations. The ones who die are usually the ones who stick to a rigid program, ignoring the fact that the circumstances have changed.' Mr Carpenter spent years travelling the Arctic by dog sled with the Innuit and that bit of advice he gave me was somewhere deep in my memory throughout the flight.

chapter 3

rumblings of a return

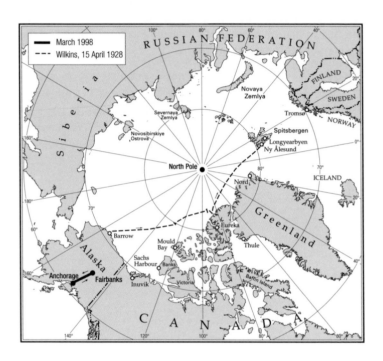

It wasn't quiet for long when I returned to Seoul. Shane was look-ing for a Lockheed Vega, the same airplane that Wilkins had flown on his long journey from Barrow to Spitsbergen in 1928. He soon found one in California, but it needed a lot of work. Ferdinand was seeking funding in Europe. Wilkins, following his return in 1927, was in much the same state. 'There was no profit to be made from the last Expedition and except for the sale of the planes there would be no money forthcoming.'

We had no planes to sell, so we started from zero. We couldn't expect Ferdinand to buy another half of an airplane of which he already owned half — although we did suggest it. Flying airplanes was very similar to organizing Everest expeditions, something I'd done more often than I cared to remember. The planned adventure may be a great one. You may be setting out to do something never accomplished before. But no one is going anywhere unless the money is raised. There was no use in talking about polishing the propellers and recalibrating a new GPS for the Pole until we had funding. An expedition ultimately relies on the skill of its adventurers. But to get anywhere near an adventure requires significant business acumen and a very large dose of entrepreneurial zeal. Luckily, Shane and Ferdinand had both these qualities.

Shane had also had time to reflect on how he had organised the expedition in 1997 and had come to many of the same conclusions as Wilkins.

> *From the beginning of arrangements for this year's flight I resolved to be my own business manager, workman, laborer, mechanic, and navigator. I did not want to be hampered with the worry of accommodating a staff of mechanics, correspondents and wireless men. Notwithstanding the fact that the newspaper men and wireless staff we had with us in 1927 were most efficient at their jobs, most amiable and likable companions, their presence added to our task far more than the publicity we received could probably benefit those of us who actually had to do the work in the field. Despite the dire need of financial help from newspaper sources, their correspondents and required revenue are an added responsibility and a scarcely justifiable hindrance to the commander of a scientific expedition.*

Shane certainly didn't want to become mechanic, but reducing the size of the team would allow us to concentrate solely on the flight. With Ron owning his plane, and Ferdinand and Shane owning the second, we had transport — the basis for the expedition was still there.

The Green Tortoise needed a complete overhaul, though. The reason for its rabid fuel consumption and spraying of oil had to be found and fixed. This had to be done by a professional Antonov mechanic, not the kind of person likely to be found anywhere near a Western Hemisphere airport. Shane and Ferdinand would have to spend time in Alaska, overseeing the work and doing test flights. A shake-down flight from Anchorage to Barrow was too late to fix anything major. They had to be on hand to fly the plane well in advance. As both lived in Germany, it wasn't a simple matter to make frequent flights to Anchorage. With a few notable exceptions, we'd had minimal support in 1997, many expenses being borne by the pilots and the team themselves. To try again may have been laudatory, but without substantial funds we'd wouldn't be able to make the preparations necessary for a serious attempt. Shane had completed a new set of budgets and it all added up to about a quarter of a million dollars to complete a flight that wouldn't last more than five days — weather permitting.

In September 1997 Shane, Ferdinand, Donny, David and I gathered in New York for a lecture at The Explorers Club. The photographs, David Hamlin's National Geographic video, and being together again renewed our enthusiasm. Flying was one thing, flying an Antonov over the Arctic was completely different. We'd become friends and we all wanted to try again. We shared rooms at the New York Yacht Club and hatched plans for a return on the backs of stationery better suited to sailing the world's oceans than flying over them. Shane's mother, Judy Stewart, also joined us. It was easy to see where Shane got his good-natured sense of humor that had prevailed right through the difficult decisions he'd faced earlier in the year. With the expedition team in tow on our rounds of New York, Judy slipped into our late-night dinner plans as easily as if she had been along on the expedition itself. I'd found that having strong family ties made expedition members more trustworthy when it came time to make the difficult and dangerous decisions that have to be taken on any worthwhile expedition. They were less likely to feel they had to prove something or do something foolish just to achieve their goal. You did what you could, then quite a bit more, but nothing outright stupid that was more likely to get you killed than get you where you wanted. With Shane making the key decisions, it was good to see he had a solid grounding and was used to being able to see our endeavors as part of a bigger picture — not a do-or-die scenario.

Ferdinand and I spent an extra day in the city, wandering in and out of art galleries and as it grew later, in and out of clubs. We'd spent time together on the expedition, but little of it alone. With just one extra day in New York, I wanted to make the most of it and found Ferdinand the ideal partner. He had a natural ability to get places and accomplish things in a relaxed manner that assumed success. On the expedition I'd been impressed with his ability to secure discounts on even the most academic of supplies, from engine oil to new window glass so our photographs would be crystal clear, by simply saying, 'We are an expedition, we are going to fly to the North Pole and we would like to ask for your help.' Nine times out of ten it worked.

We returned from New York with increased enthusiasm to find funding. A month went by, and then another. Ferdinand secured flights from Lufthansa so Shane and he could get to Anchorage and back, the first step in working on the planes. This gave us a good start. But the real money so we could actually get started on the mechanics wasn't forthcoming. It seemed more and more like a flight over the Arctic wasn't going to get off the ground. I also knew from my many previous expeditions that securing funds required three key things from a sponsor: trust, personal enthusiasm and business relevance, in that order. The first two of these rarely developed quickly and we needed funds in a hurry.

With no progress being made, Shane took off to join his father, Kim Lundgren, in the Indian Ocean on another leg of his round-the-world sail on their yacht *Metolius*. They were accompanied by Trevor Henderson, from Pembroke Capital in Ireland, an aircraft leasing and finance company. During their time together, Shane related tales of our flight, of Wilkins' own odyssey and of our interest in returning. 'I didn't try and sell Trevor on the idea,' said Shane. 'We actually spent only a short time talking about our 1997 expedition.'

Securing sponsorship is rarely a simple matter of someone writing a check. But with Trevor, the first two elements were in place — he had a long history with Shane and his family and an increasing personal enthusiasm. By convincing his colleagues at Pembroke Capital of the expedition's association with his company's activities, he was able to get us over our first major hurdle. His personal involvement and support was to evolve quickly from that of sponsor to team member to pilot as our expedition plans progressed. None of this was of course planned — but with just six people in two planes, everyone had to be prepared to fly.

Wilkins managed to sell the planes he'd used in 1927 and came up with a deposit for the Lockheed Vega. With additional support from his fuel suppliers, he was able to now equip the Vega with equipment dictated by the experience of two years of flying, crashes and rebuilds on his other airplanes. Whether it was 1928 or 1998, we had a fear of going down soon after landing with the massive increase in fuel we'd be hauling. Wilkins had a simple system to cope with that eventuality.

> To the two lower and two upper tanks were fitted half-inch plugs, on the bottoms of which were soldered strip-leaves that in their turn were attached to cables leading to the navigator's cabin. If need be these strips could be pulled off and the gasoline dumped before an emergency landing.

Our own system was a fat steel pipe extending straight through the bottom of the Antonov, with a cable leading up into the cockpit. The pilot simply had to reach down, give the cable a very solid pull and the auxiliary tank would dump its contents out in just a few minutes. It may not have been perfect, but it was dead simple, and given a little time, would keep us from having to crash-land with a ton of fuel riding on our backs.

Wilkins went a step further after his walk off the ice in 1927, remembering the leads of water they had skirted. 'A wooden, dural-shod runner was provided and made to fit the upper rear portion of the fuselage. In case of accident we could saw this section from the plane and use it as a canoe or a sled.' One of the world's most modern monoplanes of the time now also had a sled, or a canoe, as an integral part of its framework. With the Antonov's metal fuselage, contemplating getting any of it to float wasn't much of an option — we visited the local survival store and bought a pair of inflatable rubber rafts.

Wilkins had so many radio problems he was also determined to install a system more reliable than he had in years past.

Owing to the plane's design and wooden construction, we had high hopes of getting a perfect wireless installation. A shortwave built by Heintz & Kaufman had performed wonderfully well on a plane entered for the Dole flight. Its signals had been heard practically all over the world and gave us the sad details of the fate of William P. Erwin and A. M. Eichwaldt as they tail-spinned into the Pacific Ocean and to death.

It had been a great struggle to afford the extra thousand dollars for the wireless installation. But I deemed it worthy if for no other reason that it would — if it worked — give us an opportunity to send out our information as collected en route. Then, though we crashed halfway or in the water near Spitsbergen or failed to return, our work would not have been in vain.

... This year, after having consented to take it, I spared no expense to get the most efficient and reliable apparatus available but insisted that it be placed so that it would not interfere with the performance of the plane.

It was a philosophy that was to stand Wilkins in good stead — and one that Shane adopted as well. In the items we needed for the flight that were essential to our success, he didn't compromise. The first and most important element was to get the engine looked at. For that it was back to the Antonov factory, now in Poland, to fly over a Polish mechanic and put him to work on the plane.

It also gave Ron a chance to work closely with both Shane and Ferdinand. If flying the Antonov took one set of unique skills, flying it in the Arctic required an additional volume of knowledge which only experience working on and flying the plane would provide. Wilkins had a host of tricks as well, an endless amount of little extra things he did. In the temperatures in the Arctic, a mistake would quickly end any journey. In most climates, you never have to even consider using an engine cover, yet Wilkins had found he needed two to keep his engine protected.

> The reason for the two covers being that if only a canvas cover was available it might not be sufficient in a high wind; if only a water and wind-proof cover was provided the hoar-frost would form thickly on the inside of the cover during the time the engine was heating up and later melting would run down over the engine or sticking to the canvas make heavier weight to carry in the plane. With the double covering, one of canvas and one of balloon cloth, no hoar-frost to speak of formed.

On first arriving in Barrow in 1997, Ron had directed me in placing our own engine cover over the plane and on how to secure the multiple straps by looping one through the next without tying any knots. Knots freeze up quickly in the Arctic, and the engine cover would have become as tightly bound as steel cables after a storm, requiring a complete severing of all the straps and the resulting ruin of the cover if it were tied in knots. It was the simplest of techniques, but done wrongly it would ground us as quickly and simply as a major mistake.

While Wilkins had enough funding to cover the basics, additional support was beginning to fade. There were many who were beginning to doubt he'd actually be able to make the crossing. In summing up his ongoing battle for support from Bob Lavary, manager of the Fairbanks Airplane Corporation, he says:

> The first year when we had come with a glare of great publicity and were not short of funds we were loaned gratis a flying field and hangar. Last year, with four machines and equal time spent there but not much trouble, he thought it necessary for us to recompense them for the use of conveniences afforded, but this year, when I was depending upon my own resources and could least afford to pay, had only one machine and would remain but three weeks instead of three months, he demanded three times as much as we had paid before. So it goes! Unto him that hath much shall be given, but to him that hath little much shall be charged.

In March, Shane was back in Anchorage, completing a test flight to Fairbanks and back to Anchorage. All worked perfectly and he phoned to say everything was on schedule. I booked my flight from Seoul to Anchorage — one-way, I told Shane. I wanted to return home only after going over the top of the world.

I was battling a seven-hour overnight flight and the more debilitating seven-hour time change, so my friend, Dr Bill Hammel, prescribed a day of skiing as soon as I hit Anchorage. This had nothing to do with flying, but after a week of packing, making notes, cleaning lenses and testing film, a mental break seemed like a very good idea. With a pair of fat skis and two feet of new snow, it left me in little doubt that I had left the pollution and congestion of Seoul behind. That night we met for dinner with Martin Cray and Laura Thorpe. Martin had approved our sponsorship at GCI, an Alaskan telecommunications company, and I would be working directly with Laura, sending back text and images during our flight. Laura oversaw a distant-learning program that linked Alaskan schools to the Net, to provide the more isolated schools with the most up-to-date information to be used in the classroom. While Wilkins had invested heavily in radio, it was now possible to download both text and images from virtually anywhere and have them on the website minutes after they had arrived. The website contained information on our previous year's flight, team member profiles and the history on the Antonovs themselves, as well as linking into weather sites and The Explorers Club website we'd used in 1997. Backed up with daily updates and photographs, schoolchildren in Alaska, or anywhere in the world could sit down and read first hand about our expedition as it was happening.

By pure coincidence, I had arrived on the weekend of the world extreme ski championships in the Chugach mountains above Valdez. Bill Hammel and I left the following evening, driving towards the Alaska interior. At 11 pm over the mountains to the north, the Northern Lights began a visual dance before our eyes, dark green translucent colors floating along the ridge. For the next two days we'd be into helicopters, whisked up to the top of ridges and sent down steep chutes and off faces that gently avalanched around us as we skied down through cliffs and over steep bands of loose, neck-deep powder. The turns were done with a gentle lift of the skis, a minimal pressure to point them downhill and then a weightless slide as the body rode up out of the snow and swiveled to drop weightlessly straight down into another turn. In 1997 I'd been painting the Antonov and stuffing olives in jars while fighting off falling asleep. This was much better training. By the time I returned from the weekend I was ready to fly.

Shane and Ferdinand arrived rested from their own holidays and eager to head north. Shane had been in the Caribbean and we told him his photo was better suited to www.tan.com than to a site about a North Pole expedition. Gone were the endless problems of the year before and the accompanying stress. I met Trevor Henderson for the first time in the hangar helping to put logos on the plane. He was our only new addition to the team and his quiet confidence, though he was never shy of venturing an opinion, rested easily with the other members.

As I had to load new software on my computer, we went together to Laura's office, where the discussion soon moved from communications to our flight and the new survival suit I'd been issued that day.

'Do you know how to put it on?' Laura asked us. 'Follow the directions,' I ventured, having tried that the year before and finding that I had eventually managed to get into it.

'I use to teach cold-water near-drowning classes for the US Fish and Wildlife Service in Fairbanks to groups of summer field technicians before going into the wilds of Alaska,' Laura said. 'Do you want to know how to do it right?' Trevor and I were only too happy to take instruction.

'First, make sure it is packed right. Take it out and lay it flat, then roll it up. Don't stuff or fold it. You want to be able to grab the bottom of the bag, pull back sharply and have the suit fall out and unroll itself. That will work on the ground or the water.

'Next, sit down in the center of it,' and Laura sat down on the floor to demonstrate. She was obviously a teacher. If she taught us how to put on a survival suit, we were going to know how to do it right!

'You sit down because if you are on a boat or your plane is rocking, you don't want to fall over. Okay, now you put your feet in. Wear lots of socks — lots of clothes, because it will all help keep you warm. Slide all the way down so your feet reach the bottom. Then, put your weaker arm in the suit, probably your left if you are right-handed. Then use your other hand to reach back and pull the hood up over your head. Then slide your strong arm in and zip it right up to the top. Oh yes, and you should have a hat on too. Lots of insulation.

'Fifty seconds, that's how long it should take you. And you do it the same way in the water, if you have to jump out and you don't have it on. But you should have it on. They bring people in every year. The ones in survival suits are alive. The ones without them, dead. So wear it when you go over the water.

'We used to go out in Kaktovik, put on our suits and jump in the water for an hour as part of our course. The sea water is super-cooled, below freezing, just 30 degrees. Potentially, the suit could keep you alive for quite a while, maybe a few days if you are dressed right.'

I'd thought perhaps the survival suit was pretty close to jumping into a body bag to save someone the trouble later, but this gave me far more confidence. Trevor and I ran over the steps, very basic but not necessarily obvious. Maybe it would be possible to crash into the Arctic ocean and survive? At least now I was ready to at least give it a try as opposed to giving up.

We returned to the hangar — and bad news. Something was wrong with one of Ron's cylinders and the jug had to be pulled. It would take at least a day to fix. Rodney Stayrook went to work with two assistants and 14 hours later it was done. The piston rings had been installed the wrong way around and had worked for a while, but eventually began spitting oil in all the wrong directions. Rodney had spent a lot of time working on both of our Antonovs and when I asked him the obvious question, 'What's different about working on an Antonov?' he was more than ready with his response.

'Everything,' Rodney said. 'Even the two Antonovs are different in many respects.' He was speaking with the experience of someone who had been an airplane mechanic for 20 years, so I didn't hold out much hope getting anything major fixed en route if it went wrong. One of our two major problems the previous year, the leaking oil that had sprayed out and covered the windshield, had been discovered by Ferdinand almost by mistake. A single screw had been put in on a ring gasket the wrong way. Ferdinand noticed that the screw wasn't tightening properly and with his experience working on his Harley Davidson, intuitively felt that something wasn't right. He checked it with Ron and they realized that had been the whole reason for the oil leak that had so worried us. With a simple realignment, it was fixed. I wondered how many other screws were loose, how many itsy-bitsy parts hidden away that all had to perform perfectly for hours on end. I didn't think too much about this.

In the evenings we'd retreat to Mark and Susan Lutz's house for big home-cooked meals, a glass of wine and a review of the day. Their historic house, with a few extra bedrooms for guests, had become our Anchorage expedition headquarters. Situated right next to Bill Hammel's house and just minutes from town, it was the perfect base to come home to, jump in the hot tub and have a cold beer — a welcome relief from the customary hotels we were all so accustomed to. Every morning we'd be up early and into the dining room, sipping orange juice and eating our way through steaming omelets and sausages, pancakes ladled with maple syrup and bacon, with cups of strong coffee to launch us into the day. With all but Ron and Donny staying within fifty feet of one another — and they often joined us for breakfast — it was easy to keep the team moving in one direction. There was always a list a mile long of tiny things that needed to be completed, all of which had to be done and all of which took an hour or two.

One morning we stopped by the office of Trent Carbaugh from Petro Star, who was again supplying us with all our petrol while we were in Alaska. David Hamlin called there from New York to brief me on the shots he wanted for a follow-up video for National Geographic, to link into his work in 1997. Trent passed on a Petro Star jacket that, being black, had quickly turned into the jacket of choice for the team. It showed none of the oil that inevitably dripped off the Antonov and was just the right weight for the blasts of Arctic air that occasionally whistled through the cabin. As Wilkins had found, the innumerable acts of kindness we were shown, from help with the planes, a bit of advice or an extra item of equipment, popped up when they were most needed and often least expected. We were also to meet a number of Alaska'a aviation pioneers who had gone on to make real Wilkins' dream of opening up the Arctic as the fastest way between the northern continents. Trevor relates meeting one of these men almost by chance.

'A number of our team visited the Alaska Aviation Heritage Museum in Anchorage. Whilst Shane was doing an interview for one of the local TV channels, I was viewing several artifacts from the flights of famous Alaskan aviators, including Wilkins and Eielson. I fell into conversation with an older, bearded man who spoke quietly with a distinctive Scandinavian accent. We discussed our planned flight over the Pole, our preparations and some general navigational and meteorological matters. He spoke a little about his own experiences and his wife's achievements.

'It emerged that he was Nils Pedersen, who in the mid-1960s planned and navigated Scandinavian Air Services' pioneering commercial flights over the polar regions, connecting Scandinavia with the USA. His wife, under his tutelage, was the first woman to fly to the Pole.

'Some days later, when both Polar One and Polar Two stood out on the tarmac at Anchorage International an hour or so before departure, the slight figure of Nils Pedersen approached me. We chatted for a couple of minutes. Then as he turned to leave he looked at me very directly and said, "Trevor, I know you will succeed."'

Wilkins had to put the Vega together on his arrival in Fairbanks, but found even with his infinitely smaller team, this was completed with little trouble. 'Because of the simplicity of the arrangements this year we were required to hire only two men to help us assemble the machine in Fairbanks and this work was done in less than three days.'

The day before we were set to leave, Ron's wife Karin, skiing at Aleyeska, broke her leg and was put in hospital. Should we wait a few more days? It was up to Ron and after checking with Karin, he decided she would be okay and we could proceed with our plans. We wanted to leave as soon as we could, because later in the year the sea fog that had delayed us so much last year would begin rolling in. This, as well as the bigger weather picture, seemed to be pretty much unchanged in 70 years and had figured heavily in Wilkins' planning.

> *I had planned to leave Fairbanks any time after the middle of March and before the first of April. Alaskan Arctic meteorological records and my own experience show that some time between the middle of March and the first week in April there occurs a period of bad weather at Point Barrow. Last year, as has been told, we tried to take advantage of those storm conditions. This year our course lay in another direction and it was my hope to be able to take advantage of the fine period that usually follows the few days of storm. We would be glad if this clear calm period would not occur until after the fifth of April, when the sun would be above the horizon throughout the whole period of the flight.*

By Thursday morning we were all set. Ron's engine had been run up and tested and the faulty cylinder was working fine. The fuel truck came by and we filled the tanks. Even though we were going to Fairbanks and then onto Barrow if time allowed, it was still a long journey over uninhabited areas. It wasn't quite as desolate as in Wilkins' day, but I still doubted that there was anybody living on the North Slope this time of year.

> *With our spares, equipment and food to last thirty days' travel over mountains or tundra, in case we should be forced down on the way to Barrow, we had quite a load. It was just as pertinent to be well prepared on that trip for an emergency landing as for the trip*

over the Arctic sea ice. It would be almost as difficult to reach some
habitation as it would from the Arctic ice.

Shane stored the box of Antonov parts back in Bill's basement and we picked up our final load of duffel bags. A very civilized cart towed the Antonovs out of the hangar and onto the tarmac. In these surroundings the Antonovs looked out of place, hulking next to the hangar, flanked by sleek corporate jets. A TV crew arrived for a last interview and photographers milled around the propellers. Finally the way was cleared and Ron and Shane started up. We'd named Shane and Ferdinand's plane Polar One and Ron's plane Polar Two for our flight this year. The paint job on Polar One was so much brighter, the red star replaced by a Pembroke Capital Polar Bear, that the hulking Green Tortoise had been virtually reborn.

In September 1997 I joined my father in the middle of the Indian Ocean on an island called Cocos Keeling. He was sailing around the world and invited me to accompany him for the leg across to Africa. The Pole was a million miles away, literally and figuratively, and I didn't think that the funds would be forthcoming for another attempt.

Arriving in the Seychelles, we met family friends Trevor and Daphne Henderson from Ireland. During a long lunch on Round Island I told the story of the polar flight attempt. I was not actually selling the project, but Trevor was mesmerized. A few weeks later I received an e-mail from Trevor asking if there was the possibility for Pembroke Capital to sponsor another polar flight. I thought that if I sent him a budget and he looked at the cost it would be the end of the idea. Almost immediately, I received another message from Trevor to come to Dublin and discuss the project. Pembroke wanted to back another attempt.

Like Wilkins, I feel that preparation is the key to success. With Pembroke's commitment to proceed I began to organize the logistics. During the long cold month of February in Alaska, Antonov N61SL was parked inside a warm corporate jet hangar, compliments of Signature Aviation in Anchorage. The faded green biplane looked like an old Land Rover next to a shiny four-engine Jet Star.

I arranged for Jan Dziedzic, a mechanic from the Antonov factory in Poland, to come to Alaska with a few boxes of spare parts. Jan was recommended to me by Waldemar Miszkurka, the chief of the Antonov An-2 factory in Poland. I had never met Jan before and he spoke no English, but he proved to be a decidedly hard and competent worker. On his previous job he had been sent to Iran for seven months to repair fifty Antonovs all parked out in the desert. Seven months without a beer after work! He found Alaska more to his liking. Ron and I introduced him to some of the cultural highlights of Anchorage such as female boxing, the Great Alaska Bush Company and Chilkoot Charlies. Jan worked fourteen-hour days for two weeks, including weekends.

After the frustration and danger which forced us to divert during the 1997 polar flight, my top priority was to have the aircraft thoroughly tuned and inspected. With Ron supervising the engine work, I coordinated the equipment list, logistics, permissions and began the task of repainting the aircraft. Spraying the paint was forbidden in the hangar, and it took ten days of hand rolling and brushing. Fortunately I met Rodney Stayrook who joined me and whose keenness to work and good cheer made this job endurable. The polyurethane paint we used was very hard on the lungs and skin, and every piece of clothing I had in Alaska soon had green or gray paint on it.

Meanwhile Jan completed a carburetor replacement, cylinder inspection, fuel and oil line replacement, propeller removal and inspection, seal replacement, and as a complete structural inspection. It was a huge amount of work but we could measure our progress daily. It was very rewarding when on 14 February we rolled the freshly painted plane out of the hangar and into the bright sunlight. When we tested the engine it ran like a top and I'll never forget the proud smile on Jan's face.

Jan went home to Poland and I went back to Berlin to work. Ron ferried the aircraft to Merrill Field using his cellular phone to talk to the tower as the radios were broken. The extensive radio and instrument revision and installation was begun at Northern Lights Avionics. First and foremost, I wanted a way to be able to measure the fuel burn very accurately. By having an exhaust gas temperature gage (EGT) and a special fuel flow meter installed this would be possible. The Russian instruments on the panel were disorienting and I wanted to put in an interface which I was used to. The artificial horizon on a Russian plane tips the opposite direction, and is very confusing if you are flying in clouds or whiteout. I also wanted an airspeed indicator that read knots not kilometers, as well as an altimeter that read altitude in feet and not meters.

We needed radios that were reliable for communication that had the capability to make an instrument approach if necessary. Last year I had none of this and the margin of safety was thin.

To do this flight, to take these risks, I wanted equipment that I knew and that I could trust. I bought the best high frequency radio, the only way to communicate to the outside world from the High Arctic regions. The tuner and antennae coupling on these units is tricky, and I wanted the best people to work on it and test it. I heard of another Arctic flight that installed their HF hastily, and it didn't work during the entire flight. This piece of equipment could save your life and was the only way to receive weather updates en route.

When I left Anchorage, Father Anderson Bakewell, a mentor of mine in exploration, sent the following message.

'"Toil and pleasure, in their natures opposite, are yet linked together in a kind of necessary connection." (Translated from Livy's Latin poems.)
'Shane if you want the pleasure of exploration you've got to toil to keep that radial rumbling.'

Father Bakewell is 83 now and an emeritus member of The Explorers Club.

Returning to Anchorage in March I spent a week gaining flight permissions from the FAA. Then I updated and replaced much of our emergency equipment. Ferdinand joined me in the middle of the month and we set out with Ron on a series of test flights. We tested our new fuel flow meter, and recorded power settings and fuel burns at various altitudes and speeds. We tested our navigational equipment. We flew to Mount McKinley, on to Fairbanks and returned to Anchorage, as well as making many short local test flights. It was a great exercise in building confidence and I felt that the aircraft was now ready for the expedition.

We rolled back into the corporate jet hangar in Anchorage to attach sponsor logos. On 16 March, GCI of Alaska, who produced an educational website on the expedition, threw a reception at the Aviation Heritage Museum as an Alaskan send-off. I was presented with a copy of the original fur flying parka that Ben Eielson wore seventy years ago.

On 18 March we were invited to New York where Pembroke and Rolex had organized a reception at The Explorers Club. It was a great evening during which I was presented with the Club flag #61 by President Fred McLaren. Flag #7, my old companion, was now retired and hung on the wall next to Thor Heyerdahl's *Kon Tiki* flag. It was a great honor to carry it on its last expedition. I requested flag #61 as this is my birth year, as well as the number on the aircraft. Dr McLaren also pointed out that 6 + 1 = 7! There was a great deal of social activity in both Anchorage and New York and I was ready for a short rest to prepare charts, relax and think about the flight.

During this time I had a small accident and dislocated my right shoulder. I had to laugh as I thought of Wilkins with his broken arm in 1926, and that he didn't want to tell anyone about it. I too would keep the shoulder business quiet — I planned to depart Anchorage on 7 April.

chapteR 4

' ... heaDing for his Doom'

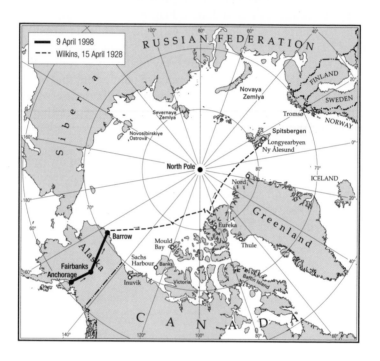

The wind changed at the last minute at Anchorage International Airport. So we set off, a twin set of waddling Antonovs, up one runway and down another, Polar Two tailing Polar One like two misfit schoolchildren. To corner, the tail wheel was turned and brakes applied, which made a huge whooshing sound like the air brakes of a big truck. I suspect the Russian technology is much the same. We were cleared for a flight of two, taking off one just behind the other on opposite sides of the center line.

In 1997 there had been so much time spent in Anchorage preparing for the journey that final lift-off was more a release from

Shane piloting the Green Tortoise on our ill-fated 1997 attempt to reach the Pole.

Pancake ice along the shoreline of Spitsbergen just outside Ny-Alesund, launching point for the historic Amundsen, Byrd and Nobile flights of the late twenties.

Trevor, an evening's work done in the minus 16°F temperatures of America's most northern point, departs the Barrow airport.

Dawn in Barrow, Alaska — on the way to breakfast a streak of refracted light circled the sun, shooting straight into the Antonovs parked alongside the runway.

As we looked straight down from the cockpit, the Antonov's balloon tire floats along over the Arctic ice 5,000 feet below.

the problems we'd faced than excitement at what lay ahead. This year, everything seemed so well organized, almost casual. Then, 100 feet off the ground, Polar One slid over in front of Polar Two, we were caught in its slipstream and suddenly we were rolling violently sideways and were flying along at a 45° angle to the ground. Ron stood on the rudder and straightened us out, but not before a quick curse. It was apparent we needed some better communication on formation flying. It also woke everybody up. The huge prop on the Antonov creates a massive slipstream that even a half mile back can practically spin a following small plane into rolls.

Escaping the city below took only minutes. Eielson's initial love affair with Alaskan flying was easily felt, the expansiveness that can only be explored from the air, the pure practicality of getting across the long distances and hopping into settlements in hours instead of days. Alaska is too large and remote to drive; jets are overkill and very limited in where they land. A small plane fits Alaska like a naturally evolved animal fits its home environment.

I hadn't been for a flight in the Antonov in a year, but it was easy to settle back in, stowing away cameras in familiar holes, hanging jackets off the coat-rack, tucking film and tapes onto tiny shelves. In the cockpit, the upgrades in equipment blinked back. The fuel flow monitoring gauge gave flow in tenths of a gallon per hour. We could still look through the sight gauge in the auxiliary tank, but it was more reassuring to know exactly how much was being burned at a given time, as opposed to seeing it slopping out the bottom of the tank, measuring it after the fact.

Shortly after takeoff Ferdinand took over the controls and set a direct course for Fairbanks. Ron pulled out the latest and one of the more welcome equipment upgrades, a portable CD player, loaded up some Tchaikovsky and soon the refined notes drifted through our headsets, the rumble of the engine fading into the background as we purred northward.

The forests below were dotted with dark trees and snowy

meadows. Lakes close to Anchorage were frozen fast. Ploughed through the snow over the ice were roads leading from one house to the next, a winter transportation system that come summer would be replaced by speedboats. Tiny roads then wove off into the forest and snaked over hills to the next homestead. Flying around Alaska, Wilkins took the first aerial footage of the state, giving people their only real view of the extent of the area they were traversing. Having trained as a cameraman and covering the Balkan War, it was just one more skill he put to use while navigating, bringing back the first moving images from the far north.

Halfway to Fairbanks we had our first good omen — ground-speed was touching 140 knots at times, a good 40 more than we usually obtained. Outside, a strong tail wind was pushing us along so quickly that the rocky ride through Windy Pass we had the previous year was so short it was barely noticeable, the Antonov being blown over the mountains and out into the plains around Fairbanks in just a few minutes. We came in sight of Fairbanks just two hours after leaving Anchorage, so quickly I was still juggling cameras to get the footage we required and finishing a half-eaten apple.

On Wilkins' arrival in 1928:

> The weather was still warm when we reached Fairbanks. The water dripped from the roofs of houses. The streets were ankle deep in slush, making conditions extraordinary. A year ago on that date we had been assembling our machines in temperatures of forty-eight and fifty below zero Fahrenheit.

Our own stop, compared to the previous year's work on minor repairs and an overnight at the hotel, was even more efficacious. We taxied to a halt, the fuel truck rolled out, Ferdy and Donny were up on the wings, fuel was poured in, oil checked and we were ready to continue north. Shane had been given a copy of the coat that Eielson had worn on his flights and he slipped into it to pose next to the plane. 'Boy, this is warm,' he said just a few minutes later. It had no zipper, no ties, no flaps and was simply, like the original, a reindeer skin wrapped in a circle and sewn tight with a hood attached. It was designed in the days when a man put something warm on in the fall and didn't take it off until spring. Shane was stuck when he tried to take it off. Eventually Trevor grabbed the hood, and by pulling hard and with the effect of a man dragging on the antlers of distraught reindeer, Shane managed to extract himself from the heavy jacket. It was a magnificent coat, but after putting it on and taking it off on our various stops, he was soon wishing the modern version had a zipper or some Velcro flaps attached.

A few journalists were escorted out onto the runway, photographs were snapped, Shane answered a few quick questions and we were all back on board. Having spent so much of my life on commercial airlines, I found a simple delight in filming our start-ups, the engine coming to life with a huge explosion of sound. Then I would rush back and pull the steps up, which were simply hooked on below the back door. The prop wash was so strong it practically blew me over as I reached the side of the plane; I'd leap inside and swing the door shut, making sure the latch was secure, and drop the bit of elastic band over it. Then I'd crawl forward, squeeze around the auxiliary tank and give the thumbs-up to the pilot that all was secure.

Wilkins did his final engine tests here on the Lockheed Vega, determining, 'Curves plotted after trials for engine speed and gas consumption showed that for the best air speed throughout our total journey we should run the engine between sixteen hundred and seventeen-fifty revolutions.' Ron's many hours in the air and Shane's test flight had determined a curve that matched manifold pressure and rpm's, figures that translated to '17 and 7' (1,700 rpm and 7 manifold pressure), the ideal setting once we were well underway, then slowly dropping back the power until the Antonov just chugged along, barely sipping fuel for the final hours of our longer journeys. This year we were also following Wilkins' dictum on the weather to try and find a more suitable weather window to fly out of Barrow.

During all our visits to Anchorage, and with Ron living there, we had made many new friends and enjoyed more than the occasional evening in the restaurants and bars. Even after an 18-hour day we would feel compelled to relax before dropping into bed. With my long friendship with my climbing partner Bill Hammel and his companion Elise Hsieh, and with Ferdinand, Trevor and Shane immediately next door at Mark and Susan Lutz's bed-and-breakfast, we could always be ensured a warm welcome no matter what the hour. Finally getting out of town in 1997, and then making a quick departure in 1998, we left the lure of the socializing that we all enjoyed behind. In the backs of our minds, we knew it would be a dangerous journey — though hopefully our friends were not quite of the same mind as Eielson when Wilkins wrote:

> *There was one very real reason for wanting to reach Barrow a few days before the flight. Eielson, who is Alaska's popular hero, has in Fairbanks as everywhere, many friends. Many of them, I know, thought that he was heading for his doom. They admired his pluck and determined that he should have a good time before he departed. His round of social obligations gave him no rest.*

Wilkins had to get Eielson out of town just so he could get a good night's sleep! Our two journeys separated by seventy years and just a few days now meshed so closely, that occasionally even our personal experiences were mirror images of the other:

> *On the morning of March nineteenth everything seemed favorable. We did not leave a stone unturned in preparation for a successful takeoff.*
> *… One hundred and thirty more gallons of gas and ten gallons of oil were filled into the tanks. With our spares, equipment and food to last thirty days over mountain or tundra, in case we should be forced down on the way to Barrow, we had quite a load.*
> *… From the start it was evident we were going to get off and at the end of the runway we left the snow as smoothly as from a concrete runway. Without more ado we headed on our course for Barrow.*

With quiet confidence we headed north in the air footprints of Wilkins and Eielson. The White Mountains rose up in front of us, but the strong tail wind and good weather persisted and we climbed higher than the previous year, taking a more direct course as we cleared the mountains with plenty of room to spare. The trees faded as we flew north, only dark patches of scrub in the river valleys persisting. I began to feel the cold and suddenly remembered the cabin heater, a three-inch round hose that fed around the engine and straight into the cabin, producing a gushing blast of hot air just behind the cockpit a few inches above the floor. Aimee Moore, a friend of Donny's who was riding with us to Barrow, traded places with Ferdinand and took the controls as we flew out of the White Mountains and towards the Yukon river. A helicopter pilot who herds reindeer as a profession, Aimee had no trouble adapting to the Antonov and was soon completely at home in the cockpit. I made sure to get her photo for our website to help allay the masochistic image of our hardy all-male crew.

The Yukon river is so broad and expansive it is like a moving sea set between banks of land. Completely iced over, it stands out from the fading forests as it loops across the wide plain between the White Mountains and the Brooks range. In the early days of exploration, it was the natural gateway to the northern regions of Alaska. Open only a few months every summer to boats, the balance of the year it was used as an icy dogsled highway into the interior. Smaller rivers radiate off, lazy twisting brushstrokes of white ice extending towards the foothills, disappearing into the valleys of the mountains. Rivers also afford pilots a natural landing strip: 'Eielson, with his usual care, swung to follow a river valley which would afford a safe landing field if necessary.'

The Yukon river faded behind us and we flew towards the Brooks range, a remote but immense range extending across the breadth of northern Alaska. The range rose east and west of us as far as we could see. In the early evening sunset, the western faces were blazing white in direct light; the eastern faces were already dark in shadow, muted and cold.

From the Brooks range we dropped out onto the North Slope, a seemingly endless expanse of white, turning gently pink and purple in the slanting sun. Our ground speed was still upward of 130 knots, a near rocket-like velocity in an Antonov; surprisingly soon we had crossed over the snow and the distinct jumbled line of ice marking the Arctic Ocean coast appeared on the horizon. As it had for Wilkins, this opened our minds to our real destination over the ice. 'My gaze was fixed toward the North and over the distant Arctic ice. I wondered what it had in store for us and dreamed many dreams.' After two years of failure, Wilkins must have known this was probably his last chance to make the journey to Spitsbergen. His support had shrunk to a point where he was surviving by selling the previous year's airplanes to fund the next year's journey and Eielson's friends were buying him just one more supper, as it could well be his last.

Ron took over the controls and we did a long slow circle around Barrow in the fading light. For an outsider, Barrow doesn't look like a place for humanity to inhabit. As we flew down off the North Slope, the tiny dark houses and solid buildings looked like square rocks dropped from a great height and embedded in the ice. The low angle of the sun cast shadows far longer than the buildings, distorting their real size. Telling which was building and which shadow from the air made it difficult to see the town as other than a hazy representation of skyscrapers laid sideways on the snow. The houses are all snuggled up next to the sea from which the village's livelihood traditionally came. Just in front of the final row of houses, the Arctic Ocean starts, a jumbled mass of ice blocks and pressure ridges forced up into strangely shaped towers. Beyond the few miles along the coast where the town lies, the beach, represented by a smooth mass of snow running into a jumbled mass of ice, weaves and twists off into the mist.

Our planes criss-crossed over the ice, Polar One rising up against the light of the sky and then sliding back below us to flit over the dark shadow of the ice. The sun shone in a long glare of dull yellow. We circled, lined up on the broad runway and dropped once again into Barrow.

> It was good to be back again. Barrow had become a second home — a spring residence for us during the last three years. The principal news was that the schoolhouse had burned down early one morning shortly after the New Year.

110

In 1997 I'd stepped off the plane and been surprised at the cold — this year I was ready for it, and it was warmer anyway, by 5°, just 16° below zero Fahrenheit. Barrow however was not a place with particularly fond memories. Getting stuck in the sea fog the previous year for five days made us all cautious. This year, however, we had a better introduction, as Donny was building a terminal for his soon-to-be-launched air service and we could pull up right in front, hook up our extension cords, throw the engine covers on and the planes were set for the night. We were also met by Laura Thorpe, who had flown up from Anchorage early that morning, so we simply had to pile into a big van and were taken off to the familiar Sam & Lee's for dinner. Trevor and I made sure nearly everything on the menu was ordered and then eaten, then it was back to a newly built hotel. Shane, Ferdinand, Laura and I gathered for the obligatory single malt while I compiled the day's log for Laura to drop onto the website and downloaded photographs from the digital camera. The camera held a computer disk, which in turn held 28 photographs. They were not of the highest resolution, but looked fine on our website and the disk allowed them to be instantly converted and loaded onto my computer and then sent downline to Laura. The ability to tell our story on the Internet allowed near-immediate coverage of our journey, but it seemed a child's fascination with flight had preceded us:

> The machine became the center of the children's playground. Around and about they ran and chased each other; dodged beneath the tail pieces and beneath the landing gear. One day we were alarmed by the story that reached us as we sat at the Trading Post. 'That crazy Eskimo boy took a gun and shot into the wing of your plane,' we were told. We hastened out to see what damage might have been done and were mightily relieved to find that the 'crazy' Eskimo was a little fellow eight or nine years old who had amused himself by shooting at the wing with a small sling and some pellets. The missiles had scarcely dented the woodwork, but as we investigated I thought what a fine story had been spoiled in the making: Eskimo, Mistaking Airplane for Evil Spirit, Brings Down Wilkins and Eielson with a Discharge from His Gun would have made a splendid headline for the sensational press.

After a 5.30 am start, we finally made it to bed at 1.30 am. A few hours later Ron was up and we were off for an early morning breakfast back at Sam & Lee's. The morning air was cold but strangely heavy. A huge streak of colored light surrounded the sun, with pinpoint bright starbursts at the 4 axis. As we passed the end of a long straight street leading to the east, the streak rose high in the sky to the side of the sun, casting a deep yellow which turned to red on the sun side of the circle. The air was thick, but not with fog, mist or cloud — just a thickness of ice crystals, a by-product of the intense cold. The light radiated through the town like bright twilight that wasn't sure whether the sun should be rising or falling in the sky. Sam & Lee's was silent, the door still locked, so we went next to the control tower and Ron looked over the weather for Barrow, Inuvik, Eureka and Resolute Bay.

There was a storm off the coast of Alaska, a big low slowly moving our way, but it was still a long way out. Where we were headed was clear, or close to it. 'We'll want to get out today, but probably better this afternoon,' said Ron. He commented that when he had been working as a commercial pilot, he'd gotten twice as much air time in by the simplest and most reliable method of weather forecasting, 'I just got up early every morning, no matter what the forecast said, and if it looked good, then I flew.'

We retreated back to Sam & Lee's, joining the others in a more civilized start to the day with French toast, eggs, bacon and coffee. The combination of hot and cold temperatures, long flights and little sleep certainly never seemed to hurt any of our appetites.

We had fully packed our planes with all our equipment in Anchorage, but for Wilkins, Barrow was a chance to finalize their own equipment. From his earlier years of traveling over the ice he had a ground-based adventurer's approach to the flight: if for any reason they couldn't fly there, they would just land and walk. Eielson had discovered the value of Wilkins' experience and his choice of equipment the year before when they had walked off

the ice, even throwing out his more modern equipment and re-
verting to reindeer- and seal-skin clothing, adapting the techniques that had kept the Eskimos alive in the Arctic for centuries.
Wilkins was very detailed in his planning, showing a depth of
experience that in reading makes you realize that his equipment
— why it was included and just how to use it — was an indication of the depth of his approach and eventual success. During
their three weeks in Barrow, Wilkins detailed their preparations.

> *My time was fully occupied. There were many things for me to do.
> First, our Arctic clothing had to be carefully inspected and repaired.
> Eielson needed a new fur shirt and so did I. Mrs. Brower, a most
> careful and skillful seamstress, undertook to make these for us, but
> first the deerskins had to be scraped by other women. Snow shirts
> and snow trousers — coverings for our fur garments — were to be
> made from the ongee silk I had brought with me. Ongee or some
> other good quality of hard-woven silk I find best for use as outer
> garments in the Arctic. Snow does not stick to silk as it does to
> cotton and silk does not absorb moisture as readily as cotton. It is
> partly wind-proof yet sufficiently porous to allow the hoar-frost to
> form on the outside rather than the inside, as it does on any type of
> rubberized or wind-proof material. Silk wears well, serves well
> and is well worth the additional initial cost.*

I'd discovered several years previous while climbing in Antarctica that in extreme cold, around –30°F and below, some of the
newest waterproof/breathable fabrics are rendered virtually useless. My state-of-the-art gaiters, come the end of a long day, would
be encased with a ring of ice rising from my ankle to my knee, as
if my leg had been fitted with an ice cast. Their normal ability to
release moisture didn't work, as it was so cold in the outer layers
of my clothing that any moisture soon turned to ice before it could
be released. I'd found that using tightly woven cotton actually
proved to work better — and if I'd known of Wilkins then, would
probably have had a set of silk windproofs made.

> *Our sealskin boots, two pairs with hair inside, suitable for cold
> weather, and two pairs of high waterproof boots were oiled, rubbed
> and made to fit by the younger women. We carried many pairs of*

insoles made of gunnysack in strips and proved to make good pads for the feet and we each had four pairs of special woolen socks made and presented to us by the Woolen Mills of Detroit. These are the most valuable of the kind I have ever used in the Arctic.

We each had a pair of Steger Mukluks, made of moosehide in the foot, with a thick rubber sole, and with canvas tops that went to just below our knees. With a number of pairs of socks, changed frequently, they were very warm and comfy, like a pair of over-sized non-slip garden slippers. They also looked the part, moosehide thongs laced up to our knees, which none of us minded. Shane had also brought along a pair of climbing double boots, slipping off the outers when he flew so he could feel the rudder pedals, while he was also able to quickly step into the plastic outer shells when he stepped off the plane. It is probably a smaller market than for expedition double boots, but the Arctic flying double boot has yet to be developed, and will probably sell all of ten pairs a year, a product we will be waiting for.

We each had a pair of fur and one pair of sealskin trousers and a double fur shirt or parka. We had two pairs of fur mittens each, a woolen pair to use about the engine as well as a pair of waterproof mittens; snow glasses and a spare pair each; a pocket knife and file were among the equipment each of us should carry.

We'd been outfitted by North Face the previous year and found the one item we all kept close at hand was our immense red down coat. If we were cold and put it on, we were cold no more. Stepping out of the plane, from 70° above into 30° below, the transition was even greater than if we'd been allowed to adjust gradually. We also had to move immediately to look after the planes wherever we were. The airplane was always our first priority and we had to step out the door ready to start work. In the midst of all our high-fashion outdoor equipment, Donny had much the same equipment as Wilkins, including sealskin pants and wolf gloves. Maybe it could be attributed to his native Alaskan heritage, but he always looked warmer and more comfortable than any of us.

Instead of the two-man half sleeping bag we had carried last year,

I had made this year two one-man half bags reaching to our hips and covered with waterproof cloth. Had it been necessary for us to carry our packs as it was last year, we could have dumped all of our gear into the sleeping bags and made packs of them.

Our own plan was simple: a very big warm down bag and a thick pad for sleeping on, with all of us snuggled up in a strong mountaineering tent. We had all spent enough time in these to jump out and settle in comfortably.

We had two pairs of snowshoes and these could be used for back packs when not needed on our feet. The snowshoes we took this year were rather larger than those carried before because there was a possibility that we would have to walk some distance over the deep snow on the mountains of Spitsbergen.

We also carried snowshoes, and Shane even had a pair of skis, which he hoped he would only have to use in a ski race he'd entered in Oslo two weeks hence.

We had far greater chance of a rescue than Wilkins — our radio contact was far superior and the weather stations dotted across the Arctic all had the ability to either mount or assist in a rescue. However, I was surprised in 1997 how sketchy the radio sometimes was, how long we would go with having no contact. In a storm, which was when we would be most likely to have problems, it would be difficult to send out anyone to assist us and Arctic storms could last for weeks. Pinpointing our location on the GPS allowed for near-perfect accuracy, but despite claims of worldwide coverage, they also would blink on with 'satellite contact lost, pls reset' as with less than three satellites, a not uncommon occurrence, they would get lost. This was assuming, as Wilkins had pointed out to us earlier, that we crash-landed safely. Hitting a pressure ridge or dumping the plane into an open lead in a white-out seemed more probable when looking down at the ice than hitting a rare clear patch big enough to land a plane on.

For food this year I decided to take more pemmican than last year and our list contained twenty pounds of it; biscuits twenty pounds; malted milk twenty pounds; chocolate five pounds; raisins five

pounds and a few tins of emergency army ration as an extra-emer-
gency — in case of temporary forced landing. I took a carton of
cigarettes to while away the time should we meet with temporary
injury. I included some chewing tobacco, for I have found from
experience that the nasty taste of it sometimes helps one to forget
other things not quite so nasty — in effect a counter-irritant.

I'd spent a large amount of time preparing food in 1997 and we'd found it far more complicated than necessary. If I was aboard, I could mix it up into something tasty quite easily, but the maze of ingredients stumped everyone else. What we really needed was an advanced snack menu, lots of drinks and sandwich foods. In 1998 Shane and Ferdy had made a quick shop and each plane had a duffel of canned drinks and water, crackers, cheese and peanut butter, a few loaves of bread, a bag of apples and once again, supplied by Donny, a large bag of spicy reindeer sausages. Ron had secured several boxes of 'hot meals' which cooked themselves by adding water and we could heat them up easily in flight when we wanted a larger meal. Ferdinand and I had been in charge of single malts and I'd also researched cigars and brought along a Hoyo de Monterrey Epicure #2. As Ron was equally appreciative of a good quality cigar, I threw in at least one more — the Antonov was just going to have to carry that little bit extra.

Wilkins noted all their other equipment, right down to: 'a bar of coarse soap for tanning and softening small skins for socks and shirts — should we land on northern Grant Land or Greenland and spend many months or years in walking home we might need these.'

We took no coarse soap. There was no way we thought we'd have to walk that far and we didn't even want to think about it.

Contemplating an adventure you are on so long you have to start making your own clothes was incomprehensible to us. It was this kind of planning, and the emotional commitment it bespoke, that set Wilkins' adventure apart from ours. We might be tracing his journey, in a single-engine plane that flew slower and had less range than even Wilkins' Lockheed Vega. But we were a few giant steps removed from the long-term commitment he was prepared to accept to complete the flight. However, I knew from the previous year and our takeoff from Barrow, flying up through the clouds while the ice build up on the wings, that the feeling of danger, of relying on the extensive experience of Shane, Ron and Donny, would undoubtedly surface more than once in the long journey ahead. That commitment, to get in the Antonov, shut the door and take off into the clouds with ten or fifteen or twenty hours of flying planned, without looking down and seeing a single sign of civilization, wasn't going to be easy. The body is naturally drawn to warmth, comfort and flat ground. We'd be leaving all of that just about as far behind as is worldly possible.

Our modern technology would only take us so far and the limitations of our aircraft kept us on our toes. On an earlier routine hop across Anchorage in Ron's Antonov, the newer and more reliable of our pair of planes, there had been, as Trevor reminded me, a sudden tense moment: '... but not forgetting that Polar Two had tried to bite Ron and myself on the short flight from Merrill Field to Anchorage earlier, when one of the cylinders quit to the tune of a rough vibration and much black smoke, sufficient to prompt an observant air traffic controller to offer us an unsolicited expedited return to the field.'

We staggered out from breakfast, Shane, Laura and I, to check again on the weather. It is so cold in Barrow that buildings all have an entrance, then a place for coats and boots and space to recover from whatever raging storm one has crawled in from, then another door, and finally you are inside. All windows are double-glazed and walls are heavily insulated, stuffed to the brim, which makes being inside both very warm and strangely quiet.

By lunchtime the planes were refueled and ready to fly, the oil topped up; the weather looked good and we retreated for a few hours' nap. It was easy to be a little nervous about Barrow — getting stuck the previous year had made us mindful of the weather and the flight out and up through the clouds is one we didn't want to have to repeat.

There were also a few niggling problems. I had become so used to riding along in the Antonovs that sometimes I forgot that things were less than perfect. Trevor, however, with his many years in the industry and as a private pilot had an eye for just how the Antonovs were performing — or not performing, as the case may be.

There were a number of incidents on my mind in Barrow, several of which are descriptive examples of the 'extreme aviation' content of the expedition.

The loss of pressure in the left oleo undercarriage leg, the unsuccessful attempts to even it out by lifting the wing, the resulting under-wing fabric tear, the duck tape repair in Barrow, releasing pressure in the right-hand leg to try and collapse them evenly to level the aircraft (partially successful), the resulting imbalance in fuel load between right and left tanks, the inability to fill either wing tank completely, the implications of that for endurance and range. (One wing tank potentially overfills then loses fuel through the vents whilst the aircraft is canted over on the ground; the other cannot be filled completely due to the position of the fuel orifice.)

The obvious dangers of an (over)loaded aircraft with reduced undercarriage compliance.

Also in a cross wind from the right one generally flies right wing low on the landing approach, so a tendency to go immediately left wing low on touchdown is unhelpful (likewise in the takeoff phase) and makes maintaining runway heading in a right cross wind after touchdown more problematical, particularly on a frozen and slippery surface.

Sometimes not knowing everything about the Antonovs was a good idea. If we had combined everybody's concerns, we probably never would have gotten off the ground.

We'd also changed our route to shorten the flight to the Pole. Instead of having to launch from Barrow all the way to the Pole and on to Spitsbergen, we were going to fly across Northern Canada and land in Eureka. This would place us a few hundred miles closer to the Pole and make the flight from the Pole on to Spitsbergen more achievable. This way we could treat Barrow as more of a way point, as opposed to the place where we needed to

118

indulge in a last supper.

We also had the immense space of the Barrow airstrip from which to launch the Antonovs. Wilkins was not nearly so lucky.

…on the afternoon of the fifth and all day on the sixth thirty Eskimo were busy shovelling the snow from the ice. With the help of men and dogs we moved the plane to the part of the lagoon from which we should start and Eielson and I filled the tanks with gasoline.

The following morning the challenges of flying where no one had gone before began to mount:

At three o'clock in the morning I was up for observations. A light wind from the South promised stronger winds later in the day and the thing to do was get off before it was too strong. I hurriedly donned my flying clothes, lit the kitchen stove and put the oil to warm. Then I went to the plane to light and adjust the stoves for heating the engine. By five o'clock the engine was warm and ready. … I turned back to the kitchen to waken the cook and Eielson. I was dismayed to find that the oil, becoming overheated, had boiled over the edge of the cans and had swamped the kitchen stove and floor. The smell of the burning oil had wakened the cook and he was now prancing about his kitchen saying little and thinking quite a lot.

Not a great start to their day. Meanwhile, we had an early dinner, wandered across the street to the runway, pulled the electric heaters out from inside the engines, dragged the heavy cover blankets off and fired up the engines, both starting first time. In the Arctic silence they were just as loud, but the sound seemed much more lonely, fading quickly in the immensity. Less than 24 hours after landing at Barrow, we headed back out onto the main runway, pointing the Antonovs on their journey north.

Anchorage – Fairbanks
9 April 1998

After the run-up test on Ron's aircraft went well, we were ready. I wanted to go all the way to Barrow today if possible as we had lost a day due to the engine problems. Getting out of Anchorage is always difficult as there are endless last-minute details. Ferdinand attended to fueling both planes and to attempting to pack Ron's airplane. It looked as if he had decided to bring the contents of his garage on the expedition, but probably had no more equipment than Wilkins would have chosen to carry.

We started at noon and made the long taxi from the south airpark at Anchorage to the north end of Runway 14. We took off in formation and made a left turn over the post office and headed north across Turnagain Arm towards Fairbanks. North of Elmendorf Air Force Base we watched a couple of military C-130s fly past us not far away. The weather was perfect and the plane was running along nicely over familiar ground. I had constructed special fuel and flight logs to measure every detail of our consumption and began taking readings every thirty minutes.

Around Talkeetna the clouds began to build and I started climbing so as to stay clear of them. It started to remind me of the last leg of our flight last year as we struggled to get up on top of the clouds. While the Antonov is a steady machine, she is no thoroughbred, and I was barely able to get on top of the weather. I radioed for a weather report in Windy Pass and heard that it was obscured in snow showers. It was absolutely necessary to stay on top, and we were just able to do this at 10,000 feet. Despite the work done to my aircraft it still seemed like Polar Two could fly higher and faster. I guess that twenty additional years of wear and tear takes its toll on an airframe.

On the north side of the pass we could see Fairbanks in the distance and began a slow cruise descent. Closing the oil and cowl flaps to keep the oil from getting cold we built speed on the downhill run. Ron landed ahead of us and I entered a left downwind for the runway. It was perfect weather again in Fairbanks and I parked in front of the tower.

I still wonder where the snowbanks shown in Wilkins' pictures have gone. We refueled both aircraft to the exact same level and noted that the amount burned on the flight from Anchorage was equal. We had each burned 100 gallons.

Flight Log   Date April 9, 1998   N61SL
LEG 1 Anchorage-Fairbanks
Polar1 Crew: Shane, Donny, Trevor
True Course 014   Distance 227.3 NM

Fairbanks – Barrow
9 April 1998

Fairbanks served as an intermediary fuel stop and an historic landmark for the flight. It was from here that Wilkins and Eielson set out seventy years ago. I wore the Eielson fur flying parka for a few photos, but it was so warm and sunny that it seemed a bit silly. Aimee Moore, Donny's girlfriend, checked the Barrow weather at flight service for me. There was a large front approaching from the west with high winds, but Barrow was still clear and calm. We could make up for the lost days in Anchorage by continuing straight through, and everything was running well.

Departing Fairbanks in formation again I took the left-hand side of the runway. When I added takeoff power the squelch on the intercom picked up the rpm increase and blasted my ears. Donny began turning various radio knobs which distracted me and as I reached over to turn down the squelch we nearly swerved off the runway. The old girl just wanted to remind me that I had to pay attention to her at all times. Flying north of Fairbanks was a reprise from last year with absolutely perfect conditions. Donny and Trevor swapped seats, as Trevor was very keen to fly and Donny preferred to work on his notes. I continued with the fuel and time readings, which would give me a better estimation of our capability on the polar flight.

121

After 30 minutes I switched over to the auxiliary tank and showed the steps of this procedure to Trevor. The Yukon river was a familiar and awesome sight.. Trevor and I cross-checked our GPS positions, readings and speeds during intervals to make sure that they were both working properly. I experimented with the astro compass and attempted to take a navigational fix, recording the angle of the sun.

The Arctic Circle slid past at 0157 GMT and I joked to Trevor that we would have to cover him with bear fat and feathers as an initiation. He reminded me he was no Arctic neophyte as we had sailed together to 78° North from Norway to Spitsbergen in 1992. As we entered the Brooks range and I thought about Wilkins and Eielson's flights seventy years ago it struck me how exciting their time must have been. These are rugged mountains and without knowing their height, they must have looked pretty scary. Fortunately for me, I used detailed aeronautical charts which showed the minimum en route altitude to be only 7,000 feet. I decided that we would overfly Anatuvik Pass this year as the day was getting by and I wanted to get to Barrow before it was too late. Anatuvik passed just below our right wing and I was sorry not to have the time to visit the friends I had made there last year.

We were carrying a good tail wind, and the fuel burn appeared to be down to about 38 gallons per hour — very good news. I remember the awe of seeing the North Slope last year, and the impact was no less now. The first hours across the Arctic basin passed blithely while I listened to Louis Armstrong and Ella Fitzgerald on the CD player, now part of our intercom system. I don't think Wilkins had one of these gadgets. In the distance I spotted Admiralty Bay to the east of Barrow, and then the Arctic shoreline and finally Barrow. The visibility was perfect and we decided to fly along the coast to the actual Point Barrow and do some aerial photography. In the golden twilight we flew low looking for polar bears and I remembered why I loved this kind of flying. The earth was a bit too cold to smell today, but it was godlike to fly the Arctic atmosphere at low level. The radial was rumbling happily and I felt prepared for the real adventure to start when we departed Barrow.

Flight Log   Date April 9, 1998   N61SL
LEG 2 Fairbanks -Barrow
Polar 1 Crew: Shane, Donny, Trevor
True Course 334   Distance 438.6 NM

chapter 5

'a mistress...not subdued by idle gestures'

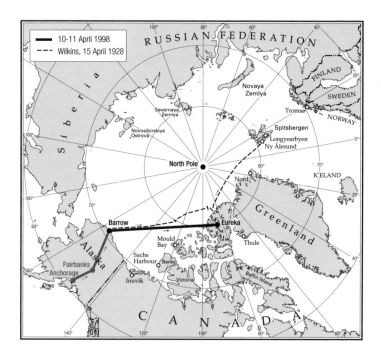

In 1997 I hadn't known enough about a fully loaded Antonov to be really nervous, I was just normally apprehensive on our take-off from Barrow.

In 1998 I knew enough to be properly scared, and with good reason. Occasionally the engines missed in the air. Not often, but they would sometimes give a big kick and backfire and spray smoke and then jump back to life. Hopefully. This caused corresponding heart arrhythmias in anybody aboard. It wasn't until later I learned that in Finland the national aeronautics control had taken one look at an Antonov and said, 'Nothing that big should fly with just one engine,' and promptly banned it from their skies.

I don't really get claustrophobia. But being in an Antonov, rolling along the runway, trying to will the thing into the air, watching the ground go past and then seeing someone on a nearby road overtake you in a small and obviously slow car, doesn't inspire confidence. I wanted off. But by this time I was always stuck. I reassured myself I wouldn't be there unless I trusted my partners. Then I'd have to change lenses on my camera and would catch sight of 390 gallons of gasoline an eighth of an inch from my back through a layer of fiberglass, sloshing in the top of the tank like the world's largest Molotov cocktail and I'd break out in a sweat all over again.

The Antonov, as if to reassure me, kept its waddling to a minimum leaving Barrow. The props dug into the air like a four-bladed shovel and we were rolling, rolling, then a very gentle sway and Shane pushed the rudder pedal down and pulled the tail back in line. We crawled into the air, the nose up, going through a bit of fog. We were what is described as airborne, no longer attached to the earth. In reality, however, we were not a very long way above it.

What was I really worried about? We had an asphalt runway long enough for a 737. We had taken off the year before with more weight. We had Wilkins' example to follow — something we didn't even want to think about. When it came to getting off the ground in 1928, he'd already parboiled his oil supply.

> It was almost too dangerous to attempt a cross wind takeoff but since we had made ready with so much bother we concluded we'd at least run down the runway and see how the machine behaved. If we did get in the air and did not like the conditions we could dump the gas and return.
>
> Eielson gave her the gun, the Eskimo wiggled the tail and we started. I was surprised at the ease with which we started. We accelerated but it was soon evident that we would not get off before reaching the end of the runway. How would our skis behave on the snow? Before coming to the end of the ice Eielson pulled back the stick to try and force her off and the tail came down with a bump that shook loose the trigger we had provided on the tail-skid for an

emergency brake. It certainly acted as a fine brake, scoring a gutter three inches deep in the tough sea ice. Our speed was considerably decreased and fortunately so, for when the machine bounced off the end of the runway the side wind caught her and flung her to one side. We landed with most of the weight on one ski. It gave way and we ploughed through the snow in a circle and came to rest.

Meanwhile we were airborne and it had actually happened with less drama than the previous year. We had no thick clouds to go through and shortly after leaving Barrow set a direct course for Eureka, just over 1,000 nautical miles away. Over the intercom Shane invited us to 'sit back, relax and enjoy the ride.' He broke out the Mozart, the cabin warmed up with a ready blast from the heating tube and the clouds passed by below as if on a treadmill. The cloud wasn't heavy, but like the previous year was too thick to see below to the ice. We floated along on the reassuring bed of clouds as the sun began its long slow slide towards the horizon. I took visual fuel checks through the site gauge every hour and we compared them to the fuel flow gauge. It was steady at 43 gallons an hour, just what it should be. After the previous year's flight, it was very reassuring to have a gauge doing nothing more than measuring fuel.

I'd spent a year asking questions of anyone who flew, and having been joined on the ski slopes of Korea by a fellow ski patroller who is a helicopter test pilot, Mike Weist, I learned there is more than one way to measure fuel. Flying Black Hawks for a living, he takes them out and makes sure they do things the way they should. 'It is more accurate to measure fuel by weight, because when it gets hot it expands and you'll have more gallons than you thought. But a Black Hawk will burn upwards of 135 gallons an hour, depending on fuel temperature.' Just when I thought the Antonov was bad — at least we weren't trying to get a helicopter to the Pole.

How much fuel can expand was soon to become very obvious. Even if this year all was going well, there were still things to learn as Trevor was finding out over on Polar Two.

126

At the commencement of the 13-hour flight from Barrow to Eureka, Ron was in the left seat, Ferdinand in the right, and I was standing in the centre at the cockpit entrance with my back wedged against the aux. fuel tank.

About 10 minutes into the flight I became aware that the back of my jacket was very damp. I touched it with my hand and realized that it was soaked with fuel.

Fuel was running down the tank side on to my jacket!

The explanation was simple. As we gained height, the inside of the aircraft warmed up from both the heat of the engine and the effect of the sun on the fuselage. Also the atmospheric pressure fell as we climbed. There was no expansion space in the huge internal auxiliary fuel tank in Polar Two, as it had been completely filled for the long flight ahead. The fuel, having nowhere else to go as it expanded from the warmth and reduced pressure, was being forced out past the internal filler inlet.

We said little and changed the engine fuel feed to the auxiliary tank. After a few long minutes the leakage stopped as the fuel level fell. It does not take much imagination to calculate the effect of some static from the movement of a passing jacket, or a spark from the activation of any one of the myriad of electric switches in the cockpit.

On Polar One, Shane and Donny ran through their post-takeoff checklist. Hopping from plane to plane, I noticed many differences in the styles of the pilots. I watched Ron after takeoff and he covered everything Shane, Donny, Ferdinand and Trevor do, and was quick to remind anyone who missed a step. Shane uses a checklist, both a by-product of his training and because flying an Antonov is far removed from flying a 737, where he could the recite the checklist backwards. I never had any qualms about flying with one pilot or another, even though the approach to the journey and flying styles were different. They each had enough experience to get where we want to go, though they may do it in different ways. The further we flew, the further we got from civilization, the more prominent became these differences — not personally, but in the way they planned and flew across the Arctic.

In this diversity was one of our greatest strengths. Both Shane and Ron visited the weather offices and looked at the maps, then conferred and made decisions. Ron may have been flying for years, but was the first to say, 'Every day you fly and don't learn — you might as well quit flying.' In the climbing, and undoubtedly the flying world, the well-known saying goes, 'There are old climbers, and there are bold climbers, but there are no old, bold climbers.' Continual learning and adapting is the key to staying alive in the Arctic.

Several hours out of Barrow the clouds broke up below us. The ice started showing through, first a misty, dark layer of shadow revealed below, then the ice itself started to come to life. The dark leads snaked through, pressure ridges rose and disappeared, huge smooth ice slabs crinkled into non-symmetrical patterns that all fitted together. The sea was moving in swells and pushing the ice in circles from below. The wind blew across and completed the sculpture from above. Then the sun rolled around just above the horizon, casting shadows extending for miles and forming ice rainbows stretching horizontally through the clouds.

The GPS measured time and distance in tenths of seconds and minutes of degrees, but mentally we were simply several hours into our journey with maybe twice as far to go. Exact measurements out here made no difference. Yet at the same time, everything was marked in latitude and longitude. It was the only way to place into perspective where we were on the earth's surface, where we were going.

When I first became interested in Wilkins' journey, I contacted a friend who had helped us with maps when we visited the remote Kangshung Face on Everest, Miklos Pinther, Chief Cartographer at the United Nations. He visited the American Geographical Society in New York and discovered deep in their files a number of articles and the original maps Wilkins had used on his journey. We were soon to learn this was an invaluable archive that had been very closely linked to the explorations, and as

Wilkins wrote from Green Harbour later, and sent by wire to the *Globe* newspaper:

> *But the Arctic is a mistress who will not be subdued by idle gestures, nor can the work of exploration be carried out without the help of many generous friends. We owe much to many people, far too many to mention individually, but to the faith upheld by and the encouragement received from the American Geographical Society and the* Detroit News *we owe immeasurably.*

Folded between two large sheets of thick black paper at the American Geographical Society's office in the heart of Wall Street was the map Wilkins had used and made notes on as they flew over the Arctic. Down the right side, neatly penciled into the margin, were the hours they had been in flight, latitude and longitude. Below this was their compass course, as recorded every hour. Now as we flew along the path they had taken, the importance of his measurements became real. The only thing to measure progress by was the slow ticking away of the latitudes. Outside, the unreality of the way the world looked needed to be counterbalanced with a mathematical precision. By taking sights, concentrating on measurements, calculating the compass direction, Wilkins not only stayed on course, but they also had a link to something simple and precise and more real than the world that was passing by outside the window. Even a map I was using prepared in the US by the Defense Mapping Agency Aerospace Center had a cluster of bold-print boxes dotted in the Beaufort Sea northeast of Barrow with the messages:

> *Magnetic Disturbance of as much as seven degrees exists at sea level in this vicinity.*

and:

> *WARNING — DUE TO PROXIMITY OF THE MAGNETIC POLE THE MAGNETIC COMPASS MAY BE UNRELIABLE FOR NAVIGATION BECAUSE OF MAGNETIC STORMS AND WEAK DIRECTIVE FORCE.*

By 10.30 pm the sun had dropped down into the horizon and

the ice had turned orange and then pink. Donny was in the left seat, taking shots at the sun with the sextant, peering through the tiny sights and tilting the arms to line them up with the sun and the horizon. This was not greatly assisted by my flying. The cockpit of the Antonov is filled with an immense assortment of dials, knobs, switches and indicators. Many do very little, but one may be the obscure lever no one has ever dared pull that activates the ejector seat. When I'd flown an Antonov for the first time the previous year, Shane had told me to quit watching all the dials and keep an eye on the sun and horizon and fly by feel instead. Both Shane and Donny did this effortlessly, while also flicking channels on one of our two radios, checking weather forecasts, charting our route on maps and GPS, comparing the two, keeping an eye on the fuel feed, rpm and manifold pressure, not forgetting to spare a quick glance over the oil pressure and temperature gauges — still munching on a bag of pretzels and listening to Mozart. Eielson would have been looking down on an equally extensive set of gauges, and while their accuracy may have improved, the key gauges were the same on our airplane as were in common use seventy years previously.

> *The instrument board in front of the pilot held besides the usual tachometer, thermometer, pressure gauge, altimeter, air-speed indicator and watch, an additional altimeter registering accurately to two feet, a turn and bank indicator, a fore and aft inclinometer, a lateral inclinometer, one fast moving and one slow moving compass.*

Wilkins rarely flew in the Arctic, even when he had the chance. On the final journey, he wasn't even in the cockpit, sandwiched behind their own massive auxiliary gas tank and the rear of the plane. But in 1926 he took the controls of the *Alaskan*, the single-engine Fokker monoplane, and indicated he was susceptible to the magic of flying:

> *I have never, in my limited experience, flown a machine so exquisite to handle. The smoothness of control, the power of the engine in the machine, making her start like a high-powered car when its*

throttle was opened wide in level flight, gave the same sensation as if in a fighting plane. Yet in turns and glides she was steady, smooth, solid and stable. I lost my heart to the Alaskan on that first flight.

Since Shane had shown me that first tattered picture in New York of the Antonov parked forlornly in Russia, what had appealed to me most about the plane had been linked to its appearance, which in itself created an atmosphere that something had to happen when you stepped into it. Universally, the same characteristics seemed to stand out for whoever saw it. It is big. Its wings are huge. The propeller, attached to the front of the massive engine, looks supremely powerful.

The sun faded and Donny folded the sextant up. Shane moved forward to the cockpit from his reindeer rug in the first-class sleeping cabin. He flipped on more Mozart, made sure I wasn't flying loops and said, 'I'm just going to shut my eyes for a little while.' I flew along with Mozart and a sunset that dipped into the horizon then rolled out again from below the clouds, faded and reappeared, until I'd lived through four sunsets in one day: orange rolling into purple rolling into red fading to gray. The altimeter settled, quit trying to rise or fall. The GPS said I was going someplace, and I was going there directly. Soon I had to look at neither, as the turn of the nose told me where the Antonov wanted to go and as we flew along a lead of black water, crossed an ice ridge and flew towards a cloud. The engine let me know if I started to climb, the bass sending back a lower note, and that I should drop just a semitone, a B-flat to a B, nothing more. The plane was talking in very low tones, easily missed, but if listened to it, it told me how to fly. So we flew along, in conversation for the first time, and the Antonov taught me that the real magic in her was in the flying.

'It's been a long time since New York,' Shane was awake and remembering a time in New York that seemed too far back to recall but equally something that could be happening through the not-very-thick glass of the windscreen, like Alice and her looking glass. The Antonov bassooned along, through the almost-night, just a bit closer to dark than we had expected, but never really quite getting there.

Polar Two was somewhere hidden behind us. We were all alone, just the occasional muffled voice on the radio, comparing speeds, fuel, weather. All was well on Polar One and Two.

Through the night the headwinds were steady. We made little better than 80–90 knots. It was not too bad, but after rocketing north at up to 140 knots from Anchorage to Barrow, not what we'd like. We flew for several more hours, which meant we were over half way, but the ever-accurate GPS estimated we would be 13 hours en route. We had tanked up on fuel before leaving, so there was no danger of running short. The weather was good. So we just kept on flying.

The sun started an almost imperceptible rise in what was now the northeast and soon land appeared. Like flying into Mould Bay the previous year, it looked like land in name only. The ice bulked up next to the shore. Overgrown rolls of pure white bread dough extended in gentle, glacially carved curves away from the sea ice, furrowed by fjords of flat ice. The fjords wove through the land, giant rivers of flat ice cutting into the side of Axel Heiberg Island. There were no markings on the map to show that anybody lived on the island. As we flew across, it was easy to imagine that perhaps no one ever will. There was no real difference in safety being over land — if anything, the hills and soft snow made it a less desirable place to land. It was still far north of what would be called 'the middle of nowhere.' It was easy to see why Wilkins told people that if he disappeared they shouldn't worry for at least two years, as they could well just be walking home.

After his first slide off the end of the runway and the broken ski, Wilkins was still back in Barrow having problems just getting into the air. Following their first mishap, he set the Eskimos to work with renewed incentives. With six dollars a day and the occasional meal they soon had the runway lengthened to 3,500 feet. It also had a bit of a kick at the end.

> *At the end of the runway the bank of the lagoon rose gradually to a height of about fifteen feet. I asked Eielson if, when he was about to take off, it seemed we were not going to rise that he either stop the engine well before we came to the end or else keep going until after we had climbed the hill. The momentum and the engine would carry us over the top of the bank and we could come to no harm on the level, soft snow but a sudden stop on a rise might cause the machine to turn up on its nose.*

Effectively they had a very long, hard-packed runway with a built-in launching pad on the end. Not particularly scientific, but with their heavily overloaded plane, they needed all the help they could get. A few days later the weather cleared again and they were back aboard:

> *Once more we slipped along the icy runway gathering speed all the time. The wooden skis seemed to slide as well if not better than the metal ones. It looked as if we might get off this time. If a light head wind had prevailed instead of the gentle breeze across our track we could have managed it. I could feel the ship getting light. She was eager to take the air and almost lifted as we came to the end of the runway. We struck the snow and careened up the bank of the lagoon and over the snow-covered tundra at the top. Right over the hill we went and down the other side. Eielson had gradually reduced the throttle when we struck the snow and we came to rest slowly.*
>
> *… I was jubilant, almost as happy as if we had taken off. We were sure now that our machine could stand hard usage if necessary and her buoyancy at the end of the runway proved that only a few more feet would be necessary to enable us to take off even in a calm; with a head wind she would be well away.*

Wilkins hitched the plane up to two dog teams and dragged it over to the larger Elson Lagoon. It would take additional time and money, but he now felt sure they could get the plane off the ground.

The advantage of Wilkins' Vega lay in its aerodynamics and speed. But the characteristics that made it fast in the air also made it hard to get into the air, particularly with a heavy load. In 1928, it was far ahead of its time, as was documented in an unattributed newspaper article.

The Lockheed Vega monoplane used by Capt. Wilkins and Pilot Eielson in their spectacular flight over the top of the world is regarded in the aeronautical world as a radical departure from the generally adopted theory of construction for commercial airplanes.

Expensive and laborious to build because of the peculiar construction of its fuselage, the Lockheed Vega embodies a cleanliness of line and lack of parasite resistance found only in the high speed and costly racing planes. The type of fuselage in the Lockheed Vega, in fact, has been used for all successful modern racing planes, including Italy's present world speed record-holder. Powered with a Wright 'Whirlwind' air-cooled engine of 220 horsepower, the Lockheed Vega, as a cabin monoplane, has a high speed of 135 miles per hour and a cruising speed of 110 miles per hour. The span of its single wing of cantilever construction is 41 feet and the length over all is 27 feet 5 inches.

Virtually the entire plane bears a covering of spruce plywood. The fuselage, round and smooth, is covered with the long strips and glued to circular ribs under a pressure of 150 tons. The wing is covered with 3-32-inch spruce plywood, which adds greatly to the general rigidity of the structure.

In the sense that planes are spoken of as 'all metal' the Lockheed Vega is 'all wood'.

Our cruising speeds were much the same, but it took an engine with four times as much horsepower to get an Antonov through the air. Speaking of 'parasite resistance' on an Antonov was incidental; the undercarriage alone was a massive drag of struts and balloon tires bouncing their way through the air. In 1997 I'd taken the stairs up on both planes. In 1998, boarding Ron's plane, he told me not to bother unlashing them. 'I can't see that it makes any difference.' It was easy to agree with him.

The turns and twists of Axel Heiberg rose and fell below us, the hills just high enough to lift and drop the plane a few times in the air currents before we were again over the sea ice leading to Ellesmere Island and Eureka, Canada. Ron came on the radio from Polar Two: 'We are just passing over the hills in front of you close to the sea. There is a herd of musk oxen on the hill just before you reach the sea ice.' We circled, glad to have something to do, something to look at, after 12 hours of straight and level flying on a constant course. The hills rose steeply up from the sea, a brush of brown tundra on the windswept heights, a dark rock poked through. We turned back to our course and started the glide into Eureka, just over the hills on the far side of the sea.

Shane had arranged permission for us to land and spend the night in Eureka. As a scientific station, they don't encourage visitors. And with a daily fee of about US$250, nobody wants to stay long. Shane brought the plane around and suddenly the winds picked up as we bounced around to line up for the runway. After this long a flight, flying the Antonov as it suddenly started bobbing, weaving and sliding sideways in the cross wind, then rising and falling rapidly through a series of up- and downdrafts, required real concentration. It woke Shane and Donny up immediately, the radio chatter seized and they got to do some real flying. Just when I was contemplating actually sitting down and putting my seat belt on for the first time, we hit clear air 50 feet off the ground and Shane took her straight in with hardly a bump.

Like Mould Bay, the strip was immense, smooth and perfectly maintained, with towering snow banks rising on all sides. A welcome committee was there to greet us, the station manager Dick Wasacase pulling up in an oversize pick-up with big snow tires. 'Welcome to Eureka,' he shouted, and shook hands with each of us. We had the engine covers out and up over the planes in minutes, the heaters strung to their electrical cords and purring away inside. We were talking excitedly, the buzz of no sleep and the cold air making us hyperactive, the storm of brain activity before the calm.

Twenty-two barrels of fuel were pulled out and dropped next to the planes, all of which would have to be pumped up into the wings. In the meantime, the need for sleep was creeping up rapidly. We had been up since 5.30 the morning before, after just four hours of sleep, and besides a catnap or two on the plane hadn't had any real sleep for a very long time. We piled ourselves and our duffels into the truck. Just outside the airport, an official-looking sign said, 'Eureka, 1½ miles.' The small set of buildings nestled just alongside the fjord, evident because it was flat white as opposed to hilly white. The buildings were squat and square with small inset windows and looked like little forts. When it seemed like we were nearly there another sign appeared, 'Eureka, $^1/_2$ mile.' Dick was pointing out the buildings and an observatory located above Eureka on a hill. 'Guess how far that is away from here,' he asked. 'A mile, two, four?' we guessed. 'No, nobody ever gets close,' said Dick. 'It's nine miles. Clear air, Arctic air, makes everything look closer.'

We dropped our big red coats, hats, scarves, gloves, piled jackets and boots in the entry of the main building. Inside, it was toasty warm, wood on the walls, dark carpet, big sofas, like an oversized house. We'd flown through three time zones and it was early afternoon, Eureka time. We were shown to our rooms and then back to the kitchen for toast and coffee. Dick cleared us through customs, a reminder we had actually changed countries. He stamped our passports at our request. The stamp is a miniature map of the top of the world, circled by bold print stating GARDEN SPOT OF THE ARCTIC, EUREKA N.W.T., 80 00 N 86 56 W. Eureka is marked with a big star and above it a rather mad-looking musk ox stares out. It is the kind of stamp that takes up a full page and will drive serious-minded customs agents, intent on knowing where one has been, a little crazy. Dick printed up our bill — six people for the night, a bit of fuel for the planes, three meals, just over 10,000 Canadian dollars. An Antonov holiday doesn't come cheap. 'Hey,' said Dick, 'we get all kinds of people here. A King Air with a few people stopped in once, and didn't have quite enough money to pay their bill from a briefcase they had brought in from the plane. So the next morning I went out with them to the plane, they pulled out a second briefcase, opened it up and it was filled with rows of cash, just like in the movies. They were circling the world via the polar regions and that was the way they traveled, their own aircraft and a few briefcases full of cash.'

A nap was called for since non-reality was setting in from lack of sleep, the Antonov roar still echoing in our heads. But too much time awake precluded sleep and after 15 minutes in a small dark room, the black-out curtain pulled over the tiny inset window, I got up and typed up notes from our Barrow-Eureka flight and sent them off to Laura to load on our website and update all the schoolchildren following our progress. The description may have been a bit surreal, but if the kids were looking for real life, they were assured of that. 'Laura,' I wrote, 'please feel free to edit.'

At 5 pm dinner was served, a large roast of beef, potatoes, gravy, well-cooked vegetables. Flying the planes and eating infrequently made us all ravenous, so a few donuts and a piece of pie was added for dessert. Sleep seemed like a good idea, but the planes still needed fueling and getting it done before a new day would make us that much more efficient in the morning. We walked back to the airport to wake up. Just over the hill from the airport was a wide valley and at the far end some dots of brown had been pointed out to us as musk oxen.

'Come on,' said Ferdinand. 'We can't all fuel the planes anyway, let's go see if we can get close to the musk oxen.' Like the observatory tower, they appeared not too far away, little more than a mile. But in between were drifts and snowbanks, hills and tundra that could be difficult to cross. We loaded up our cameras with big lenses and stuffed our pockets with film and off we strode. We went up and down hidden rises, skirted a wind-packed snowdrift and dropped into the valley. The airport disappeared behind us and suddenly we were very much alone on the island. As we drew closer, the dark dots disappeared.

'Are they there?' asked Ferdinand. We had been walking over an hour and they were nowhere in sight.

'A bit further,' I said, 'I think.' It was hard to believe they could be close and we couldn't even see them yet. We walked up a final rise and directly in front of us, in a small dip, brown hummocks appeared above the snow. The musk oxen looked like dark rocks, only their humped, rounded shape defining them as anything different. It was hard to believe they were alive. We crept closer, taking the occasional picture of little more than a dark hump. We were under 100 feet away. Maybe they weren't musk oxen? Suddenly there was a huge upheaval, the brown blobs rose out of the snow, massive faces covered with ice lifting and steam shooting out of their nostrils. They came up onto their knees then lurched suddenly to their feet, immense faces capped by their distinctive horns framing their furry heads, sharp points curving out at their base in sharp relief to the white background. They formed a line immediately, the larger musk oxen at the ends, smaller ones in the center, babies behind. It was like a phalanx of defending warriors. The big ones were stomping their feet and looking unhappy. A lot of snorting of air was going on, great clouds of steam rising above them, more dragon- than mammal-like. It crossed my mind that I knew nothing about musk oxen and what they might do. They were twice as big as I expected and through my camera lens filled the frame. Ferdinand had walked a little closer to them on a short rise off to the side and they suddenly started milling around, the big ones still facing us.

'What are they doing?' I asked.

'I don't know,' said Ferdinand. 'Do musk oxen charge?'

We had no idea. Suddenly the big ones, with a final snort and a shake of their huge horns, turned and led the nine of them away from us and up the hill.

The closeness, the sudden leap from being small furry brown rocks to large and fierce creatures with big horns, had left our hearts pounding. Like previous encounters I'd had with wolves, bears or lions, the absence of a fence had completely changed our relationship with the musk oxen. The feeling of being alien while the animal was at home and could do with us as they wanted, play with us on their home ground, while we stood by, inadequate, unknowing and defenseless, was all-pervasive. Ellesmere Island wasn't a people place, but a wild place. Eureka was an artificial outpost, like a fort in the Wild West surrounded by Indians. But unlike the Wild West, there was so little of value here, that hopefully it would stay this way, an earthly place where people only visit.

Ferdinand and I wandered back through the valley in the for-ever-setting sun of evening. The planes were fueled and oiled, the covers checked, wings tied to fuel barrels in case the wind came up. We retreated to the warmth of Eureka, down the long empty hallway past the Polar Bear Room filled with books, fossils and posters from previous expeditions. Forty hours after getting up in Alaska, we were all in our beds in Canada. The weather looked good — tomorrow was Easter. We could skip church and go to the North Pole for the endless sunrise instead.

Barrow, Alaska – Eureka, Canada
11 April 1998

On first glance out the window of the King Eider Inn this morning it looked like visibility was down. After the experience of being fogged in for a week last year I was praying for good weather. I checked with flight service, and also had some assistance from GCI, our communications partner, in getting detailed weather reports, and forecasts from the Internet. It looked pretty good to the east, if only I could get airborne in front of the approaching low pressure. The low seemed to have stalled to the west of Barrow which bought us valuable time. We didn't want to depart Barrow until early evening. Because of the four-hour time difference to Eureka combined with the calculated twelve hours en route, an evening departure would put us into Eureka around noon, local time.

The left strut on my airplane had lost some of its pressure and the wing was down. The Barrow search-and-rescue maintenance staff loaned us their nitrogen bottle and we refilled the strut and then refuelled both planes to their fully loaded maximum, including the auxiliary tank. Laura Thorpe of GCI organized for a school class to come visit the aircraft as part of the educational project, and we entertained some 5th graders for about an hour. I took particular care to carefully pack and tie down all the equipment before returning to the hotel for a nap. It was going to be a long night.

The Alaska Airlines crew came over to have a look at the aircraft and to wish us well. Laura was returning to Anchorage on their flight. We started our engines at 1925 local time but in the cold of Barrow it took a while to warm the oil and we ran for about 15 minutes on the ground. In the meantime the Alaska flight departed and the pilots reported good visibility above the shallow layer of blowing snow and thin cloud which lay over the coast. I took the runway and was airborne first as I didn't want the added challenge of a formation takeoff while fully loaded. The plane had no trouble taking off and we climbed up to about 500 feet and picked up our track of 032° true. Crossing the Arctic coastline the clouds thickened and I decided to climb through them immediately this time. We popped out on top at about 1,500 feet with the sun beaming above the horizon on our right and great visibility above an overcast layer. It took Ron quite a while to catch us, and after about 15 minutes he realized that he had forgotten to retract his flaps after takeoff, thus slowing him considerably. I changed to the aux. tank once things were stabilized, and after an hour of flying the clouds disappeared and we could see the pack ice below. A full moon rose into the purple twilight to our right and the sun slowly touched the horizon on the left. It was perhaps the most exciting and blissful moment of my flying career.

I was not certain if the sun would disappear completely below the horizon, but as it slid lower and lower the cockpit began to get dark. The old An-2 lights are not the best and it was tricky to see all the instruments. Also, if I used the back-lighting on the GPS the screen washed out making it impossible to read. I hoped that the unit was not quitting, but after cross-checking our bearing with the other aircraft's readings, it seemed to be on track. This leg of flying would take us to the north of the magnetic pole and south of the geographic pole and the compass would be useless. It was interesting to note that as we flew east, the true bearing swing from 03° to 102° over the twelve-hour period.

Donny had the first nap while Robert and I stayed up front sipping tea and eating dried apricots. We watched the sun slowly rise again in our 10 o'clock position. The sky remained clear, but it looked periodically as if clouds were building ahead of us. After eight hours I was down to the last 50 gallons of fuel in the aux. tank. I had made this mark on the tank with a black marker to let me know when I was down to the last hour of fuel. We were maintaining about 7,000 feet of altitude over the ice and had the mixture leaned back to give about 38 gallons per hour of fuel consumption. After 10 hours 30 minutes I was weary and decided to wake Donny up.

Once we got some hot tea into him, I went back and stretched out on the reindeer skin and covered myself with my down parka.

The back of the airplane receives scant heat from the engine, and with the outside air temperature somewhere around minus 30, it gets pretty chilly in the economy section. I woke two hours later and we were nearing Axel Heiburg Island and 80° North. Donny and Robert were in radio contact with Ron as well as the base in Eureka. It was great relief to see good weather over our landing area, and as we passed over the last stretches of island, huge herds of musk oxen were visible below us. The airstrip lay along the north side of the inlet on Ellesmere Island. I throttled back to let Ron land first. During the approach he reported turbulence and wind shifts. Coming in after him I had the same problems and on short final there was a stiff cross wind from the right. I hoped that we would not be blown off the icy runway, or spun around. The landing went well, and I taxied to the end of the runway and shut down the engine after 13 h and 22 m airborne. It was great to be here and great that our first long leg had gone well.

Flight Log   Date April 10, 1998   N61SL
LEG 3 Fairbanks -Barrow
Polar 1 Crew: Shane, Donny, Robert
True Course 032-102
Distance 1090 NM

chapter six

easter at the north pole

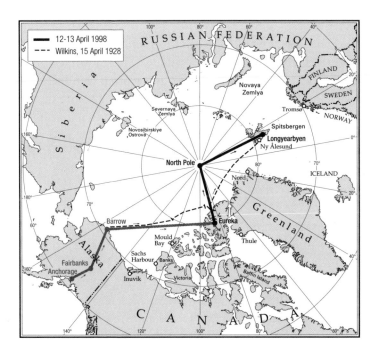

At 3 am I awoke in a warm, dark, airless room. I was thirsty and jet-lagged, though getting jet-lag from flying an Antonov is a contradiction in terms. Ferdinand breathed quietly on the other twin bed tucked up against my feet, sound asleep.

The long hallway led down one corridor, past a bookshelf loaded with well-thumbed paperbacks, a victim of the occupants' six-month work stints. The long shelves in the bathroom were lined with soap and cleaners, toilet paper and tissues. With infrequent resupplies, the bases had quantities that would last for months, if not years. Every shelf I saw, from the kitchen to the reading room, was stacked with row upon row of stuff. It wasn't just a few extra bottles or cans, but 48 or 64 or 128, the base obviously being subject to case-lot orders. I wandered farther along to the kitchen, the light outside the wide window glaring through, the white snow reflecting off the white clouds. The industrial-size fridge held yoghurts, fresh fruit and juice and I took it all back to the window and pulled up a chair for an Easter morning snack.

Suddenly there was a flash of movement from behind a building immediately in front of the window. Then a wolf popped its nose out, had a casual look around and trotted into full view. It was smaller than the wolves I had seen the year before in Mould Bay, but still a 100 percent wolf. The statement that a wolf is like a dog can have only been made by someone who has never seen a wolf in the wild. Its eyes cast around, confident and dark. It was young, evident by its playful saunter as it practically skipped across the snow. Obviously right at home, it moved up between the buildings at a trot, its feet clipping along over the snow with an effortless movement. It was pure white, darkening around the face, with upright triangular ears and a small black nose. The thick fur looked like wire standing out from its face. It glanced at me in the window, then as quickly as it had appeared, it disappeared around the corner and was gone. Easter morning, a wolf and no Easter Bunny. The Arctic was showing its true colors.

The clouds had come down over the fjord in front of Eureka and an orange boat sitting alongside a dock frozen into the ice looked very out of place, like any boat far from the sea. It was snowing very lightly; it didn't look like good flying weather. Midnight snack complete, I snuck back to bed for some serious sleep.

'Hey Robert, it's morning, we should get up,' said Ferdinand from the depths of his small bed. He was elegantly clad in pajamas, something I haven't worn for years, but an item that looked like a good addition to any polar flight. Nothing can be that serious if you are sleeping in a good pair of pajamas.

It was now 10 am and officially we had missed breakfast, but soon found we were the first of our crew to get up, barring Ron of course who had already been down to the planes. The cook, happy to oblige us after our sleep-in, soon had the grill smoking with bacon, eggs and potatoes. Out the dining room window the wolf was nowhere in sight, but the clouds were sitting close down over the hills. An occasional large snowflake drifted past. It definitely didn't look like flying weather. Shane had stopped by the weather office, conveniently located 30 feet down the hall, before breakfast. 'It is good weather everywhere but here. North of Ellesmere, Nord, Spitsbergen, all clear. We are just sitting under a big cloud on Ellesmere Island.'

It was similar to the situation we had faced in Barrow the year before. But instead of just getting off the ground and flying out over the flat sea ice, we had the additional problem of mountains in all directions. While they weren't too high, the fully loaded Antonov would climb very slowly, and directly between us and the Pole was a peak that rose to 6,300 feet. Ron and Shane talked it over, reviewed the maps and weather charts.

'We can fly out along the fjords,' said Ron. 'Plot the GPS to take us out the middle of the fjords all the way to the sea. From there the clouds should clear.' Shane set to work, the master navigator, with his charts laid out in front of him. In principle, it wasn't that difficult. But flying in low or no visibility with everything in shades of white, up narrow fjords, turning at exactly the right time, setting a new course, didn't allow for even a single minor error. The sides of the fjords rose steeply out of the sea ice and it would have taken only a small nudge to put the plane off course and into the mountains. The other problems that caused a few worries — an engine failure, a fuel problem, having to turn back in the narrow fjord — didn't bear thinking about. Ferdinand passed out chocolate Easter eggs and we munched away reflectively. Was Easter fortuitous or fatalist?

If our problem was flying once we got off the ground, back in Barrow in 1928, Wilkins was still trying to get airborne. He had finally cleared the new runway on Elson Lagoon, working day in and day out, and was set for yet another attempt to get into the air.

At three on Friday morning the weather was still fine and appeared likely to remain so. There was scarcely any wind. I was afraid to trust the weather too long and decided to try once again, knowing the runway was not long enough but hoping to gain such speed by the time we reached the end of it that we could career over the loose snow for some distance and finally get into the air. We tried this but found that as soon as we struck the loose snow we lost speed. There was nothing to do but shut off the engine, take the ship back to the end of the runway and clear the snow from the ice for a greater distance.

That was attempt number three to get off the ground. Wilkins remained undaunted and unafraid of hard work.

All Friday and Saturday we slaved. I hired every man and boy that came within hailing distance. The pay and the food attracted them. I am certain that these good fellows worked much against their will but for the sake of their friendship for us they worked well. By Saturday night we had a runway a mile long, perhaps longer, I was too dog-tired to measure it. I was forced to dig and shovel with the men to get them to keep up the pace. Hands blistered from the use of the saw would find relief in handling a shovel and when new blisters appeared it was a chance to get back to the use of the saw and pick again. I was satisfied that if the wind still held — it had freshened to a breeze from the northeast during Saturday — we would be able to into the air in the morning.

Shane spent the morning with Donny going over the charts and inputting all the way points in the GPS. We anxiously watched the weather, but frequent glances out the window only revealed a white glare. In the back of our minds was the thought of getting marooned. Last year we'd waited in Barrow for better conditions that turned out to be marginal when we finally flew. It seemed important to keep the momentum as long as conditions were flyable. Ron was particularly calm and unconcerned. He was in his element — none of the rest of us had been here before and flying out iced-up fjords with a 500-foot ceiling and little visibility seemed just a bit frightening. The year before I knew we wouldn't have flown, but this year everyone was more experienced and more committed. Shane and Ferdinand had spent the last six months preparing the Green Tortoise and had more confidence in it. Ferdinand had another year of flying and was now also working on his helicopter license.

Ron had more time to get to know us and probably felt that even if we were pretty green at times, we hopefully weren't going to do anything downright stupid. Trevor had over 500 hours of air time, weighed points from both sides and wasn't afraid to speak up which provided a valuable added perspective.

We hardly noticed the cold any more. When we went outside, we put on all our clothing and then we were warm. I think we all secretly coveted Donny's seal-skin pants — an environmental heresy but in practical terms, ideal for the conditions. Several years earlier, after ascending Mt McKinley, my photographer, Joe Blackburn, had purchased us both beaver-skin hats that had a large fur fluff on the front and fur flaps that pulled down over the ears. It had been partially on the recommendation of a bush pilot and partly a post-climb celebration. But I found it left modern fabrics for dead, wearing it on subsequent expeditions to the top of Antarctica and to Everest. It was far warmer, windproof and never iced up, just like Donny's black and white spotted pants.

The gas tanks were topped up with a last squirt of fuel and the oil was brimming at the top of the engine — nearly 100 liters. The loads were lashed as far forward as possible, anything heavy squashed up towards the front of the plane. Trevor and I were in Ron's plane, Polar Two, and Shane and Ferdinand were in their plane, Polar One, with Donny, for the flight to the Pole. Both Ron and Donny had experience in landing on the ice, as well as the most Arctic experience, so keeping one of them in each plane was essential. Donny was also a doctor and carried the reassuring traditional black doctor's bag with him wherever he went. On Polar Two, the only reassurance Ron and Trevor had was me and my National Ski Patrol badge and belt. If we hit the ice, I just prayed it was very gently.

The only major problem we still had was that Polar One lost nitrogen out of its left strut in the cold. It leaned at an angle that made it look quite drunk. More importantly, in a cross wind landing, it would have been very tricky to bring the wheels down onto the runway simultaneously if the pilot had to compensate for the wind. The solution was to let the other strut down as well. This left the Green Tortoise with a noticeably bow-legged appearance and with no bounce in its shocks for a rough landing. But it wasn't an insurmountable problem — we'd be flying for a very long time and only planned to land once, at the end of our journey, so it was worth the risk.

Back in Barrow, 21 April 1928, after three failed attempts to take off, Wilkins and Eielson lined up on the end of an ice strip they had carved out that was a mile long.

> 'Switch off?' to Eielson.
> 'Switch off,' he answered.
> 'Gas on?' I asked.
> 'Gas on,' he said.
> I swung the propeller sharply through three or four turns to suck gas into the cylinders, placed the blade at an angle marked previously to show when one piston was in firing position, then shouted:
> 'All clear?'
> 'All clear,' Eielson answered and snapped on the switch. He swung the booster magneto and as she had done each time we asked her to start, the engine coughed once, kicked back, coughed again and then emitted a steady purr. My heart swelled with thankfulness. The engine sounded fine and though the direction of the wind was not perfect it was still pretty good.
> The weather forecast, as I understood it, was in our favor for the greater part of the journey. We must chance what we might find at Spitsbergen. The only regret was that five gallons of gas I had intended to pour into the tanks before starting had leaked out during the night. There was no more on the field and without time to send back to the hanger we were forced to leave with the tanks not quite full. However, I felt we would have sufficient to cover any flight.
> I climbed into the Navigator's cabin and shouted, 'Let's go!' to Eielson. The Eskimo men yawed the tail of the machine and we

slid off the boards we had placed beneath the skis to prevent them from freezing to the snow. Away we went quickly gathering speed as we passed down the runway. The floor of the track was slightly undulating and as our speed increased Eielson had a difficult task to keep the fast moving plane within a width of fourteen feet. Thirty, forty, fifty miles an hour we gathered speed as we progressed, the machine behaving like a proud horse tugging at a load. From the cabin window I could see the tail planes swaying and missing by no more that a foot first one bank and then the other. I marveled at Eielson's skill and courage. An error of a few pounds pressure on the rudder, a swing of a few inches one way or the other and we would have hurtled into the snow bank, our skis would have buried themselves beneath the blocks we had thrown from the runway and disaster would have surely followed.

Eielson kept his nerve. I prayed. Sixty, seventy miles an hour. We lifted, swung sickeningly, touched the ice again — then soared smoothly into free air. Never has there been a more fervent prayer of thanksgiving than the one I uttered.

Wilkins was finally airborne on his audacious journey, yet the world was not without those who thought him crazy. As a fellow explorer in the Arctic and head of the Zenith Radio Corporation, Eugene McDonald, had stated after he met with the engineers from Ford, the great Arctic explorer Stefansson and the President of the American Geographical Society in New York:

At first, they could not understand why I refused to provide the radio equipment. But I was steadfast in refusing to have a part in a venture the end of which could hardly end otherwise than in sure death.

Our engines fired first time, the portable heaters having been whirring warmly through the night. Dick and the crew from the station were up to see us off with hearty handshakes. Polar One looked particularly low-slung as it taxied out and rolled down the runway, the fuel squashing it down close to the ground. Both planes turned and lined up, the engines dug into the air and we started our slow roll. It seemed to take even longer than usual to get off the ground, the plane climbing so slowly and the engine laboring under the immense load. Even so, we were soon up under the clouds in minutes, the ground hazy below us, spots of tundra and rock plainly visible. But the light was diffused, mist floated in and out, ice and hill and sky was all a mix of off-white color. There was nothing from which to gain perspective. Icebergs in the fjord below loomed large as they were the only thing on the ice. Cliffs on the side of the hill beside us appeared tiny and then grew to be hundreds of feet high as we drew near. Polar One looked like it was hovering along in front of us, so slow did we move.

'Just keep a lookout on your side,' Ron said to Trevor. We were passing close along the hill on the right. 'It's just here,' said Trevor a few minutes later, a trace of nervousness in his voice, mirroring my own feelings. Ron glanced over, 'Yes, that's fine, I was just trying to get some lift off the hills.' Here Trevor and I were getting worried about the hills a wingtip away, and Ron was surfing for wind currents!

Trevor, who was sitting in the right seat in the cockpit, recalls:

> Our initial track as we made our way along the coastline of Ellesmere Island was a series of dog-legs between the mountains, often only a few hundred feet or less from the sides of the inlets and valleys. The heavy aircraft was reluctant to gain height. The GPS on Ron's side of the aircraft was not reading correctly and Ron positioned by holding a loose formation to the right, higher and behind Polar One. Meanwhile in the right-hand seat, I watched my own GPS and called out the estimated distance from the sides of the fjords close on our right, and warned of the several protrusions and icy rock masses as they emerged out of the gloom a short distance ahead.

A few miles from Eureka, Shane called out new coordinates and we turned and headed north. Looking out the side window, it was as if the ice was rising up, the bergs getting bigger, then the hills growing straight out of the ice. The fjord looked like a glacier, ice tumbling and falling down, instead of a flat expanse of land-bound sea. Along with Wilkins, I was praying we would just get out of here. If I could have willed myself back on the ground at Eureka, I would have done so in an instant. Looking through the camera lens only made it worse: solid white, cloud rushing by, shadowy ice looming in the glare. Below us, Shane was navigating, voice calm and precise over the radio, '...five miles to turning point, bearing...two miles to turning point, bearing...'. We were skipping along behind in Polar Two as Ron tailed the Green Tortoise through the clouds, disappearing and then reappearing as we dodged from one white patch to the next. It seemed to be taking forever to get away from the clouds, they were so all-pervasive it was difficult to believe they would suddenly break up. In the midst of the clouds, Trevor and I were heartened by Ron's 'Things are pretty good, it's not as bad as it looks.' At this point I could see absolutely nothing out any window, except some very cold and brutal-looking ice ridges rushing past close below the plane, so I just took his word for it.

Forty minutes after takeoff, the first tiny spot of brightness appeared far to the north. It was so indistinct it could have been a mirage, but as we continued it grew lighter in color. Shane came on the radio — they had seen the clearing too and we set course to escape the clouds. Polar One moved up off the ice and started climbing, cresting a towering dark red-brown cliff of rock in front of us and breaking out over the sea ice. We broke out of the clouds, the sun came out and we were free from the Ellesmere Island weather.

Ron set the GPS and it inspirationally read 'North Pole' at the top. Trevor took over the controls and almost immediately was treated to another harsh lesson about Antonov flying:

> After we broke into the clear about forty minutes out of Eureka, Ron gave me control. Initially, I positioned the aircraft about half a mile directly behind Polar One. Serious wake turbulence is normally something associated with much larger aircraft. The wake turbulence behind a heavily loaded An-2 has to be experienced to be believed, as even at that distance

it is quite disproportionate. We nearly capsized as we made a couple of massive excursions with close to a 45° bank to the left, then to the right, then back again. I wrestled with the An-2's heavy ailerons to gain level flight. My flight instructor during my Antonov conversion had chided me on my habit of flying with one hand, and insisted I use both hands on the yoke in the Antonov, now I saw why. Thereafter I maintained a healthy offset from the course centreline if we were behind Polar One.

I have since learned that a number of light aircraft have been severely damaged from wake turbulence when following behind an Antonov.

After that quick wake-up, Trevor settled into his seat for what was to be a virtual non-stop stint of piloting that took us all the way to the North Pole.

Despite the claimed reliability of GPS systems, when Ron moved back for an afternoon nap and I moved to the cockpit, I soon noticed the system begin blinking. Suddenly the screen went blank and then stated: 'Only two satellites available, reset.' So much for modern technology! In bold print the map reminded us:

Because of weak directive force and magnetic storms, the compass becomes increasingly unreliable approaching the magnetic pole from a distance of approximately 1,000 miles.

With three GPS's, we hoped they didn't all suffer this problem at the same time. If they did, we'd be falling back on Donny's sextant readings. The importance of Wilkins' notes on the corners of his chart became more relevant, as their own course had to be charted hour by hour, as reflected in his careful script detailing their 'TRUE', 'VAR', and 'Compass Course', which he then scribbled on small bits of paper and passed forward to Eielson. Compared to our own convivial arrangement and onboard intercom, allowing us to talk freely on each plane or from plane to plane, Wilkins and Eielson had to scream down a tube which seemed to be rarely used, or pass notes back and forth. Shortly after takeoff Wilkins passed a note forward:

Dead Man's Island, where Wilkins and Eielson landed and were stranded for five days before just managing to get airborne and fly on to civilization. The rock is where bodies were laid in days past and covered with stones, but nonetheless 'sometimes eaten by the white bears.'

Shane sprints for the cockpit as Polar One's engine stutters at the North Pole, threatening to leave us stranded a million miles from home.

The tower in Ny-Alesund (Kings Bay) where Amundsen tethered his dirigible prior to his successful flight over the Pole. Shane wears a reindeer coat like the one Eielson wore for his 1928 flight.

The musk oxen herd Ferdinand and the author approached to within a 100 feet of, before they erupted from the snow like snorting dragons, forming a defensive phalanx nine strong.
Right: *An Arctic Hare alongside an Eskimo marking post set high on a hill above Mould Bay, Prince Patrick Island.*
Below: *One of a pair of Arctic wolves alongside the Mould Bay runway — lured closer by a tempting frozen pork chop by our French-Canadian hosts.*

'Wonderful takeoff. How's everything?'

'Everything great!' he shouted through the speaking tube. 'She handles fine. Engine turning seventeen twenty-five. Temperature hundred and twenty.'

... Ground speed was 108 mph. Drift ten degrees to the left. Wind at low altitude was slightly north of east, a little against us, but that I did not mind.

We knew we would be moving slower with our heavy fuel load, but as the evening wore on, rarely could we get above 65 knots, an infernally slow speed. At this rate if there was a half-decent road we could drive to the North Pole almost as quickly. But if we had a head wind going to the Pole, as we would be making over a 90° right turn at the Pole to reach Spitsbergen, we should have a tail wind for our final leg. So we chugged along, chalking off the degrees, another degree, another 60 miles, from Eureka at 80° North to the Pole at 90°. Trevor tailed Polar One, clocking up hours like a transcontinental jet pilot — the big jets occasionally reminded us of their presence as they came on the radio from 30,000 feet above us, 'Lufthansa cleared out of Anchorage, next stop, Frankfurt.' Only a few meals and two movies away from their destination, unknowingly living part of Wilkins' historical opening of the polar routes between the continents. Trevor and I had traded planes and not flown together before this sector. He piloted the plane confidently, though later related he had more than a few concerns in '...flying a relatively unfamiliar aircraft in an unfamiliar environment, concerned about mechanical reliability, particularly with respect to Polar One, dodgy undercarriage and all the implications of that for operational capability and fuel loading...'.

We had climbed slowly up to 6,500 feet, still not finding favorable winds. On the leg to the Pole, a decrease in speed of 35 knots meant over two extra hours of flying time. Last year's failure was in the back of all our minds and aboard Polar One, Shane kept casting anxious eyes over their fuel gauge as the auxiliary tank visibly drained towards the floor. With all the challenges of flying the Arctic, simply running out of gas again wasn't a problem we wanted. All the planning, the test flights, the change of route to start our journey from closer to the Pole, shouldn't lead to this. Besides, if we had headwinds going one way, shouldn't we have tail winds going the other?

I was always surprised how much there was to do when we were flying — the ever-present need to take video, stills and digital images, record notes, listen in on the radio or take the controls while Trevor reset his GPS, all balanced with a need to make the occasional sandwich and keep an eye on the fuel tank. The endless ice we passed over was an ever-changing kaleidoscope. With all the time Wilkins had spent on the ice, he had learned to read its every mood as they flew along. The ice we flew over would have appeared the same as in Wilkins' day, but he looked at it with a far different eye.

> Each snowdrift and ice ridge had a story to tell. To watch them as we passed above was like reading a familiar tale.
>
> The larger snowdrifts on the ice a hundred miles north of Barrow had been formed as the wind blew back from the East or West. There were smaller drifts running in various directions and this condition interpreted showed there had been winds from both East and West during or immediately after snow storms. The winds might have been more constant or equally strong from some other direction, but they had blown at lower temperatures and after the fresh fallen snow had hardened.
>
> … It is probable, though not necessarily positive, that the thick old conditions were the result of the peculiarities of the air-currents in that vicinity. The ice conditions indicated active, frequent changes in the air and directional movement of the old ice seemed to be restricted in its drift by converging currents of wind and water. It might be this ice accumulation is the result of snow in a comparatively calm zone, in which temperatures varied frequently. For, roughly estimated, two hundred miles after passing the old ice we crossed young ice, leads and ordinary pack such as is common on the edge of the Arctic Seas — where winds are variable and strong and sea currents forceful. By the look of the ridges on the ice in that area the drift and pressure had been alternately east and west with some pressure from all directions. Next we came to old heavy, ridged ice again and almost at the same time a cloud bank.

154

Wilkins didn't have a GPS. But his knowledge was so great that he could read the wind by watching the way the snow drifted across the ice, watch the color of the ice itself and see how and why it had formed and even look below the ice by watching the way the currents pushed and shaped the ice above it!

The weather was astounding clear, the sun blazing well above the horizon, but a layer of frost against the glass at the back door window belied the real outdoor temperature. The final few hours ticked by, headwinds holding our speed to a crawl, occasionally slipping up to 70 knots, then drifting back down to 65 again. We were getting there, but we sure weren't setting any speed records.

The GPS clicked through 89°50' North, then clicked through the final few minutes. The ice looked exactly the same, but the atmosphere somehow changed, we seemed very far away, very removed. It was easy to imagine riding the final few miles in a fairytale biplane, flying up the lines of longitude towards the very top of the globe. We clicked a back-up GPS off just to make sure we had one that didn't get confused once we circled the North Pole. Going around the world every five minutes when we circled the Pole would be apt to drive their computer brains mad.

There was nothing at the Pole that made it look any different than anything else we had seen in the last 500 miles — just ice and sun and long shadows cast by the pressure ridges rearing high over the ice. Ron took us on a lazy circle, dropping down towards the ice. Ron had been to the North Pole three times previously, twice in the fifties and again in 1968, landing somewhere in the vicinity. The exact location of the Pole with a GPS is now without question. Getting down on the ice on the right spot is a bit more problematical. We circled overhead, going around the world again, before Shane and Ferdinand, a few thousand feet above us and with a wider range of view, recommended a spot further out from where we were circling, just over the Pole. Ferdinand, sitting in the cockpit with Shane, took the controls for a celebratory loop around the world, lapping through every latitude and time zone in just a few minutes.

Several thousand feet below, Ron turned Polar Two and we

flew out to their location, dropping lower. Ron tipped the wings and flew along close over the ice, following our projected runway. 'Could you drop a flare?' he radioed across to Polar One. They flew in low behind us, Donny opened the back door and tossed out the flare. We saw nothing. They circled and Donny opened the door again for another eye-opening blast of –20°F air. This one dropped virtually straight down onto the ice, a light orange stream of smoke trailing vertically above it.

Ron had explained what he was looking for to land safely. He wanted a lead of ice that was relatively new and flat, a lead that had opened, then refrozen. If it was still darker than the surrounding ice, it was too thin, probably only up to a foot thick. If it was over a foot thick, the ice had usually consolidated and it would be clean white ice. What we needed, however, was two feet of ice. So Ron would drop down, make three gentle bumps, then pull up and circle round to see if the tracks turned dark and water had seeped into them. If the ice remained white and unchanged in color, it was solid enough to land on. We also needed enough space to land and park both the planes.

Ron pulled around again and we lined up for the ice strip, dropping low over the ice. Suddenly the pressure ridges grew from being indefinable ripples into towers of ice pushed up from the flat ice resting between them. We came over the ridge at the end of the flat ice, dropped down and touched the ice ever so gently, the tires just kissing the surface. Then the Antonov rose and settled again immediately, touching with a small bump. We skimmed the surface, then dropped again, bouncing hard against the ice, the engine roared and we climbed back into the sky. The perfection with which the plane had been just so lightly skimmed over the ice, then touched and finally bounced, was a precision bordering on the magical.

Just reaching the Pole was the goal we'd set. Getting down on the ice had always been discussed, but never really seriously contemplated by any of us except Ron. There were so many factors that made it difficult — cloud cover, wind, finding a place to land, using the added fuel, not to mention the landing itself —

that it was a plan that popped up only after a few beers in Anchorage. But here, with the stark reality of the surrounding ice, it seemed an even more remote possibility. After those three touches on the ice, I realized again not only Ron's depth of experience, but also the natural flying talent that backed it up.

Ron cut a tight corner and looked out the window. 'Looks good and the ice is at least two feet thick. See how it has curled up on the edges of the old ice where it has expanded,' he said. 'I'll take her in.' He turned the final corner, lined up and we set down on the carpet of white ice. We came to a quick rolling stop, I pulled open the door and jumped out. The ice wasn't hard, but had a cushion of frost overlying it which crushed underfoot like a thick carpet. The tires of the plane had sunk in little more than a few inches before hitting the solid ice below. The ice was absolutely flat. Ron spun the plane, turning the nose and lining it up exactly as I had requested for my photos. It was perfect. I was aware of a euphoria, the intense cold, no wind, the glare of the sun, the soft ice crystals underfoot, my breath erupting in steam clouds from my mouth and nose, the plane rumbling nosily and the sound disappearing into the expansiveness.

Polar One came around behind us, lined up and Shane brought it in next to our tracks. It touched the ice further along the ice runway and Shane saw the end of the strip and a drop-off rapidly approaching; he hit the brakes, the plane skidded, then skidded again. The end of the strip was looking like the final resting place for Polar One. But he hit the brakes again and spun the tail wheel and they turned. He pulled Polar One up to park alongside us. We were at the North Pole.

Trevor and Ron jumped out of Polar Two behind me. It was minus 22°F and we'd stepped from the warm, familiar surrounds of our planes right into an ice wonderland. The emotion seemed to be universal, as Trevor, the most reserved of our team, recounted.

> I was quite unprepared for the intensity of my inner feelings, I was absolutely elated and it felt as though a huge cloud had suddenly lifted, and the sun shone through. I gave Ron the benefit of some well-meant congratulatory impromptu Irish

adjectives which are not really printable. I thought Shane and the rest of the team were for that moment truly 'Masters of the Universe'. The modesty considered proper on such occasions had gone from me.

Once we were on the ice and out of the aircraft, I was absolutely elated and hugely impressed by Ron's performance. Not only had he executed the whole surface testing and landing like the masterly Arctic fox that he is, but he even had sufficient reserves to discuss and contemplate the best photo lighting angles during the process.

We posed for photos, dragging everybody into line in front of Polar One. I proceeded to snap away. I was on the third shot when suddenly Polar One coughed loudly behind us. Everyone turned their head and even as I watched through the lens, Shane sprinted from the line, around the prop and the far wing, and dove through the rear door. We'd left the engines idling and his engine had dropped back just a notch, causing it to miss and cough, a prelude to it conking out completely. While it may have started again, the risk if it did stop was too much to even think about. He reset the throttle and jumped back out to rejoin the photographs. We were on a perfectly flat platform, surrounded by ridges, the ice leading off over the horizon. It was a magical place. With the ice movement, we were undoubtedly the only people to ever step on this particular piece of ice, and as it would soon drift away from the Pole, it would fade into obscurity. Not only did we have the Pole, we had exclusivity.

Ron and Trevor were calling before I knew it. I shook hands quickly with Shane, Ferdinand and waved at Donny, who'd wandered off to the far end of the ice strip. I pulled the door shut and knelt to peer out the window as they reboarded Polar One and Ron swung us around to taxi down to the end of our runway. The decreased fuel load meant we were off the ice easily and rising back into the blue, Polar One following close behind us. With the longitudes inches apart, Ron reset the GPS and watched the directional gyro and astrocompass closely to set us off on our new course to the south. A short time later Trevor turned his

GPS back on and we started a slow steady climb back out over the ice.

Just like reaching the summit of Everest, being at the North Pole was an emotional high, but climbing back down from the geographical top of the world and reaching Spitsbergen was going to be the real challenge. We had 709 nautical miles to go, further than on our route in. We'd already consumed over half our fuel supply. But we'd had head winds all the way and now the planes had shed over 2,000 pounds of fuel weight. We should be skipping through the air. A hundred miles out and an hour later we were still dragging along at little over 70 knots. We had turned just over 90° and were now headed straight south on the 16° East meridian. What was the wind doing?

The GPS didn't allow for any maybes. Not only did it show location and distance, it also indicated very plainly 'time to destination'. Our time to destination was greater than our remaining hours of fuel. Spitsbergen often had open water extending out from the island, the most dangerous place to land — or splash, as the case would be.

Wilkins, after having been in the air eleven hours, had also begun asking the same questions and looking for answers, some which didn't augur quite as well as they would have liked either.

About this time Eielson, who could see the gas gauges and the tachometer which I could not, handed me a note reading: 'Engine been turning about sixteen fifty. We are using approximately eighteen gallons an hour. Now about forty gallons left in wing tanks. Oil temperature hundred and five.' This showed that our gas consumption so far was high. We should soon be consuming less gas as our load was getting down to normal. By rough calculation I figured that if we could get the consumption down to even twelve gallons an hour on the last quarter of the journey we should have enough to complete twenty hours flying. We were averaging more than a hundred miles an hour over the ice. The distance over our course was about twenty-two hundred miles. We had see-sawed over the

159

clouds and we would probably see-saw again. We had also, from my observations, swung a little to the right on one leg of our journey and a little too much to the left on the next leg. It was not possible to keep accurate within a mile or so. I felt certain that if my interpretation of the meteorological conditions were right that we should have no violent head winds and that we could make it, but I knew it would mean piloting with strict attention to the job and most careful navigation.

Trevor and I were watching the gauges and neither of us felt too comfortable. Ron had slipped back for a midnight snack and a nap. The euphoria of the North Pole had well and truly faded. Had we pushed out too far? Did we have any alternatives? Unlike Wilkins, I wasn't so sure I could walk home. Trevor's piloting would have put an autopilot to shame — hour after hour — straight down our course towards Spitsbergen.

Over on Polar One, Shane, Ferdinand and Donny were in worse shape than us. Ron's tank held about 20 more gallons of fuel as he had moved the filler cap to a higher location and it allowed him to top it off right to the brim. Polar One, even after its overhaul, had always seemed to consume just a little more fuel than Polar Two. Their estimates for time versus fuel were falling well short of reaching Spitsbergen. Three hours out from the North Pole, Shane came on the radio: 'We are diverting to Nord, our fuel is an hour short of Spitsbergen.' We had been on the radio to Spitsbergen, but had been unable to reach Nord. When Shane informed Spitsbergen they were diverting to Nord, the only response was, 'It is forbidden to land at Nord, repeat, it is forbidden to land at Nord.' About that time Shane's radio began breaking up — he was going to Nord, it was the only airport he felt they could reach.

I'd stepped back out of the cockpit and woken Ron. 'Everything's fine, but I think they need you on the radio for reassurance.' Ron can be a bit gruff at times, but it is a very effective way to communicate exactly what needs to be done quickly in tense situations, leaving no room for doubt as to the best decision.

There were several weather stations/military bases in Northern Canada and Greenland that provided us with alternative landing sights, but they were for emergency use only and don't allow visitors. Even so, with its fuel levels dipping low and headwinds increasing, Shane felt their was little choice for Polar One but to shoot for the closest possible landing point. There was also another imponderable — should we stick together or not? Trevor and I were mulling over much the same thoughts:

> Shane's decision to divert because of inadequate fuel raised a whole lot of dilemmas — should we have followed? After all, I thought the whole idea was to operate a buddy system rather as scuba divers do … should I have 'debated' the point more vigorously with Ron? Would us following merely, as Ron implied, be likely to put both aircraft on the ground at the wrong place, with the possibility of there being no fuel there, or fuel insufficient for two aircraft, at the diversion landing place? Was the buddy system really quite illusionary in many respects anyway, in many cases if one aircraft got into trouble all the other aircraft could have done was to watch helplessly?
>
> However in other cases a swift rescue off the ice would be a distinct possibility. Would us diverting also merely satisfy a sense of obligation, without adding anything useful in real terms, and perhaps even compromise the expedition?
>
> When Shane reported substantially increasing headwinds, whilst ours marginally reduced, when Spitsbergen reported CAVOK and the Nord area weather mentioned poor visibility and white-out conditions … my concerns further increased.

Though the plan had been to stick together, Ron had been to Nord two years before and they had no fuel. Going there could mean we were really stranded and would have to fly fuel in, probably on a special charter flight, at a cost that would have been astronomical. If we were both there and there was no fuel it would be even worse. If Polar Two carried onto Spitsbergen and Polar One reached Nord, we could always ferry fuel over to them. As Trevor has pointed out, it wasn't an easy decision. Ron would have also had a feeling that even though Polar One was low on fuel, they had a very good chance of making it into Nord and having us beside them would have been little more than psychological assurance.

We had a few increasingly distant and difficult-to-read radio calls from Polar One. Things were definitely not improving. They had no weather report from Nord beyond a faint 'overcast…not good'. They were hitting increased headwinds and their speed was under 60 knots, while ours was now touching 90 knots. At that rate they would be lucky to make Nord at all, never mind the weather. Then their radio faded completely. Trevor continued to take us on over the ice. Ron edged the throttle back by millimetres, listened, then edged it back some more until we were just chugging along, sipping fuel. Fourteen and then fifteen hours passed. The world seemed all ice, the horizon filled with hazy fading cloud that disappeared as we flew closer. I crawled back from the warmth of the cockpit and dozed and woke, forgetting the day, the time, waking to immense shivers in the back of the plane.

How long could one live aboard an Antonov, how many peanut butter and honey sandwiches could I eat, when would I again be able to bite into an apple that wasn't frozen hard with ice, why did a thermos specially preheated and cooked to boiling just before take off now hold only frosty coffee syrup?

Wilkins had his timepieces all freeze up on an earlier journey — something we didn't have to worry about with a mechanical Rolex on our wrists. We'd set one time to the international GMT clock (Zulu time) so that if we went down on the ice and the digital devices failed, we still had a foolproof way of knowing where we were.

Wilkins had sailed along through increasingly bad weather, busy making observations of his own.

> Vision ahead was bad. We ploughed through several cloud banks. I was hastily writing a note to inform Eielson of my estimate of the exact position, and to say that we could not afford to go into the cloud to look for Grant Land [Ellesmere Island] and suggest that he swing due north to clear the cloud when I heard him shout. I looked out of the window and saw slightly to the right and not far — perhaps less than twenty miles away — the rugged mountain

162

tops of Grant Land piercing the clouds. It was a fleeting glimpse we had, but served to stir deep emotion in our hearts.

'Robert, we are coming in over land — you may want to get some pictures.' The dark line of mountains rising from the ice marking Spitsbergen with the clouds formed halo-like overhead were a homecoming after more than fifteen hours over the ice. Land, what a novel concept! The peaks rose jaggedly from the sea, immense faces, snow-filled valleys cast like rolling streams of white, cotton-candy softness set between black cliffs. The afternoon sunshine cast immense shadows and hues of muted white over the landscape, primeval in its isolation.

Wilkins, after crossing the Arctic Ocean, had finally arrived off the coast of Spitsbergen in a major blizzard. They spotted a twin-spired mountain in the cloud, so dropped down low over the sea and just narrowly missed crashing into another mountain that suddenly appeared out of the clouds.

It soon became evident that what we had missed was a small mountainous island, also that it was useless for us to remain over the water. Back we turned towards the land only to be rewarned by the steep mountains. We were like an imprisoned bird beating against a window pane.

Wilkins spotted a small patch of white through the mist and began passing Eielson notes:

'Turn right.'
   'Now to the left.'
   'A bit more.'
   'No, we have passed it.'
   ... It was impossible for Eielson to see but with steady nerve braced for all eventualities he levelled the ship until lost in the swirling snow.
   We came smoothly to rest.

We flew up the fjord over a belching coal-fired power generating plant and around past a village set at the head of a wide, U-shaped valley. Trevor describes our final moments in the air:

Ron took the controls and demonstrated an expedited approach Alaskan bush pilot style which is as expeditious as it is different from the air traffic controller's instructions, but then air traffic control don't have our view of the fuel gauges.

We dropped without a bump onto the expansive runway. We'd been journeying for 17 hours, 15 minutes. We were on land, we were in Norway, we had been to the North Pole and we had walked on the ice. Physically, our bodies were relieved, happy, even though Trevor mentioned later that his epic sojourn in the cockpit was not without some penalty. 'Amongst other things my right buttock had gone numb some hours back and it took nearly two weeks to recover.'

We stood there on flat ground, swaying a little with the stability of it all. But there was no euphoria. We had not heard from Polar One in over three hours and had no idea if they had managed to make it to Nord. Somewhere beyond the mountains and the ice and the rocks of Spitsbergen was a huge expanse called the Greenland Sea and the Arctic Ocean and somewhere out there still was Polar One with Shane, Donny and Ferdinand aboard.

Captain's Log
Polar One's Southbound Solo Flight
North Pole – Nord – Spitsbergen

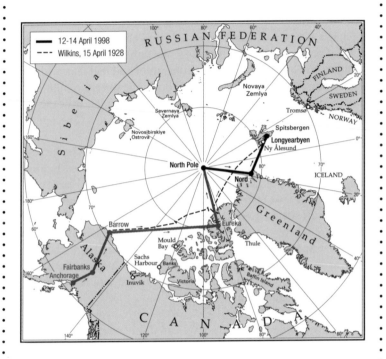

Whatever you can do or dream you can, begin it for boldness has genius, power and magic in it.

Goethe

Landing at the North Pole was a dream. I had given it about ten-to-one odds. After years of thoughts, efforts, and dreams here I was.

Flying to the Pole had always been the spoken objective but with such perfect weather conditions a polar landing was suddenly within our grasp. I crossed directly over the Pole and banked the aircraft to the left, flying a circle around the top of the world. Circumnavigating the world in thirty seconds confused even the GPS as the bearing and track numbers swam around hopelessly.

The conditions were perfect. The trick was to find a smooth piece of ice that was long enough to get the plane stopped, and thick enough to hold the weight. I was still holding a higher altitude than Ron and had a better perspective of the open areas but the scale was deceiving. How much of a runway was enough? Ron flew low over an area that I spotted from above and said that it looked pretty good. 'Let's drop a smoke flare and check the wind conditions,' he radioed. I circled the target and had Donny drop an orange smoke bomb out the aft door. We were too high and missed the target. On the second pass, I came in low over the ice hummocks.

Donny hit the landing area perfectly and the orange smoke rose almost straight up. There was no wind. Ron followed behind our smoke drop and landed first. I could see Polar Two touching down, snow blasting up behind her. It was awesome to see the aircraft sitting down there alone on top of the world. I began to configure for the approach, giving myself plenty of room to stabilize speed and landing attitude. I still could hardly believe it. I had spent over twenty years landing aircraft on terra firma, but this was my first landing on ice. There was nothing like starting at the top of the world!

Touching down on Ron's tracks, I eased the power back and began to apply the brakes. There was a large fissure in the pack ice on my left side which I was being careful to avoid. I tried to ignore the fact that 14,000 feet of Arctic Ocean lay beneath me. I thought that the powdery snow on the pack ice might help to slow me down after landing, but the brakes were useless. I pumped them a few times. I was not stopping, I didn't even think I was slowing down.

A large ice ledge, about a two-foot drop-off, lay just ahead. It seemed like slow motion as the plane slid towards the ledge. I could see Ferdinand squirming in my periphery, his feet pushing on the pedals trying to use brakes he didn't have.

At the last moment I gave the plane full right rudder and locked the right wheel brake to try and swing the tail round. We finally spun around and were facing the opposite direction. I goosed the throttle to power out and away from the ledge. I taxied up to Ron's aircraft, my legs shaking. If I had gone over the edge it probably would have meant abandoning the aircraft.

Ron and I had decided to leave the engines of the aircraft running. If we shut them down and were unable to get them restarted, it would mean that everyone would have to pile into one aircraft...or worse. Ferdinand and Donny jumped out to chock the wheels with spiked ice-gripping chocks. I sat alone in the cockpit for a moment, awed by where I was. My Antonov at the North Pole. It was the culmination of a lifetime of childhood dreams.

The stiffness in my body after more than eight hours' flying made it awkward to squeeze past the fuel tank to the back of the aircraft and put on my mukluks and parka. It was so cold with the door open to the Pole that I could barely get my laces tied. I jumped out the door into the prop wash, and realized how cold the air was as my ears began to sting. According to the thermometer it was –25°C. The team was completely exhilarated. Rolls of film were shot in the first few minutes. We all congratulated each other heartily, and there was a certain exuberance, a wild look in everyone's eye, which said it all. The hummocks and pressure ridges which surrounded our landing place seemed improbably high, the place improbably surreal. We were surrounded, sitting on a patch of smooth ice which was our world. The brightness of the light on the snow was intense, the cold biting.

When we lined up to take a photo of the team, the engine of my aircraft suddenly started to sputter. I sprinted back and dived into the cockpit. The throttle lock had loosened and the vibration of the engine was working the throttle back to idle. It was about to die as I slowly fed in fuel to revive the sputtering engine. I reset the throttle and tightened the lock before returning to the ice cap.

We spent forty minutes at the Pole. When we reboarded Polar One, it took a few moments to calm down and then go through the checklist. Flaps reset to 15°, cowl and oil flaps set for take-off, and the flight control trims set. Once airborne, I did a 270°

167

turn to the left and pointed the aircraft towards Spitsbergen. The GPS needed a bit of an offset for a starting point as otherwise all points on the planet were south of us.

In celebration of the polar landing Ferdinand poured a wee dram of single malt scotch for us to share. I knew that I now faced the challenge of getting home, but I hoped the sip of whiskey might relax me a bit. When the airship *Italia* arrived at the Pole in 1928 its crew toasted their success with a shot of avocaat, a thick yellow egg nog drink. I wanted to remain true to form and a toast seemed only appropriate.

Departing the Pole, I already had a gnawing doubt about having enough fuel to make it to Spitsbergen. I was trying to think where to divert to in the sparse regions of the Arctic. Ferdinand was very happy, but he had not really been watching the fuel situation, and was unaware of my concern. Donny had been asleep in the back during much of the flight to the Pole, which I encouraged, as it meant that he would be fresh when I needed him to assist in flying at the end of our journey. Because of this he also didn't know what the fuel situation was. After our short celebration I wanted to get together to see if we all came to the same conclusions on the numbers — if perhaps I had miscalculated. The mood quickly became subdued as calculations were checked and crosschecked. I spoke with Ron on the radio and again this year he had more fuel than me. On each previous leg we had been even, but now he had about 40 gallons more. Part of this was because of our deflated strut in Eureka didn't allow us to fill the tank full and part of it was because of the fueling point on the aux. tank. Whatever the reasons, Polar Two had an hour and a half more fuel than Polar One. I needed some luck to make it to Spitsbergen. I decided to climb up to 6,000 feet to try to save gas and in the hope I'd pick up more favorable winds.

Although the weather in Spitsbergen was reported to be good, I was concerned about the possibility of open water around the islands. It would be a bad ending to have to ditch into Arctic waters. While we carried survival suits and a life raft, the idea of finishing in this manner was unappealing. When Wilkins approached Spitsbergen in 1928 he had the same thoughts: '...the

168

sea held for us no haven of rest or safety unless, forsooth, it should be a long, long rest.'

I continued flying towards Spitsbergen for two hours in the hope that I could get some tailwind, that the fuel burn would drop. It was eventually evident, no matter how I ran the numbers, that continuing on to Spitsbergen was a long shot. It didn't look possible to make it to the airport in Longyearbyen. My background is in commercial air transport, where I am used to plenty of options, multiple alternates, familiar surroundings. This was different. I had one alternate airport which I had never been to, and no information as to the weather. At least if I was forced to land short of Greenland, I could land on the pack ice and stay in the aircraft. I have never run out of fuel in an aircraft and I was not willing to accept this as an option. In a Boeing, if you run out of fuel you have bought the farm, and this mentality is pretty well ingrained in my flying.

The only option was to divert to Greenland and the Danish military base at Station Nord. Longyearbyen airport lay at N78 and Nord at N81.36, a difference of 216 nautical miles. Greenland was no cakewalk, but it was closer and the odds looked better. I spoke with Ron about my decision, and was surprised when he informed me that he intended to continue on to Spitsbergen. He didn't think that there was enough fuel in Nord Station for both aircraft. He also thought that he could coordinate an air rescue for me out of Norway if I was forced to land on the ice. There was not much I could do about his decision. I had to get my aircraft going on a different course, the GPS coordinates had to be carefully inserted and checked, fuel notations made and an alternate plan attended to.

We stayed in close radio contact and tried a number of HF radio frequencies to contact the Danish military, advise them of our plans and to try to get a weather report for Nord. I expected high terrain in Greenland and if the weather was tricky it could be a difficult approach. I had been given a photocopied approach chart of the airport prior to leaving Anchorage, but had never thought I would need it. Strange how small pieces can end up being so important! Turning the aircraft to the right we said goodbye to Polar Two and began our own little adventure. Not long afterwards, clouds began to build. As I approached them I climbed up — up to seven and eight thousand feet and the clouds were still above me. It was useless. Flying through the clouds I could occasionally see the ice below, but mostly I was in a solid whiteout. It was extremely fatiguing and we took turns flying as I was tired after the long flight to the Pole. Wilkins and Eielson faced a similar situation: 'We had been thirteen hours in the air, long enough to be tired and cramped. The gas consumption had been more than we expected during the early part of the trip.'

Once we were headed to Nord, I needed to get some rest so that I would be alert for the approach. In the back I made tea for Donny and Ferdinand before wedging myself onto the floor next to the fuel tank. I wanted to stay up forward where they could wake my up in an instant if I was needed. When I thought about Eielson and the fact that he stayed on the controls for twenty hours in 1928, I was happy to have a few extra pilots on the aircraft. During my polar attempt in 1997, the longest leg of flying had lasted eleven hours and forty minutes. This flight was well beyond that already.

I woke up to turbulence. We were flying through clouds and the air was unstable. The groundspeed had dropped as a headwind dogged us again. The GPS showed an ETE (estimated time en route) of 3 hours 30 minutes to Nord, which was what it showed an hour ago when I had gone to sleep. The only thing dropping was the fuel level. I climbed back into the cockpit. I was starting to expect the worst.

Seventy years ago Wilkins had run into much the same conditions north of Spitsbergen: 'The air was turbulent above the clouds; beneath them it was boisterous. Our now almost empty plane was tossed like a cork on a stormy sea. Loose things in the cabin tumbled and rattled. With nothing to get a grip on I tumbled too, if I didn't rattle.' We were all rattled, as the conditions deteriorated. Ferdinand disappeared to the back of the aircraft and when I went to look for him, I found him smoking a cigarette on the toilet. Not a good idea in our flying fuel tank, but at least the aux. fuel was burned.

Donny was silent and looked like a scared owl, his brows arched in concentration. During this time I attempted to speak with the Danish military to advise them of my intention to land at Nord. They requested my position. It was very difficult to hear them over the radio static but I gave them my coordinates. Over the radio crackle it sounded like they advised me that I had no permission to land at Nord. I thought about this for a moment before answering. If I acknowledged that I had no permission it might present problems to go ahead and land there. On the other hand, I couldn't really hear them very well...so I gave them my position again, and advised them that their radio transmissions were coming in unreadable. It was fortunate that the words *position* and *permission* sounded alike over the airwaves. In a worst-case scenario if the runway was actually closed for some reason I could land on the ice next to the station. I was willing to keep going without permission. We really didn't have any other option.

In 1928 Wilkins wrote a note to Eielson:

There are two courses open. We are above the storm now. Down there we can land and wait until it's over. Can we get off again? If we go on we will meet storm at Spitsbergen and perhaps never find the land. Do you wish to land now?

Ben with his solid courage and calm considering mind wriggled in his seat. I could see a few inches of his shoulders above the gas tanks, his head being hidden by the wing. In less than a minute he replied: 'I'm willing to go on and chance it.'

Two hours passed as the Antonov struggled along. The ground-speed dropped to 58 knots. Then ever so slowly, almost imperceptibly, the sky lightened. Our speed began to increase and it looked like we might make it to Nord. Fifty miles out I radioed the station on the VHF radio and they advised me that the weather was good and that I was actually cleared to land. The shore lead of black icy water at the north end was very wide and I kept my altitude so as to glide across if the engine quit. From ten miles out I still could not see the field and I began to wonder if I had inserted the correct coordinates into the GPS.

Finally, Ferdinand spotted the radio antennas and from there I spotted the dark mounds of snow around the huts. It was the most insignificant-looking place I have ever seen at first glance. The snow hid practically everything and the massive scale of the undulating ice cap in the distance dwarfed the tiny outpost. I circled the station and lined up on the runway, but they had dyed a huge red stripe down the center which made it look like there were two runways. I wondered which one to land on. There was a stiff cross wind from the right and high snow banks along the sides, and by now the orange fuel low warning lights were on. I needed to get her down soon. The Antonov settled back onto the earth and her big balloon tires took up what little cushion we had left in the struts. As I rolled towards the end of the runway, a Mercedes jeep appeared and I was escorted, along with a snowmobile, one on each wing, to where I could park.

I was so relieved to be on the ground, but I now expected to have trouble with the Danish military for landing at their base. Fortunately they were very friendly and pleased to have our company. They offered us dinner and accommodation for the night. And best of all they had aviation fuel available. They told me a story of an American who had been here with a similar plane a few years back and needed fuel. Since then it had been ordered from Denmark. When I looked at the photos of the American and his airplane, I was surprised to see Ron and Polar Two — Nord's last unannounced visitor from two years before!

chapter 7

'sometimes eaten by the white bears'

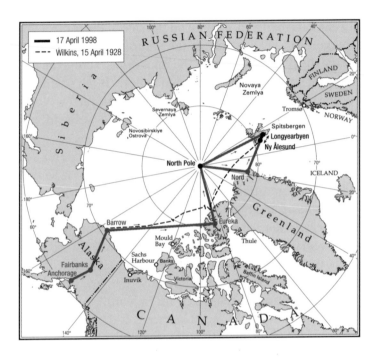

Trevor stepped out of Polar One in Spitsbergen onto the short ladder and stood there a moment before touching his foot gingerly on the ground. After over 17 hours in the Antonov and endless white, even the black asphalt of the runway was disorienting. There were no trees in Spitsbergen, only a towering hangar, a flat ice-covered fjord and rolling mountains in all directions. The town and coal mill were a few miles away. There wasn't another airplane in sight, only a five-story control tower and a small airline terminal. The ground underfoot was strangely solid and the brain was hyperactive, taking in all the new sights and sensations after being immersed in the world of the Antonov for so long.

Then we were straight back to business, remembering the airplane, as Ron followed Trevor to earth and we blocked the wheels, secured the flaps and tail rudder. A few mechanics appeared from the hangar and strolled over, welcoming us to Spitsbergen. The one question we all had — where was Polar One — they couldn't answer. We paused under the sign 'Svalbard Lufthaven Lonyearbyen' printed on the side of the control tower. Spitsbergen had been sitting at the end of our polar charts for two years, the place to which all the lines drawn across the Arctic led. Now we were here, it was hard to believe. It felt so different, so European, yet a large pole pointing with long arrows to London, Tokyo and New York made it seem as if we were still a very long way from anywhere.

At the entrance to the control tower we removed our shoes. 'You always take your shoes off here. The coal dust is so bad, it has been a long tradition,' commented Ron. The top of the tower was five floors up and there was no lift. My legs were heavy. When we got there, a lone man, dark hair, brusque but distinctively soft Norwegian voice, welcomed Ron, known from his annual sojourns in Spitsbergen. We exchanged pleasantries, then the traffic controller remembered suddenly, 'Oh yes, your friends, they called ten minutes ago. They are in Nord.'

At last we could be happy. Now we could celebrate! Smiles came on our faces; the team, if still separated, was at least intact. There was no longer the horrible silence, the message 'Well, we last heard from them...'. Our success was assured now we didn't have to drag our worries around in a frozen wasteland until we would have had no more joy from our accomplishment. Inside the tower it was warm and we grew sleepy. We had the news we wanted. The taxi took us the few miles to town, Trevor booked us all rooms at the Svalbard Polar Hotel, and we wasted a lot of hot water.

A few hours later we resurfaced. We adjusted our watches and the date. We were feeling a little more civilized. It was dinner time, or more properly, the cocktail hour. Large tall beers were poured, glasses clinked. The hotel was an oasis of culture and sophistication surrounded by snowdrifts and snow machines. There are 700 cars in Longyearbyen and 1,400 snow machines. They have more snow trails than roads, as roads only cover a grand total of 45 kilometers. In the Nansen Room Restaurant, two-story picture windows framed the view over the frozen fjord. White tablecloths, white napkins, tall wine glasses which needed to be filled and refilled. The menu was crowded with scallops and caviar, Arctic char and reindeer steaks. We ordered all of it and a good dose of cloudberries for dessert. Twenty years previously I'd lived and worked in Norway with relatives, spending days in a factory and Arctic twilight nights climbing rocks along the fjords — Norway was a second home and returning there from the Pole was like sneaking into heaven through the back door.

We talked until our eyes fell shut on our desserts and our wine glasses looked emptily back at us, then we crawled off to lie flat and toasty under fluffy down comforters and crisp starched sheets. We'd been up for close to two days and the 17 hours we had been en route was like a year of experience. At least we were in a warm bed and we knew where we were — Wilkins had finally landed, but was still trying to figure out where he was.

Our coast to coast, non-stop flight had been ended. We had been twenty hours and twenty minutes in the air. It was less than half an hour since we first sighted the twin mountain peaks yet it seemed like an eternity to us. After a short rest Eielson began to regain his hearing and we commenced to figure out our exact position. From dead reckoning we reasoned we should be in the neighborhood of Kings Bay but the island we had seen in flight was confusing. There was no such island on our chart. True, the chart we had was on a small scale, twenty miles to the inch, and small islands may not have been included in the drawing. The snow-covered mountains gave us no clue as to position for they were not indicated on our chart. There was nothing to help us until the sun shone and even then our method of navigation was not considered to be accurate within ten or fifteen miles.

He was also overwhelmed by the distance they had flown crossing the Arctic.

We had flown just about half way around the world in one hop. We tried to make it seem real that at Barrow Fred Hopson and Charlie Brower, whom we had left twenty hours before, could be eating breakfast while the inhabitants of Spitsbergen would be having their evening meal.

In an hour or so our strained nerves relaxed and we slept.

I was up at four, my body indecisive as to whether it should be day or night, the eternal light outside reviving me. I dropped the photos off our digital camera and onto my computer, just to make sure. They were all there, the North Pole on a pixel, ready to be sent off around the world. Outside Spitsbergen was quiet, the snow machines at rest, a hazy but bright twilight covering the snow. The tourist brochure stated in bold print that a walk could be dangerous.

Polar bears: Longyearbyen is usually not visited by polar bears. Thus hiking in this area should be relatively safe, but a chance encounter should not be ruled out. It is strongly recommended to carry firearms on trips.

When words like 'usually' and 'relatively safe' are used in the same paragraph as 'polar bear,' you don't have to be too bright to realize a midnight stroll is not such a good idea. As the coal industry, Spitsbergen's only real business, was dying, they wanted to attract more tourists. When talking to my climbing partners in Norway about climbing in Spitsbergen, they had related how a European expedition had a polar bear pull one man from his tent, drag him across a thin open lead of water and proceed to eat him in full view of the rest of the party. As they had no gun, there was nothing they could do but watch — and hope the polar bear wasn't still hungry when he finished. News like this hadn't helped the adventure travel industry and brochures and posters now erred on the conservative side.

176

Three hours after I awoke, typed up the latest segment of our journey, sorted the photographs and read all the tourist brochures, breakfast was finally served. Platters of jarlsberg and gjetost cheese, baby salamis and pickled herrings, cloudberry jam and loaves of thick wheat bread graced our plates. Ron and Trevor were up early as well, the buzz of the Antonov still echoing in our heads.

Trevor had begun Pembroke Capital's sponsorship with a strong personal interest and a belief in the value of its corporate potential. He'd joined more as passenger than pilot, but had been quickly elevated to the front seats — and would have spent more time at the controls than anyone else by the time we landed in Spitsbergen. More importantly, his personal contribution had been in many ways greater than his financial one; sweeping wings free of ice, offering a reasoned and experienced outside perspective on our plans, while also fitting comfortably into a team that had already formed a year before he had a chance to fly with any of us besides Shane.

As part of his corporate support, he'd also promised not to spend too much time out of the office and was already due back at work. He had managed to arrange a commercial flight back to Norway and on to Ireland for that afternoon. He was reluctant to leave with Polar One still having to make the long crossing from Greenland to Spitsbergen, but as they had found fuel and reported good weather, the flight shouldn't be too difficult. I was in much the same situation, having taken an optimistic week from work — but my return to Seoul with a combination of time change and distance wouldn't have seen me reach home until the end of the week anyway. I faxed Stephen Fraser at Ogilvy and Mather, Seoul, with claims I was being chased by a polar bear, and visited the office of the world's most northern newspaper for a local update on Longyearbyen from the editor, Nils Lorentsen, and to download my latest entries to Laura.

Wilkins was not quite as comfortable, though they had crashed just around the corner.

All the next day the southerly wind continued, to later swing sud-
denly north again and beat down with a fury bringing icy chill.
Our thermometers had fallen to the floor and broken and we could
not register the temperature except by feel. Until we knew exactly
how much gas we had we could not afford to burn gasoline for fuel,
so in a cup we burned some alcohol and melted snow for drinking
purposes. We could have nothing hot in the plane, for the same
principle would apply as regards the snow-house or tent. If we raised
the temperature in the cabin the hoar-frost on its walls would make
it uncomfortable. Another reason we felt that we did not need to
heat our food. We had learned last year that we could manage very
well with cold water, dry biscuit, chocolate and pemmican.

Ron walked back from the airport that afternoon, having checked the plane over completely after the long flight. 'They'll be in late this afternoon,' he said. 'The tower talked to them on the radio and they have already taken off.'

We went back out to the airport and were on the runway an hour later when we heard the familiar distant throbbing of the Antonov. A few years previous a Russian jet had made a mistake on the approach and crashed into a hill on the far side of town, killing everyone aboard — a story Shane knew well. He planned his approach accordingly, locking onto the approach beacon, then circled straight down through the clouds over the airspace above the fjord well away from the hills.

Above was heavy cloud, up to 6,000 feet. Ron described what they were doing, following their path simply by the ebb and flow of the engine noise.

'They are coming in on the landing beacon, above the clouds, turning now, heading around, coming back. Now they have the beacon, they are circling down.' The sound ebbed and faded, then returned full and low as far out over the fjord the landing lights of Polar One suddenly sparkled like tiny stars over the ice, flying low and straight towards us. It seemed to take them a long time to arrive, the sound growing, echoing off the steep mountains surrounding the fjord, the wings straight and level, flying in over the landing lights at the end of the runway and dropping softly onto the far end of the landing strip, slowing within feet. The Antonov ambled down and around the corner to where we stood. Normally the Antonovs looked so large, but now, with the ice from the Pole still clinging frozen to their wheels, they seemed quite puny and insignificant, tiny capsules that had somehow carried us over the top of the world.

We were all safe and in a sense we were all home. Shane and Ferdinand pulled the window back in the cockpit and peered out, faces flushed with the heat of the cabin, talking excitedly. They had a great flight, a challenging flight, dodging through the fog and clouds over the Barents Sea to Spitsbergen. There was a lot of hand-shaking, a lot of hopping excitedly from foot to foot. Little needed to be said and a lot of smiling was done. Rare is the adventure where one has had grand plans and managed to surpass them.

Polar One was tied down, ropes strung through icy steel loops set in the asphalt, and we were off to the luxury of the Polar Hotel and more hot showers.

Back around the corner, Wilkins was enjoying less than ideal conditions.

> *We had sighted Spitsbergen 6.15 pm, local time, on Monday, April 17th, and landed twenty minutes later. It was not until Saturday at three am that the weather was again fit for flying. At that hour we climbed from the machine and cut and shoveled snowdrifts for six hours to clear the machine. At the head of the runway we made a downhill start. We planned if we had no time for more accurate sights, to rise in the air and from an altitude observe the coast, definitely fix our position and then choose our course.*

Where Wilkins had landed may have been one of the few flat places around — but it didn't have a particularly inspiring history, as this unattributed article from 1928 shows:

> *Doedmansoeri (Dead Man's Island), where Wilkins' plane stopped five days, is in the strait between Danes Island and Amsterdam Island, a location which was known to Arctic whalers as a haven. A voyager of 1671 wrote of it:*

*'In this south haven the ships ride at anchor, between high moun-
tains; on the left as we sail into it is a hill called the Beehive; close
to it lieth a large and high mount called the Devil's Huck, com-
monly covered with a fog, and if the wind bloweth over it, it
darkeneth the haven, and seemeth as if it smoked, filling the heavens therewith; on the top thereof are three small, white hills covered with snow; two of them stand near to one another.*

*'In the middle of the harbour is an island, which is called the
Dead Man's Island, because they bury the dead men there after
this manner: They are put into a coffin, and covered with a heap
of large stones, and notwithstanding all this they are sometimes
eaten by the white bears.'*

We more modern pilots stayed inside the walls of the hotel,
sloping around in thick socks. Dinner was an expanded version
of the previous evening, Ferdinand ensuring we started on the
right note with a bottle of champagne. We told stories until we
were the last in the restaurant, the twilight hovered outside the
windows and the cigars melted down to their bitter ends. Finishing an adventure in a European hotel had distinct advantages
and we'd soon recovered enough to notice that our waitress, long
pigtails plaited down her back, was providing Shane far better
service at the table than the rest of us. 'Yes, I am the captain of
the Green Tortoise,' said Shane — and at that, it was time to cut
our losses and go to bed.

Longyearbyen had one small mall, a few shops and many well-
bundled-up people strolling the arcade. Small children played
in overstuffed playsuits, their faces surrounded by fur ruffs. Babies were perambulated along the street under so many blankets
that only a breath of steam indicated they were in the basket
somewhere. Arctic summer had officially just arrived, 24 hours
of daylight, the sun circling the horizon, rising through the day
in the south and just dipping behind the hills at night in the
north. Despite whaling tales from 1671, no country had much
interest in Spitsbergen and an unattributed article from 1928
detailed its short history before Wilkins' arrival.

The Svalbard Archipelago was a no-man's-land until 1919, when it became officially Norwegian territory by virtue of the acceptance by the Oslo Parliament of the Paris treaty of 1919 conferring the sovereignty of the islands on Norway.

Scattered over the Kings Bay plain are the little wooden shacks of a mining village which is operated by a Norwegian coal company. During the brief summer months it is the home of from 300 to 400 miners who come from the European continent for the mining season.

Wilkins was well past Kings Bay however, where the small village of Ny-Alesund now sits. He didn't know exactly where he was but thought perhaps they could see buildings on the far side of the fjord they had landed on. They were however too indistinct and he was too used to mirages to hope that they were so close to civilization.

We spent a day of rest in Spitsbergen, checking over the planes and preparing for our onward journeys. From here, Ron and Donny were taking Polar Two back across the Arctic to Anchorage, while Shane, Ferdinand and I would continue onto Tromso, Norway and then across Europe to Germany. The left strut on Polar One was still losing nitrogen, but with a refill in Spitsbergen we hoped it would last into Europe and with the warmer temperatures, stay sealed until the plane was safely in Germany. The weather remained cloudy the following day, but on Friday 17 April we were up early, munched our way from one end of the breakfast buffet to the other and were out at the airport in Polar One for the quick hop north to Ny-Alesund, staging point for three historic polar flights, as noted in the article filed by AP in the *Detroit News*, 21 April 1928.

The North Pole has twice been crossed by air, the first time by Lieut. Comdr. Richard E. Byrd, who flew over the Pole in an airplane from Kings Bay, Spitsbergen, returning to that place in May, 1926, and the second time only a few days later by the Amundsen-Ellesworth expedition in the dirigible Norge, *which flew from Kings Bay, Spitsbergen, across the Pole, landing at Teller, Alaska after 71 hours.*

Shane and Ron shared the cockpit for our tourist flight, taking us out the end of the fjord and on a diversion south, over Green Bay, where Wilkins had finally reached civilization and radioed the world of his success. We then turned north, flying low along the beach, spotting the dark outline of seals next to their holes and then groups of small whitish-brown reindeer wandering along the flat shoreline. At the head of the fjord we flew in low over the renowned Dead Man's Island. 'There it is,' said Shane over the intercom. 'It's really just that bump there and they would have landed just below us somewhere.' The sun was slanting low across the ice of the fjord and a long shadow cast by the rocky bump was all that marked the island, which wasn't really an island at all, but more a mound of stones on the end of the peninsula. Exactly 70 years previously, Wilkins and Eielson would have been huddled below us, wind whistling around the Lockheed Vega, munching cold pemmican and sipping water, waiting patiently for the weather to clear. Finally, on 21 April, they would get the break they had been waiting for:

We placed the stove beneath the engine. It was difficult to do this in the wind, but once in place, it gave no trouble. I heated the oil on the primus stove in the cabin. We were soon to find that our decision not to land on the pack-ice with half a load had been very wise. The tanks now held only twenty gallons of gasoline. With that little for a load and two of us aboard the machine would not budge an inch. When I got out and pushed the tail she started fine, but to climb in as she moved was not simple.

The story of trying to leave Dead Man's Island would have been well suited to a children's cartoon:

Because the machine would not move with the two of us in it, I needs must get out and push on the tail. As she started I clung to

the step and tried to climb in, but soon fell off. Eielson, unable to see
behind, thought I was in the machine and took off. When he turned
he saw me forlorn on the ice. He circled and landed.

But after five days camping on the ice, Wilkins was undaunted.
If pushing a plane to get it started then running along and jumping in the door had proved impossible, he had a simple solution:

I slung out the rope ladder I had prepared in lieu of the block and
tackle, but I wasn't too sure that my ability as a sailor would en-
able me to gain the cockpit with the aid of a dangling rope in that
low temperature.
... We started again and as the machine gathered speed I climbed
to the tail and from there struggled desperately to gain the cockpit.
I had thrown off my mittens in order to get a good grip of the
ladder. My hands were soon numbed with the cold and I could not
readily grip the rope, so I grabbed hold of it with my teeth. A fool-
ish thing to do, perhaps, but it seemed imperative that I cling to the
machine. We had gathered much speed and Eielson, feeling the
weight still on the tail, thought I was safe and took off. Just before
he left the ground I realized that my chances of gaining the cockpit
in the air was much too small and I slithered from the smooth,
shiny fuselage, being struck by the tail and thrown to the snow. It
was fortunate for me that the snow was soft. I was half buried and
partially stunned from the fall. When the snow was freed from my
eyes and mouth I found that I had escaped other injury, but every
front tooth in my mouth was loose.

Eielson circled around and came back once again. Wilkins
was now contemplating taking the tent, a rifle and some food
and letting Eielson go on alone and come back with a boat. But
as he admitted:

That would have been a desperate move. It would have been un-
wise for a party of two, situated as we were, to split. There was no
forecasting what might become of either of us, but ours seemed to be
a desperate plight. We could possibly have found our way to the
mainland and along the coast to some habitation, but that would
have entailed leaving the machine behind.
... The third time might be the charm. I would hook one leg in
the cockpit-opening and with my foot against the fuselage push

with all my strength on the log of driftwood we had found and thus try to move the tail. Then I fixed myself and the stick, gave Eielson the signal and he shoved the throttle wide open.

For a full minute we hung. I pushed and strained every muscle. The tail swayed the inch or so allowed by the play in the skis, but seemingly would move no further. Suddenly, with a slight lurch, she was free. I dropped the log and with one hand in the cockpit and with hands on its open rim I dragged myself up and regardless of bruises tumbled to the bottom of the cabin. Utterly exhausted, I was unable to answer Eielson's shout of enquiry, but he took off hoping I was safe. Before he had time to circle I had let him know that I was aboard.

Moments later Eielson spotted the radio masts and houses that they soon identified as Green Bay.

We crossed about five miles of open water, swung across a mountain top and then planed down close to the ice. The snow surface on the harbor-ice was smooth and we flew beyond the radio masts for a mile passing the immense surface machinery of a coal mine. Then circling over the ice we came in to land at the foot of the radio masts. Our flight from our base in Alaska to a town in Spitsbergen was ended.

Thus ended a journey hailed in an article from New York by Russell Owen on 21 April 1928.

... in the eyes of men who have made journeys of equal daring, the flight of Wilkins in a small plane over an unknown sea is destined to go down in polar history as one of the greatest achievements of them all.

Shane circled Dead Man's Island again. It was completely desolate, an icy covered beach on one side, an ice-strewn fjord on the other. The clouds were floating overhead, passing back and forth over the sun, casting a dull yellow haze across the snow. It looked like one of the world's most inhospitable places to spend even a few minutes. We continued north, still flying low, looking for the elusive polar bear. But while there were plenty of seals tucked up next to their holes and reindeer wandering the ice, the distinctive yellow-white of the polar bear was nowhere to be seen.

184

The mountains of Spitsbergen after 15 hours en route lay at the edge of the Arctic ice pack, looking more like a rolling extension of the sea than any land we had seen before.

Left: *Flying from Barrow, Alaska, to Eureka, Canada, we passed through a land of perfect purple sunsets, the sun rising and setting four times in the late evening hours as the full moon rose over the ice.*

Below: *The further north we flew, the less distinction there was between earth and sky. The ice was a reflection of the clouds, the clouds a reflection of the ice as we chased the sun over the top of the world.*

The mountains of Spitsbergen set out below us as Ferdinand, Shane and the author flew the final leg across the island and out over the open ocean to Tromso, Norway.

Ron, Donny, Ferdinand and Shane at Longyearbyen airport, Spitsbergen, following our flight over the Pole and before our respective flights back to Alaska and on to the European continent.

Flying in over land in Spitsbergen, the first solid ground we have seen in 15 hours of flying, the shadow of Polar Two chases us along the mountainside.

Half way to Ny-Alesund, we passed over a wide lead of black open water. With icebergs bouncing on the waves below and the shoreline rimmed by ice, any thought of an engine failure on our tourist flight was particularly unpleasant. I calculated whether we were high enough to glide over the water and reach the ice on the far side — probably not. The engine sounded the same as ever, throbbing away confidently, but it didn't hold much of a guarantee. I thought of the long flight from Spitsbergen to Tromso in the Antonov — when I got back to Longyearbyen, why shouldn't I just go jump on a big jet and be gone?

Shane circled around the ridge at the end of the fjord and we turned into Kings Bay. Ny-Alesund came into view, a small cluster of distinctive dark houses against the snow, on the far side of which the dirigible tower still stood, black against the white snow. We dropped onto the runway and were greeted by the local manager. The airport was only an asphalt strip in the snow, no terminal or tower anywhere in sight. The town was equally tiny, the tallest building two stories, a small village encased in snowdrifts. Twenty people bustled about, Europeans coming north for courses in glaciology, Arctic meteorology, astrology and, before they ever went into the field, polar bear defense. A van took us to a tiny museum, with a small mining exhibit. A general store sold souvenir T-shirts with 'Verdens Nordligste Nordmenn' (the world's most northern Norwegians) and seal-skin vests, mittens and pants. It was like a ski resort with far too much snow.

We walked out a thin snow machine track for five minutes to the base of the dirigible tower. Black steel girders rose 100 feet into the air. The picture of Amundsen's dirigible tethered at the nose before setting off to fly over the North Pole and on to Teller, Alaska, was easy to imagine. But the harshness of the surrounding landscape and the fact that a major expedition had to come this far north just to get started, was difficult to comprehend. In 1998 it felt like the end of the earth. In 1928, it would have been the end of the world. Shane had crawled back into his reindeer suit and looked right at home — he was certainly the warmest of us all. At the same time he commented, 'Let's get these shots and get out of here, the clouds are moving in.' Even though we were on little more than a tourist jaunt north, flying around Spitsbergen was as potentially dangerous as any other segment of our journey. We certainly had no desire to have to land at Dead Man's Island and wait for the polar bears to come looking for us.

The house Amundsen had stayed in was still in place, a pale yellow, two-story, barn-roofed structure, little changed in the intervening years — bar a few high-powered snow machines pulled up in front. Two short hours after our arrival we were back at Polar One and rolling down the runway, headed back to Longyearbyen. Twenty minutes later and a few hundred feet off the ground the clouds closed in and we were flying blind through the mist, in and out of the clouds, wondering if things might get more exciting. Before the weather broke, we curved around the scary-looking black water and back into the fjord leading up to Longyearbyen. There was something very reassuring about having Ron and Shane both up front in the Antonov, like having two fighter pilots, both completely competent in their own right and with a wealth of experience, controlling the airplane.

On the way back we passed a reindeer we had seen on the way up, tossing itself wildly about, thrashing it horns. Impaled on its horns was a green fishing net, about a meter square, with tendrils steaming off it. Somehow the net had attached itself to the animal, perhaps as it took an inquisitive stab at the net, and it had become tangled in the mess. Now it was quietly and forlornly going berserk, tossing its head, shaking its horns, stamping its hooves, the net waving about overhead like a bad nightmare. It would die — perhaps not soon, but in a day or two, of madness, or it would fall into a crack in the sea as it went slowly crazy and forgot to watch where it stood — or a polar bear would happen along and find it easy prey. Here, in this infinite wilderness, it was particularly disturbing seeing a manmade mistake, a fishing net gone missing, drive an innocent creature nuts and then to its death. It stuck in my mind, though I would have preferred to have left it behind.

We were back in Longyearbyen in less than an hour after

leaving Ny-Alesund; the fuel truck under the wings pumped the wing tanks full, with an extra hundred gallons into the auxiliary tank for our flight to Tromso. Shane and I rode into town for a quick last meal. Norway had been a very comfortable introduction to Europe — our evenings at the hotel and Norwegian hospitality unchanged since Wilkins had arrived.

> *Presently we were comfortably seated in Manager Ihlen's sitting room sharing bountiful hospitality. Rare wines and liquors were offered. 'Skaal.' 'Skaal to you. Your very best health and future success.' A toast to our accomplishment must be drunk with everyone on his feet.*
>
> *… The steward at the radio mess, Oscar Bergh, prepared steaming hot coffee for us; the first really hot drink we had had since leaving Alaska six days before. We thoroughly enjoyed the Norwegian delicacies set before us but that was not enough. We must accompany Her Varming to his house and partake of his hospitality there. He had some special liquor made according to a famous old Danish recipe and with that all must drink to our success and the success of future enterprise.*

Shane had a long association with Norway and my relations and youthful working and climbing experiences here had left us in a surprisingly similar state of mind to Wilkins — it was an ideal and pleasurable way to wrap up our trip over the Pole.

> *However, the mannerisms were more after the fashion of my youthful experiences and after three years' absence from European customs, they charmed me.*

Polar One was fueled, and had been checked over by Ron, followed closely around by Ferdinand, as this was our last chance to glean any last-minute tips on Antonov maintenance from the master. We shook hands and said gruff farewells. We all knew the journey was far from over. Ron and Donny were going to attempt a reverse of Wilkins' flight, going non-stop all the way from Spitsbergen back to Barrow. We were flying over more open water than on any previous portion of our journey. We now knew we could land on ice. Landing on water was something none of us relished learning about.

I wondered if I wasn't pushing my luck. I'd been to the North Pole. We'd landed on the ice. I was safe in Spitsbergen. I could jump on a jet and be over the sea in little over an hour. The Antonov flight would take at least six hours. But the Antonov hadn't missed a beat in our entire journey. I had complete confidence in Shane's abilities — he wouldn't be flying unless he felt confident. Ferdinand had gained many hours of flying experience in the last year and had a perspective that helped balance out our decision-making. And I wanted to make the journey all the way to Europe in the Antonov — it seemed that then it would be truly finished. Like setting off on a big climb, I went through the rationale, then the emotional arguments, then got down to the bottom of the question — was I happy taking the risk for the reward of the experience? Shane started the engine, I went to the rear door and pulled the steps free and tossed them inside. I made the big leap aboard, secured the door, went forward and gave Shane and Ferdinand the thumbs up — we were on our way to Europe.

chapter 8

'our engine, faithful every moment'

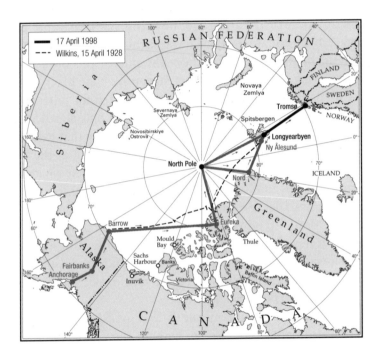

Shane and Ferdinand looked very elegant in their bright orange survival suits, sitting in the cockpit of the Antonov. The suits, of thick rubberized neoprene with a woven plastic cover, looked impregnable by any earthly element. At the cuffs they had a very tight band of thick neoprene and gloves which fitted snugly over and around the wrists. For flying, the gloves were left free, secured back against the arm with a Velcro tab. The large insulated hood could also be left off, saving one from complete internal asphyxiation. But otherwise the body was in a very hot plastic bag in a warm cockpit. This would be their home until we arrived in Tromso.

As a first-class passenger, I kept my suit close by, but decided not to put it on until we flew out over the sea. Sealing myself into a heavy orange plastic bag for any longer than absolutely necessary had no appeal. 'If you fart, you will probably kill yourself anyway,' commented Ferdinand.

There were light clouds overhead when we took off west into the wind before turning and heading back around past Longyearbyen and up the fjord towards the mountains of central Spitsbergen. Running along the right side of the fjord above Longyearbyen, a massive cable car structure, huge black towers and cars dangling from a thick cable, stretched for miles up to another big coalmine. Shane had the Antonov on a steady climb all the way up the fjord, heading for a deep valley that extended cloud-free up into the sky. The mountains rose up at the side, steep ridges and faces forming to pinpoint peaks. The rough texture of the land, the low sun angle and the soft lighting on the snow gave it a fairytale appearance. The peaks popped straight out of the fjord, up into the sky, then dived back down the other side to a series of glaciers curving back out to sea. But there was no open water anywhere so all was white and shades of white, with the occasional long thin ridge blown clean of snow, cutting the white in a striking black line.

We dodged a few clouds up one valley, crossed over some peaks and down the other side. Flying without the company of Polar Two, we felt very much on our own. Shane, Ferdinand and I had become good friends in our journeys — we liked many of the same things and had much the same sense of humor, so we chattered happily away on the intercom. Shane was now on his own in his role as captain — with no expert advice on the Arctic or the quirks of an Antonov from Donny or Ron to guide him. If anything went wrong, it was all going to be in his hands very quickly. This lightened the atmosphere but also sharpened our emotions — adding an edge to the flight that hadn't been there before.

'This is probably where the most polar bears live and we left both the guns with Ron and Donny,' commented Shane. 'Oh well.

Best to stay in the air.' When the ice broke up we'd be over the freezing waters of the Barents Sea. In between would be an area of broken ice where the polar bears also lived, so if we didn't freeze in the water, we'd probably be chased down and eaten.

In 1997, trading Antonov stories in Anchorage, I'd heard about a Russian crew ferrying Antonovs across the South Atlantic, hopping across the ocean, through the Canary Islands and then dropping in to refuel at obscure islands en route to South America. They would spend the majority of their time over the sea. It had sounded crazy at the time, flying long distances over huge expanses of water with only a single engine, something I'd never contemplated and thought best left to crazy Russian pilots. Now here we were, sun setting behind us, leaving the coast of Spitsbergen for the sea ahead. Fortunately it was still covered in ice. Not very solidly, but some of the floes looked big enough to land on, or at least crash onto and then jump out quickly, dodging the polar bear, inflating the tiny raft and rowing for Norway.

As we flew out over the coast, I retreated to the wide cabin to put on my survival suit. Affectionately called a 'gumbie suit' it had one huge zipper with a palm-size tab on the front. Unlike Shane and Ferdinand's, it had no detachable paws, so I slipped my feet, already clad in a few extra pairs of socks, into the moonlike treaded foot sections and secured the ankle straps. Then I had a quick practice encasing myself in the rest of the suit, as Laura Thorpe had instructed Trevor and myself back in her office in Anchorage. Left arm in, pull the hood up and flat across the forehead, right arm in, zip it up tight. Two and a half minutes. Not exactly the 50 seconds Laura expected of her students, but now I was half in the rest wouldn't take long, I figured.

Getting into the suit changed the atmosphere — it was impossible to ignore the fact that this was an action one would take only when dire consequences could be faced at some very close time in the future. Nobody would wear one of these for any other reason. I struggled back up to the front of the plane and Ferdinand waddled back. 'I'm going to take a nap, that way I don't have to look at all that water that's coming up,' he joked.

I'd noticed that pilots had the ability to sleep anywhere and lose consciousness almost instantly. Ferdinand was obviously gaining this ability to assist in the long hours of flying he was logging. If pilots weren't flying they quickly reverted to resting.

Two days after the event, A.P. filed this brief report on Wilkins' arrival and quick adaptation to life in Spitsbergen:

> On arriving at Green Harbor the first thing Wilkins and Eielson did was to cover the airplane with a double canvas cover to avert too fast refrigeration. This had to be done in extreme cold and without gloves.
>
> Captain Wilkins is making himself perfectly at home and becoming more talkative. He is walking about in trousers of reindeer skin and seal-skin boots for such outdoor exercise as he cares to take. Every morning at 5 he receives bunches of telegrams, which he accepts smilingly and peruses, disposing of them later. He puts in most of the day working hard indoors.
>
> Eielson, in contrast, spends most of his time resting on a sofa, smoking his pipe and reading. As he is of Norwegian origin, he loves to talk the language and the people have found he retains the dialect of his fathers, although even his parents were born in America. He is delighted at the idea of going to Norway for the first time to meet the members of his family there and to see the birthplace of his grandparents.

Wilkins had closeted himself away and was obviously busy writing, as over the next few days he would have lengthy articles published in major papers around the world. While they were able to claim no new land, another part of their work was the opening up of the Arctic as a potential aerial route for generations to come. On 25 April, he wrote for the London *Times*:

> We ruminate on the incidents of our journey, speculate as to the future of Arctic flying, wonder what we might have done and what we have done. Who can tell?
>
> The flight we made might be the forerunner of transarctic transportation, a scenic air route which in years to come would serve curious tourists speeding from Alaska's sea-level tundras to awe inspiring Grant Land, glaciated Greenland and Svalbard's jumbled peaks, a trip perhaps in future not more unusual than now

from the plains of Lower California to the high Sierras.

But the possibility of that is not yet. There is still much progress to be made in aeronautical engineering and still much advance to be made in weather forecasting. The book of Arctic exploration is not by any means closed. Many more chapters may still be written.

As we had passed over the Arctic, the voice of the Lufthansa jet pilot five miles above us, signing off from Anchorage and headed non-stop to Europe, was a more-than-ample reminder that Wilkins' ruminations had truly come to fruition.

With even more enthusiasm, the famous explorer and statesman Vilhjalmur Stefansson began an article on 29 April from New York with:

Romance is now on every tongue, but when history is calmly written the Wilkins-Eielson flight from Alaska to Spitzbergen will come to be looked upon as the final necessary pioneer stride toward the realization of the Elizabethan dream of a practicable highway to the East Indies.

… For, if you can rise above a small hill you can eventually fly across the highest and widest mountain range; if you can cross a river by mechanical flight, the greater perfection of the means will eventually cancel the oceans from the transportation problems of the world.

The sun started its long descent into the sea. We hadn't left until early evening as fueling had been delayed. As we would fly straight south for the duration of our journey, we'd actually be moving back onto a planet where it got dark again. Shane turned over the controls to me while he reviewed his charts — he'd sailed up on *Metolius* in the early nineties, stopping off at Bear Island.

The current pushing up from the south was blocked by Bear Island, so the ice extended in pancake chunks right down to its shoreline. It made the island look like a huge ocean steamer with froth tailing off its stern. Bear Island was white, windswept, and held a weather station but had no real permanent population, so inhospitable was the land. We were over the island and then back over the black sea on the far side in minutes. Clouds built up after our crossing, but they were low over the sea. 'Good,' said

Shane, 'I don't want to look at all that water anyway.' He put the Mozart CD on and checked my course. 'Looks like you have nailed it. I might just close my eyes for a few minutes.'

The clouds rolled away below, orange, then purple, then fading to nearly black. Boiling up on the horizon, they gave me something to shoot for. For some reason, Polar One was just a little easier to fly than Polar Two, a little less sensitive. But it was still all a matter of feel, sensing the drift before the compass moved, hearing the engine rise and fall if the nose went up or down, steering with minimal tweaks to keep on course. The clouds opened up in holes below. If I looked down, the sea was a black hole through the dark gray clouds with only a few whitecaps for relief. I'd considered anyone flying an Antonov over the sea crazy — now I sat in a thick orange plastic bag, 7,000 feet over the water, contentedly chugging along. Having accepted the reality of the flight, it was now simply a matter of doing it, even enjoying it. All was running perfectly; I'd learned enough to glance over fuel gauges, manifold and oil pressures and listen to the engine to know the plane was happy.

An hour passed and then another. Shane changed the CD, Ferdinand rose from his sleep, passed a Coke forward and on we hummed. I felt conscious that any deviation from our course would make the journey longer and if the engine did conk out, every inch made a difference, so it wasn't difficult to concentrate. The sun sunk into the sea behind us and it became darker, the purple going into the shadows. The CD ran out and I was all alone, flying over the ocean, the Antonov telling me its secrets to help me keep it on course.

A bank of clouds on the horizon marked the continent and we approached ever so slowly — 100 knots can seem very slow at times. The Antonov droned on and we finally came in high over the land. At our elevation, if anything went wrong now, Shane could glide it in and crash us in Norway. Finally we were actually above a finger of land jutting out between fjords. I suddenly had to get out of my survival suit; the feeling of heat and claustrophobia overwhelming. Ferdinand came forward, rested from his stint in the first-class cabin to take us down the long glide-path into Tromso airport.

In 1928 Wilkins may have enjoyed superb hospitality in Spitsbergen, but he was still a very long way from home. Newspaper articles were hot on the topic of how the heroes would get to Europe, with one report from the International News Service in Oslo, Norway, claiming:

> As Capt. Wilkins' airplane is in good condition, it is thought here that he will not tarry long in Spitsbergen, but will take on fuel and supplies there and continue his flight southward stopping at Oslo and London.

But in another update on 2 May filed by A.P. from Green Harbor it is more accurately reported:

> They plan first to fly their plane over to Advent Bay, another Spitzbergen harbor about 100 miles distant, for shipment aboard the steamer Inger Elisabeth, due to leave for Norway on May 15. They will take off on the ice and doubtless land on the ice.
>
> Wilkins himself hoped to be able to leave on board the steamer Hobby within five or six days and Eielson may possibly accompany the plane, although nothing definite has been decided about that.

And finally on 11 May it is reported by A.P. from Green Harbor, Spitsbergen: 'WILKINS QUITS POLAR REGION'.

> Capt. George H. Wilkins and Lieut. Carl B. Eielson, who flew across the top of the world, several weeks ago, left Spitzbergen today aboard the sealing vessel Hobby, bound for Tromso, Norway.
>
> The departure of the two aviators from Green Harbor was almost as spectacular as their arrival in Spitzbergen from Point Barrow, Alaska. The aviators left Green Harbor in the gleam of the midnight sun and landed some distance along the iced border of Isfjorden at Bjoerndalen, where the aviators boarded the sealer. The plane was taken aboard and it is expected the Hobby will reach Tromso Tuesday.

Tromso was dark, lights twinkling along the fjord as Ferdinand took us over the outskirts of the city, across the final fjord and towards the long stream of landing lights blinking up at us. Shane took over as we flew in low over the lights, the Antonov leveled out and the bubble tires squished quietly down onto the European continent.

Spitsbergen – Tromso

I landed in Longyearbyen at 1400 in the afternoon after our tour of the historic places visited by the early polar flyers. All I needed to do was organize fuel and pay the airport and landing fees. I parked directly under the control tower and went up to obtain a weather briefing from the meteorological office. I was informed that there might be multiple layers of cloud up to 10,000 feet around Bear Island. Possible turbulence, icing and instability. Tromso was clear, however. I looked closely at the weather charts and could not detect any great pressure or temperature gradients between Spitsbergen and Tromso. I figured that I would give it a try. The Store Norsk Coal Company was good enough to sell us fuel that is normally reserved for their own operations, and they delivered it to us in a tanker truck.

It was time to say adieu to Ron and Donny who would be headed back across the ice pack to Alaska. Polar One and Polar Two were going their separate ways. By the time we had fueled, paid and repacked it was late in the day and I wanted to get headed south. It would be dark at night further south, and with the poor instrument lighting in the biplane I hoped to land before night. Ferdinand, Robert and I all donned our bright orange survival suits. If we were forced to ditch, there would be no time to put the suits on. They were not very comfortable, they were bulky, and I began to sweat as the suit fit like a plastic bag. Taking off from Longyearbyen I turned to the east and flew up the fjord where the sky looked blue. The weather was closing in to the west, and I had to either get on top of the clouds or be able to stay below and avoid the mountains. Flying the Antonov in this environment always presented challenges.

I found a nice spot to climb up into the blue sky, around a mountain and up a snowy glacier. Soon the sunlight was back in the cockpit and I pointed the plane south. The scenery below was spectacular and I shot too many pictures of snow-covered mountains, each indistinguishable from the next. The view of the southern end of the Spitsbergen was perfect and as we passed to the east of Hornsund I remembered making landfall there with Trevor in 1992 after sailing up from Tromso. We had held a race to see who could slide down the mountain fastest.

It seemed like a long time ago. Ferdinand moved to the back to rest and Robert moved up to the right seat. It was a perfect evening, and I could see Bear Island from a long way out. There was no sign of the cloud, turbulence, or ice mentioned in the forecast. I spoke with the weather station on Bear Island radio as we flew over head. It looked like a small supply ship sat off her western shores, and this is where the open water began. From Bear Island south the sea was clear of ice. An overcast developed and we flew on top at about 7,000 feet. Occasionally there were breaks in the clouds and I could see frothy whitecaps below in a dark sea. I preferred to look at the puffy pink clouds, which combined with the music of Mozart on the CD gave me a nice sense of security. The sun was dropping fast, and it was actually getting darker than I had seen it for the past ten days. As we approached the coast of Norway I could see numerous fishing boats. Finally I could see the lights of what looked like a town along the shore. I lined the plane up for a straight-in approach, and was rejoined by Ferdinand in the cockpit. In Tromso it was dark. The instruments pointed us right down the track to the runway and we touched down on the European continent just before midnight.

As Wilkins said, 'Our work of exploration was really over. We were cheered immeasurably by the fact that our machine had performed wonders, our engine faithful every moment.'

conclusion

antonovs over the antarctic?

Northern Europe. Coffee bars, late-night twilight, cobbled alley-ways, peaked buildings with gray slate roofs. Bistros, tall beers and much taller women with long blonde hair.

Tromso, 1 am. The plane is put to bed. The fire station/customs welcomes us. 'We'll do the paperwork in the morning, we'll call a taxi for you, have a pleasant evening,' and we are footloose on the streets. The hotel clerk is asleep so we wake him. 'Ja, here are yar room keys, ja, here are some sandwiches from my fridge, ja, the nightclub is open.' The nightclub would have been popular in 1974. The bartender and her friend sit beside the door talking of customers they would have rather not met. We order our beers, frothing and tall and cold.

The Antonov ring is still in our ears and Ferdy asks for the music to be turned down. We have our own stories to tell. We are like a late crew exiting the factory — the night feels old in hours but too young to go to sleep. Our senses spiral down out of the sky, into the fjords of the wider world and finally onto the continent. All the land, the darkness, after a week with never more than a light duskiness of gray, feels large and a little frightening. It is our first real night. We tell tales until the sun threatens to sneak quickly back up on the other side of the horizon and wander off to beds laden with feathers that cushion the weight of darkness around us.

The sun is up far too early, light creeping through a crack in the heavy curtains. The Pole seems a very long way north but we haven't even reached below the Arctic Circle yet. I have to check the map to verify our latitude — we are just under 70° North. Geographic location has returned to being a place and a country and is no longer simply a GPS reading. I think it must be cold out still and start looking for a clean suit of long underwear. Ferdinand wakes up as I dig through my duffel. 'Hey, you don't need to wear that any more, it's like Italy here.' He's right, a pair of jeans will suffice.

The window of the hotel looks out across a small city to the airport. A hundred thousand people are tucked away up here at the top of Europe. At the far end of the runway, the Antonov is easily visible, backed into a corner. It looks an oddity again, out of place with streamlined jets taking off over it and small sleek planes tucked under its wings. Planes to fly the Arctic are most happy in remote places, surrounded by wolves and flying over ice, and seem uncomfortable in their return to civilization. As Wilkins related in a dispatch to the *New York Times* from Spitsbergen on 25 April 1928:

> *Our slim, eager-looking plane rests safely on the harbor ice. During the warm days since we arrived here the tail has settled in the snow. She seems to have lost something of the eager and spirited look she had and now appears much like a tired seagull dozing on the snow.*

Shane, Ferdinand and I are alone at the breakfast bar and quickly decide to move hotels — there is no gjetost or cloudberries. The new hotel in the center of town has rooms tucked away amongst the rafters, its five-story height looming right over the harbor. Out the expansive window a sweeping bridge leads across to a singular, soaring, A-framed church. Gray filigreed trees lace the side of the hills above, quickly fading into the white of the surrounding snow-covered mountains. The water is still an icy black in the harbor, but is devoid of the familiar ice coating. Not even a small iceberg dots the surface. Fishing boats strung with nets are tied up to a heavy wooden dock in their sturdy dark red, while green warehouses curve around the edge of the water.

It would be easy to sit in the big comfy chair in front of the window in the hotel room and gaze out the window all day. The feeling of being home, being on land, sinks in quickly and feels solid and reassuring. The dangers fade into humorous stories and the quiet enjoyment of endless sunsets. At lunch, over a rather old bottle of white wine, we recollect flying through twilight nights. The ice that slipped past below settles into the forefront of our thoughts like daytime dreams. In the same article Wilkins mentions his own relief, recalling the storm on Dead Man's Island.

> *Throughout the main journey, the delay and the second short, quick flight we were deeply conscious of our good luck, but only now, as we gather news, is the magnitude of that good fortune evident.*
>
> *During the storm in which we landed the radio operator at Kings Bay lost his way in passing from the radio station to the village and froze to death in the blinding snowstorm. Two other men, experienced trappers, in a shelter cabin on the coast nearby, were unable to move from their shelter. Without food or fuel or suitable clothing, one froze his feet and the other's hands were badly frostbitten.*

We have no frostbite, no frozen toes. But the glass-walled sauna set into the attic of the hotel lets us superheat our bodies and melt off any residual ice left in our brains.

The whole of Europe now sits at our feet and Shane and Ferdinand are already plotting their course south. Mine is far simpler — SAS to Oslo, Lufthansa to Frankfurt and on to Seoul. We plan dinner and nightclubs, but as dusk settles in at 11 pm and we are still at dinner. We find our own company and a final beer more to our liking. Nightlife can't compete with the North Pole.

We await news from Ron and Donny, heading back over the ice to Barrow. With their extra fuel barrels and sights set on a reversal of Wilkins' journey, they will be attempting what must be one of the longest flights ever contemplated in an Antonov. I have spent so much time with Ron in his plane I can feel them out there over the ice, droning away.

Throughout Wilkins' quest, he had stressed the importance

his scientific studies played in their flight. Crossing the Arctic was simply a means to that end. In a commentary from Quebec on 24 April a journalist commented:

> It is plain that, in the view of Captain Wilkins, compass varia-
> tions, meteorology and the mapping of the Arctic Sea were of more
> importance than the achievement of flying 2,200 miles over the
> 'top of the world'. He was seeking new land, so he set his course
> away from the Pole, and sighting the peaks of Grant Land, he
> changed direction for Spitzbergen.

Even today there is still much to be studied in the Arctic, but there will never again be the interest generated by the simple goal of finding new land. Wilkins undertook the last journey that could have potentially yielded up a significant new parcel of territory on the earth's surface. In itself, this lifted the exploration well above the basic scientific observations that he made. Wilkins was also exploring in a time when simple adventure for adventure's sake wasn't encouraged. One needed a significant reason to spend time on a grand adventure and the funding to accomplish it. But reading Wilkins' book one recognizes that at heart he was a classic adventurer, a man challenged by extending the horizons of the possible. Even before he left Spitsbergen a story was filed by A.P.

> Capt. George H. Wilkins, scarcely landed from his great feat of
> flying across the top of the world by airplane, already is planning a
> new air venture, this time over the Antarctic at the other end of
> the world.
> The Captain has received a telegraphic offer from Commander
> Richard E. Byrd, who also is planning an Antarctic expedition, to
> sell the Wilkins polar plane for the Commander's south polar trip,
> but Capt. Wilkins replied that he was unable to accept the offer, as
> he himself is planning a new expedition, this time to the south.
> He hopes to start on his new venture as soon as possible, prob-
> ably at the beginning of September, and has roughly drawn up a
> program for the projected exploration. Beyond this he refuses to
> give out any information.

Wilkins had barely gotten out of one plane in the Arctic before he was already packing it up and shipping it to the opposite end of the world for his next flight!

In 1997 in Alaska, Shane and Ferdinand had talked of selling the Antonov. In Tromso, the topic never surfaced, as if the thought had been banished. They had the excuse that the Antonov would be closer to their homes. We would also be flying it across the English Channel to exhibit at the Farnborough Airshow in the United Kingdom later in the year, so there was no immediate reason to consider selling it.

More importantly, the plane had become a part of them — carrying them to the Pole and then across the open sea to Tromso. It had developed more personality than any of us could have imagined. And it was still probable that just getting it started was a greater challenge to Shane than piloting a journey across Europe in his 737. Ferdinand also had his perfectly restored 40-year-old Cessna, but as he said, 'Robert, it is like a Mercedes — it never makes a mistake.' After flying the Antonov, the Cessna would be like stepping into a well-tuned sports car.

Continuing with his world explorations, Wilkins would go on to other great adventures. He became one of the pioneers of flying in the Antarctic, then returned to the Arctic to float under the polar ice cap in a submarine.

Eielson returned through Europe and America to Alaska to continue building his commercial airline business. Then, tragically, a year and a half later, still in his early thirties, he flew out off the west coast of Alaska over the Bering Sea on a rescue mission. On 9 November 1929 he disappeared. His plane was eventually located in Siberia, having flown into the ground in a presumed whiteout. His body was discovered after many days of searching in the deep snow, and returned for burial in Alaska.

Wilkins' life was set in a time when exploring the world by air was opening up the remaining areas of remoteness and breaking new boundaries. He may have led the headlines, but records were being broken as soon as they were set.

A review of the outstanding aviation achievements of 1928 establishes the first four months of the present year as the greatest flying period of the world's history.

With the summer flying season in prospect, the following aerial accomplishments have been recorded:
- *An airplane in which rode Captain George Wilkins and Carl B. Eielson flew over the top of the world from Point Barrow, Alaska, to Spitzbergen, remaining in the air 20½ hours.*
- *Baron Gunther von Huenefeld, Captain Hermann Koehl and Major James Fitzmaurice made the first westward crossing of the Atlantic by plane.*
- *Major Debernardi of the Italian Air Service established a new airplane speed record at 318.53 miles an hour.*
- *Eddie Stinson and George Haldeman established a new sustained flight record of almost 54 hours.*

Pushing the boundaries of men and machine was the driving force behind Wilkins' adventures as much as the advancement of science that he pushed to the fore. In 1998 we still had the challenge of exploration, but by limiting our outside resources we forced our emotions inward. Our expanded knowledge was of ourselves, gained from probing the Antonovs' capabilities in the Arctic and thus learning more about our own abilities. Mistakes carried the same penalty air exploration always has and required us to plan and execute in ways that demanded perfection. The resulting satisfaction was as close to complete as we could experience. As Shane stated simply in Tromso, referring to the entire journey, 'That was the best flight of my life.'

My final challenge has been in telling our story. Luckily, Wilkins was still a good guide as to how best to proceed, as noted in an article filed from Spitsbergen on 8 May: 'Capt. Wilkins is working day and night on his new book describing his polar trip, and is writing it on a typewriter, hoping to get it ready prior to his departure.' Even when it came to recording his adventures, Wilkins was using the latest technology! His work was further detailed in an article filed for the *New York Times* on 15 May:

During the voyage from Spitsbergen on the steamer Hobby, *which reached Tromsoe yesterday, Captain Wilkins was busy on the last third of his book on the flight. He hopes to complete his writing before he gets to Oslo. After visiting Oslo, he will go to Berlin and thence to Paris and London on his way to America, where he will begin preparing for his Antarctic expedition.*

It seems the true interest for explorers, as one journey winds down, is a brief reflection and a rapid move forwards, chasing the sunset over the horizon and catching a new day before it even starts. As we wandered back to our hotel through the twilight streets of Tromso, talk was of where else the Antonov could be taken — at least to Moscow, to finish its flight around the world, then perhaps off to Mongolia to trace the route of the Great Wall of China from the air.

On my return to Seoul, Ron Sheardown, back home in Alaska, forwarded me an invitation he'd received from a friend in Poland:

> ... I would like to know your advise regarding flight with An-2 in which I will like you to take part, through boths poles, concerning technical and financial by your past experienced...

I have found a directness in men of action that can be very abrupt, but have discovered it stems from their desire to move ahead quickly backed by the confidence in knowing what they state will happen, will actually occur. This supersedes the need for smalltalk, yet rarely takes the gentleman out of the adventurer when you catch him for a story in an obscure pub somewhere north of the Arctic Circle.

As our own plans followed Wilkins out of the Arctic and towards the Antarctic, and as he rushed through his last chapter, 'Hail and Farewell', his final paragraph in *Flying the Arctic* moves off the ice, away from the planes and back to what in the end was at the heart of our exploration and what made it most worthwhile:

> *Whatever else we may have accomplished through our efforts we will learn only as time goes on. Eielson and I have learned, at all events, the sincerity of friendship.*

appendix I:

easter lake on banks island
by Dr Donald (Donny) Olson

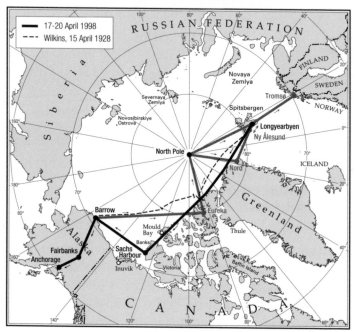

Legend on map:
— 17-20 April 1998
- - - Wilkins, 15 April 1928

Spitsbergen – Barrow – Anchorage

Our worst fears became reality as the orange glow of the village lights appeared when we were 4.5 miles out of Sachs Harbour on Banks Island in the High Arctic of northern Canada. Fog. It reduced forward visibility to zero, could precipitate on the wings and might cause icing in the carburetor and on the wings. Now what did we do, where did we go? We had been in the air for almost 20 hours, our fuel was running extremely low and Cape Perry, 125 miles south, the only alternative with the fuel we had.

Earlier that day we had left Spitsbergen and were headed nonstop across the polar ice cap to Barrow, Alaska in Polar Two, a straight-line distance of some 2,000 miles. Ron and I had decided to retrace the exact Wilkins-Eielson polar route in reverse for the return leg of our commemorative flight. We had their route coordinates as recorded from Wilkins' aeronautical sextant. We studied the weather patterns and determined we would need to plan for a 20-hour flight. On 17 April we had filled the main tanks of the Antonov, the internal auxiliary tank and four extra steel drums — a total of over 900 gallons of aviation gasoline. Carrying so much gas we were very conscious of fire. Taking off with this explosive load is like piloting a live bomb.

On the morning of our departure, we noticed that one of the drums was leaking and had to be replaced, which caused a considerable delay. We finally took off at 4.30 pm local time from Longyearbyen Airport. The airplane was loaded to capacity but it still performed well using its superb aerodynamic designs and STOL (short takeoff and landing) surfaces to pull itself airborne.

We flew southwest to Green Harbor, where Wilkins' Vega had been loaded onto the steamship and brought back to America by way of Europe. From Green Harbor we flew northwest, passed Barentsburg, an active Russian coalmining settlement, to Dead Man's Island, near Wilkins Bay and Eielson Point where they first landed in the eastern hemisphere. It was a beautiful day with the sun shining and a calm sea below with gentle waves rolling over the surface and a slight tail wind. We flew further northwest over open water dotted by small pieces of broken ice, then set our course to the next coordinate en route to Barrow.

As we approached the pack ice, clouds began to gather and we were soon beneath an overcast. We continued on at our low level until it appeared weather conditions were deteriorating and could become such that we would be unable to proceed and might even have to turn back. Ron pushed the throttle full forward and like a person pulling himself up by his boot straps, the solid Antonov clawed itself skyward, barely clearing the surrounding billowy clouds.

We droned on, ever northwest. The radial engine rumbled faithfully, never missing a beat.

After a number of hours flying we had burned enough fuel that we could now transfer the gas in the drums into the internal auxiliary tank. I had the flight controls while Ron went back to the cabin. Using a battery-driven electric pump, he moved 200 gallons of gasoline into the aux. tank. This was a sensitive undertaking as a spark from static electricity or any other source would have us instantly knocking at St Peter's Gate.

With the critical fuel transfer completed and good weather all around us, the remainder of the flight would be rather monotonous. We only needed to keep the plane straight and level and grind out the rest of the flight hours. Ron and I had a combined experience of over 30,000 hours flying time, mostly in the Arctic, so our idea of adventure and good flying were the challenging periods in takeoffs and landings, and navigating through adverse conditions, treacherous terrain, strong winds and the situations demanding our expertise, skill, and cunning. What we really needed now was an autopilot, or pilots eager to build time in their logbooks for this straight and level flying.

This was an ideal setting for the sandman to play his little tricks. Our greatest challenge was to fight off the weariness of the tedious task of holding altitude. I used whatever excuse I could to have Ron handle the controls while I went into the cabin to do whatever frivolous activity I could think of so as not to be compelled to fly the plane. Once when Ron sneezed I offered him some of my vitamin C. Assuming I had it right there he said yes. I told him to take the controls while I scampered to the back to look for the medicine bottle hidden deep in my pack. But as soon as I returned with the vial of vitamins he promptly turned the flight controls back to me. This unvaried grinding away of flight time continued on throughout the first 16 hours.

Radio contact was maintained on our high frequency radio with the station in Bodo, Norway and others scattered throughout Europe, Iceland and northern Canada. Weather updates and personal messages were conveyed through our contact Lee

Wareham in Anchorage. In the long run, contact with Lee proved the most helpful since he was in Alaska and could get us up-to-the-minute weather conditions for the North Slope.

Some 14 hours into the flight our trouble started. Weather at Barrow went bad with dropping visibility due to falling snow and possible icing conditions. Barrow could no longer be our destination. But we were not alarmed since we could just as easily divert to Deadhorse in Prudhoe Bay, some 175 miles east of Barrow. Within an hour the Deadhorse weather went sour, reporting an indefinite ceiling, sky obscured and deteriorating conditions. Still no problem. We would now head for Kaktovik on Barter Island, another 100 miles to the east near Demarcation Point. In less than an hour of receiving the Deadhorse weather, the Kaktovik automated weather system reported ice fog with less than a quarter mile of visibility. The fog was moving in fast and covering the entire North Slope region.

US Customs had already been notified of our proposed arrival times and were expecting us, so would have to be made aware of our new intentions. But what were our intentions? Ron and I discussed our options. These included landing on an ice floe in the polar ice cap and camping out until the weather cleared enough for us to proceed, or diverting to Tuktoyuktuk or Inuvik in the Northwest Territories of northern Canada. However, the weather forecast for both of these places included a large chance of fog with extremely low visibility prevailing prior to our estimated time of arrival. Because of the impending darkness, we decided against landing on the ice and since the forecast was not in our favor we opted to head for Sachs Harbour on Banks Island in the Canadian High Arctic.

Our main concern was that we had no current weather for Sachs. The only report available was six hours old. It was reported as 'clear of clouds and visibility unlimited'. Through our HF radio link, a nurse was called in Sachs Harbour. Although she was not a pilot and had no training as a weather observer, she stated that the weather was 'good'. Sachs Harbour was still 3–4 hours away, so we decided to divert to Banks Island as our best alternative considering the weather and rapidly approaching darkness.

Ron and I had now been awake more than 27 hours and flying almost 19 hours. We'd flown through the night and all the following day and were now approaching Banks Island at 2 am their local time. We were both tired and were well aware of the dangers of fatigue when challenged by unplanned obstacles and complications. The only sleep we had was what we could get sitting up in our seats in the cockpit. It might even have been possible that our short sleep periods overlapped. As we approached where we thought Sachs Harbour should be we decided to begin our descent even though we could see no lights. At 7,000 feet and 30 miles out we could not find the welcome lights indicating the village. Twenty miles — still no lights. Ten miles out — not even a flicker of a light. We were plenty high enough that we could see a long way and should be able to observe any grouping of lights.

The sun had long since set and we were afraid to descend into the horizonless dusky dark since the surrounding terrain was unfamiliar to both of us. I had never been there and it had been some 30 years since Ron had last landed there. The GPS indicated 8 miles to the airport and not the slightest hint of a light shone where we thought the tiny hamlet should be. Surely we should be able to see some light from our altitude? Something was very definitely wrong. Did we put in the wrong coordinates for this High Arctic settlement? Has there been a power failure in Sachs so that no one was able to have any lights except candlelight? Was our GPS malfunctioning? Were our minds going flat from sleep deprivation or were we reacting with anxiety to the unexpected significant obstacle of no town where we desperately needed to have one due to our diminished fuel levels? At 5 miles out we were still unable to explain why no lights were sighted and unable to explain the confusion. Then at 4.5 miles distance an orange glow began to form and as we got closer we confirmed the street lights of Sachs Harbour emitting a faint luster through the dense fog that now besieged our destination.

Like a moat around a fortified castle, the fog was going to

prove impenetrable to our futile attempt to land on the only maintained runway within 100 miles. It was 2 am and the sky was dark, but darker still was the atmosphere in the cockpit as two polar pilots began mustering every resource of energy, experience and skill to overcome this rapidly deteriorating set of circumstances that we now found ourselves facing. Like Arctic warriors in our blue chariot armed with our GPS and charts, we rallied to come up with a plan to overcome the enemies that now faced us: dense fog over the runway, low fuel reserves and darkness.

Our first plan was to find the runway and make a normal landing approach with minimal visibility. We circled above the fog and lights in the clear dark night trying to find the runway's vicinity by activating the electronically controlled airport lighting. Normally turned on by clicking the microphone button seven times and controlled by a timer, the lights refused to come on. Realizing that in every village there is some type of VHF receiver or scanner we transmitted over the radio 'in the blind' for someone to manually turn on the runway lights. As we did flight circuits overhead we could finally see the airport lighting through the dense fog. At last assurance that we had correctly identified the general area of the runway and proper lighting was available.

The task now was to try and line up with a runway we essentially could not see. I used the GPS moving map screen like a operator uses a radar screen, calling our directional heading and distances as best I could to Ron who was flying by instrument reference and occasionally looking out the window for indications. Since our visibility was so limited we tried a couple test patterns above the fog. We could only see two sets of lights at a time, indicating a forward visibility of about 200 feet. As we circled overhead we could also see the power lines and the telephone poles around the airport posing serious dangers to low-flying aircraft. There was also a non-directional beacon tower just a mile from the airport that stuck up several hundred feet in the air and whose only marker was a red blinking light on the top with our ADF (automatic direction finder) tuned into it. This tower was situated near the runway and was lined up with the centerline.

Not only that, but the level of the fog was above the red light on top of the tower, so we could only see it when we were very close to it or when we were right over the tower.

The other physical obstruction was two-story terminal building that was situated just off to the side of the runway. With all these things sticking up in the air trying to snag us out of the sky I had the feeling that we were flying around a bumper crop of Venus fly traps. Naturally, after flying over the town at low levels with our 1,000 horsepower engine for a considerable amount of time we woke pretty much everybody up. We could see down through the fog vertically but not horizontally. What we saw were people on the ground walking and driving snow machines, all headed toward the airport. Soon Brad Carpenter introduced himself on the radio and wanted to know how he could help. We had now established contact with the local Inuit. When asked what the weather was he reported less than a quarter mile of visibility — not overly encouraging. He then stated that it seemed that the fog was getting thicker since it had just rolled in an hour or so before our arrival.

As we slipped from the clear cold sky into the slurry layer of moisture below it was like swimming around in a milk bottle, groping for a visual reference. All my training in Braille had not prepared me for this type of mixed VFR/IFR flying. During our initial approaches we could find the airport all right, but runway lights which we could only see when we were right over them would be angling off to the side at about 60 degrees. We would immediately turn toward them but as we turned we would lose sight of the few lights we could see and when we found them again we could not tell how much runway length we had available. Not knowing if we would run off the end, go up on our nose or possibly flip over, we did the conservative thing, added power and went around. Climbing back up into the clear air like a great whale surfacing, coming up for more air, we would take a deep breath, relax for a few seconds and mentally prepare for another dive down into the murky condensation, trying to find that elusive needle in the haystack.

On our third approach we felt like everything was going right. And sure enough it was. We could see runway end identifier lights right in front of us and we were perfectly lined up. With 4,000 feet of gravel runway ahead of us we could now relax, we had as good as made it, beaten the odds, we were home free — or so we thought. As Ron pulled the throttle back, the engine slowed and he prepared to pull the yoke back to start the landing flare. Just as he was beginning to commence the landing the runway lights suddenly and mysteriously were turned off. With the lights on we could barely see 200 feet down the runway; without lights we could only see a gray monochromatic haze outside the windshield. It was too dark and foggy to see even the outline of the runway. Since it was so foggy we had not turned our landing lights on to avoid the glare that they produced and to try and maintain the night accommodation of our vision.

Instantly adrenaline started recirculating through our vascular systems and just as quickly the throttle was poured to the 1,000 horsepower engine and it came roaring back to life. It was demoralizing, coming so close yet erring on the side of safety so far. The fuel gauges were now getting low, and with no other airstrips nearby we were running out of options.

On our next approach, down through the fog I could see what appeared to be a road. Assuming that it went to the airport premises I kept an eye on it until suddenly it made a 90° right-hand turn away from our flight path. But the runway lights appeared just to our left, again not exactly lined up. Our fear was that not knowing where the two-story terminal was, the chances of becoming intimate with it were too much of a threat so we aborted another landing attempt. As we flew overhead the radio operator stated that they could see the belly of the airplane when we suddenly appeared out of the fog and flew directly over them. One could only imagine the number of people gathered at the airport intently listening for the sound of our engine in the fog, trying to pinpoint our position relative to the airport, only to be startled by the sudden appearance of the massive underbelly of the Antonov.

Trying to maintain a sense of equilibrium took a fair amount of concentration. The airplane was turning back and forth, climbing and descending. Without a visual reference for the horizon it was hard to tell how steep the angles of bank or attack were getting to be. We were not just tired now, we were bone-weary. If we continued in this futile attempt we had a good chance of being the first to the site of an accident — our own.

We made one last try by extending our outbound segment and making a long final approach, which allowed us to stabilize our directional heading. We made contact with the runway lights, but the fog had gotten noticeably thicker during the last hour so that now we could only see one set of runway lights at a time, indicating less than 100 feet forward visibility. The worsened fog conditions and extremely low fuel, combined with our level of fatigue, made it imperative that we go to plan B. What was plan B? What we did not want to do was add our name to the local list of unfortunate explorers whose wreckages still appear around Banks Island. Sachs Harbour is named after the ship *Mary Sachs*, which had met its unlucky demise just a couple miles to the southwest while searching for the famed Franklin Expedition. McClure had abandoned his ship *Investigator* where it later sank in Mercy Bay just a few miles to the north of us while on the same search.

We had to find some place to land. But where? As we scanned the horizon we could see a reflection in the distance. Thinking that it might be a lake we headed toward it. Once overhead we confirmed that it was indeed the glare ice of a frozen lake, swept clean by the prevailing southeast wind. The obstacles to our landing on the ice were intermittent ribbons of snowdrifts, compounded by not knowing how high or how deep or how hard they were, all impossible to determine in the dark. But this was our only chance of making a controlled landing.

On one side of the lake was an area about 1,500 feet long that had fewer snowdrifts than the rest of the lake. After flying over it a number of times, we set up for a landing to the southeast, a direction we hoped was into the wind as this was the wind direction at Sachs Harbour (160 degrees at 10 knots). There was no

214

way to tell which direction the wind was from or how strong it was. We could only guess and leave the rest to God.

As we lined up on final for our intended landing site we braced ourselves for whatever may come. We flew low over the tundra bank on the north end of the lake. Ron cut the engine and we glided down close to the ice surface, he pulled back on the control wheel and we experienced that uneasy feeling of the tires contacting the glare ice. Directional control evaporated and we were at the mercy of whatever the strongest force on the aircraft happened to be at the time; whether it was wind, momentum of the airplane, or the landing surface. Sideways movements were just as probable as going straight forward. About that time we hit a solid snowdrift and felt the tooth-jarring jolt from our right landing gear. We could feel the oleo strut compress down against the tension of the spring as the hydraulic fluid squeezed through the tiny pores as it tried to cushion the solid block of snow we had just hit. The violence of the shock combined with the angle of the snow mound launched us back into the air. Just as quickly, the landing gear strut went into full extension. We were now airborne and there was no weight on the tire. Bang. We could feel the mechanisms forcefully pushed out to their steel stops. We came down on the glare ice on the other side and continued to slide along. Thankfully the landing gear had maintained its integrity and was properly situated under us and not in the partially retracted position as frequently happens to less robust airplanes during rough landings. There were a few more snowdrifts that jostled us around a bit, but since we had slowed down the violent action and reaction had been tamed to a much more tolerable level.

When we finally skidded to a stop we idled the engine for a while to cool the cylinders. We still had radio contact with Brad Carpenter in Sachs Harbour, so we gave him our position and told him we could camp out until the weather improved. He suggested that he send snow machines out to get us. Many people were buzzing around offering to help in whatever way they could. We had landed on Easter Lake, 9.2 nautical miles northeast of

Sachs Harbour at 72° 07' N, 124° 58' W.

Much like the Rolaids commercial, 'How do you spell relief?', we spelled it 'Easter Lake on Banks Island'. The relief was so profound that I could not carry on a conversation. Rather, I felt like giggling to relieve the tension that had been built up during the last part of the flight. We had been in the air for 20 hours and 12 minutes and neither of us had been particularly well rested when we had taken off from Spitsbergen.

As we sat there looking out over the radial engine cowling, reality returned. We could not rest on our laurels. The cold Arctic wind was carrying away the last remaining heat that had been scavenged from the engine exhaust stacks. We still were a long way from being home and events could still take place that would jeopardize our health and welfare.

We gathered our strength, put on our winter clothes and prepared to tie the plane to the lake ice. To secure it we had a hand auger that we screwed down into the ice, making a seven-inch hole, four feet deep. In this hole we placed the 'duckbills', a cable and steel bar set-up made specifically for this type of anchor. We were so tired that just walking on the glare ice was a challenge. Operating the auger, twisting its handle while trying to get a good bite on the ice with the blade, took a fair amount of dexterity and stamina.

Within an hour the light of the snow machines appeared on the horizon and they were soon alongside the airplane. Wayne Gully, Richard Carpenter and Andy J.R. Carpenter had come to pick us up and take us into town.

We went to Bill Slade's home on arrival, where we were fed breakfast and went to bed. Restful deep sleep came quickly as a welcome guest. We slept until afternoon and by then the fog had cleared and a nice spring day reigned overhead. After eating again we got ready to go back out to the airplane and fly it in to the elusive local airport.

At 2 pm we started out for Easter Lake by snow machine, both Ron and I in a plywood box lined with musk ox hide, on top of the tethered sled. After traveling three miles from town, the engine started making a clanging sound. This latest mechanical development warranted a shutdown and an inspection to determine what was making all the racket. Looking at the engine we quickly determined that 2 of the 4 head bolts holding the cylinder on were broken off at the shank. The snow machine driver, Richard Carpenter, said that he would walk back to town for another vehicle, while Ron and I decided to start walking toward the plane. We parted at 3 pm.

As Ron and I walked along, we reminded ourselves that we had no firearms to protect us if a polar bear came across the tundra in search of a fresh protein source. I thought of the accounts of earlier explorers like Stephenson and others looking for the survivors of the Franklin Expedition; they had hiked over these same bald hills whose soil was devoid of any shrubs or even willows, mapping, observing and searching. Some would eventually succumb to the ravages of scurvy, the madness of the High Arctic, or the ever-present threat of freezing to death. At 6 pm, after three hours of trudging through the soft snow, we finally arrived at the lake where the Antonov was anchored into the ice. We untied the plane, pulled the prop through and started the engine.

On takeoff, we slid over the glare ice and rolled over the score of snowdrifts that made the lake runway feel like an obstacle course, driving over some of the smaller drifts while trying to steer around the more ominous ones. The flight to Sachs Harbour took less than 10 minutes

The following morning we searched for several hours through a morass of steel drums buried in snow, looking for aviation gas. From the several hundred drums, most of which were empty, we managed to find eight that had 100-octane gasoline of sufficient quality to use for the plane. We used a monster Caterpillar loader to clear a road, dig out the drums from their snowy confines and carry the barrels, three at a time, to the parking apron. After fueling up, we filed a flight plan to Barrow where the weather had cleared and family and friends were expecting us.

After an eight-hour flight we received the airport advisory of a cross wind over 25 knots, gusting to 35, and were told that braking on the runway was poor in places. When we landed we did not roll far, but soon found that we could not turn onto the taxi way since the runway was so icy. The brakes weren't holding and the large vertical stabilizer made it impossible to rotate into the wind. This would not have been quite so alarming if it weren't for the Alaska Airlines jet close behind us and already cleared for the approach into Barrow. The only solution was for me to disembark, get a truck and pull the plane backwards off the runway. Dano Bollman, the airport manager, who was cleaning the runway with a plow, came by and gave me a ride to the airport garage and let me use the airport truck. I drove back out to the windbound plane where Ron was already securing the leading edge slats so that they would be less apt to get one or both wings airborne and cause the plane to become light on its wheels or go out of control. We used a tie-down rope to join the tail wheel assembly and the truck bumper. With the airplane engine running and the truck pulling the plane backward we exited the runway with a minimum of control. The Boeing 737 landed seven minutes later. We then had to use two trucks to anchor our plane. Even so the wings strained at the ropes, tightening the knots we'd used to secure the aircraft.

Our next challenge was the engine cover. Getting it over the top of the cowling was like trying to erect a tent in a windstorm while standing on an icy ledge. While one of us stood on top of the stepladder on the icy ramp holding the heavy engine blanket and leaning into the gale, the other climbed up the back of the airplane to stand on top of the engine cowling. With both of us struggling to not fall or get blown off our precarious perches we finally managed to get the cover on. We plugged in the electric heater and headed for shelter ourselves. That night we went to bed with our faces weathered and windburned.

We had completed the Wilkins and Eielson commemorative flight in reverse, having been challenged by the same elements and having to divert to a less-than-optimum alternate just as they had done 70 years previously.

appendix ii

antonov an-2 specifications
(Excerpts from *Jane's Encyclopedia of Aviation*, 1997-1998)

PZL Mielec (Antonov) An-2

Nato reporting name: Colt

TYPE: Single-engined general purpose biplane.

PROGRAMME: First flight of An-2 prototype, designed to specification of USSR ministry of Agriculture and Forestry, 31 August, 1947; went into production in USSR 1948, with 746 kW (1,000 hp) Ash-62 engine; over 5,000 built in USSR by 1960; license rights granted to China where first Y-5 completed December 1957 and limited production continues since 1960, apart from few dozen Soviet-built An-2Ms continued production primarily by PZL Mielec; original license agreement provided for An-2T and An2R versions; first flight of Polish An-2 on 23 October 1960. Unofficial Polish name Antek (little Antonov).

CURRENT VERSIONS: An-2P: Passenger version; 12 adult passengers and two children; improved cabin layout and comfort, better soundproofing, new propeller and spinner; weight-saving instruments and equipment compared with Soviet model; entered production in 1968.

CUSTOMERS: Over 11,950 An-2s built by Mielec for domestic use and export.

COSTS: $105,000 to $125,000 (according to equipment) for delivery in 1997, meeting FAR pt 23.

DESIGN FEATURES: Unequal span single-bay biplane; braced wings and tail; fuselage circular section forward, rectangular in cabin section, oval in tail section; fin integral with rear fuselage.

FLYING CONTROLS: Dual controls and blind-flying instrumentation standard. Mechanically actuated differential ailerons, elevators and rudder, using cables and push/pull rods; electric trim tab in port aileron, rudder and port elevator; full-span automatic leading-edge slots on upper wings; electrically actuated slotted trailing-edge flaps on both wings.

STRUCTURE: All metal, with fabric covering on wings aft of main spar and on tailplane.

LANDING GEAR: Non-retractable split axle type, with long stroke oleo-pneumatic shock-absorbers. Mainwheel tyres size 800 x 260 mm, pressure 2.25 bars (33 lb/sq in). Pneumatic shoe brakes on main units. Fully castoring and self-centering PZL Krosno tailwheel, size 470 x 210, with electropneumatic lock. For rough field operation shock absorbers can be charged with compressed air cylinder installed in rear fuselage. Interchangeable ski landing gear available optionally.

POWERPLANT: One 746 kW (1,000 hp) PZL Kalisz ASz-62IR nine-cylinder radial air-cooled engine, driving an AW-2 four blade variable-pitch metal propeller. Six fuel tanks in upper wings, with total capacity of 1,200 liters (317 US gallons; 264 Imperial gallons). Fuel consumption 120 to 170 liters (31.7 to 45.0 US gallons). Oil capacity 120 liters (31.7 US gallons).

ACCOMMODATION: Crew of two on flight deck, with access via passenger cabin. Standard accommodation for 12 passengers, in four rows of three with single aisle. Two foldable seats for children in aisle between first and second rows, and infant's cradle at front on starboard side. Toilet at rear on starboard side. Overhead racks for up to 160 kg (352 lb) of baggage, with space for coats and additional 40 kg (88 lb) of baggage between rear pair of seats and toilet. Emergency exit on starboard side at rear. Walls of cabin lined with glass-wool mats and inner facing of plywood to reduce internal noise. Cabin floor carpeted. Cabin heating and starboard windscreen de-icing by engine bleed air; port and centre windscreens electrically de-iced. Cabin ventilation by ram air intakes on underside of top wings.

SYSTEMS: Compressed air cylinder, of 8 liters (0.28 cu ft) capacity, for pneumatic charging of shock-absorbers and operation of tailwheel lock at 49 bars pressure and operation of mainwheel brakes at 9.80 bars. Contents of cylinder maintained by AK-50P engine-driven compressor, with AD-50 automatic relief device to prevent overpressure. DC electrical system supplied with basic 27 V power (and 36 V or 115 V where required) by engine-driven generator and storage battery. CO_2 fire extinguisher system with automatic fire detector.

AVIONICS: Comms: R-842 HF and RS 6102 or Baklan-5 VHR lightweight radio transceivers and SPU-7 intercom.
Flight: A-037 radio altimeter, ARK-9 radio compass, MRP-56P marker beacon receiver, GIK-1 gyrocompass and GPK-48 gyroscopic direction indicator.

DIMENSIONS EXTERNAL:

Wing span: upper	18.18 metre (59 ft 7$^{1}/_{4}$ in)
lower	14.24 metre (46 ft 8$^{1}/_{2}$ in)
Wing gap	2.17 metre (7 ft 1$^{1}/_{2}$ in)
Length overall	12.74 m (41 ft 9$^{1}/_{2}$ in)
Height overall	6.10 m (20 ft 0 in)
Propeller diameter	3.60 m (11 ft 9$^{1}/_{4}$ in)

DIMENSIONS INTERNAL

Cargo Compartment: Length	4.10 m (13 ft 5$^{1}/_{2}$ in)
Max width	1.60 m (5 ft 3 in)
Max height	1.80 m (5 ft 10$^{1}/_{4}$ in)

WEIGHTS AND LOADINGS

Weight empty	3,450 kg (7,605 lb)

| Max. fuel weight | 900 kg (1,984 lb) |
| Max T-O weight | 5,500 kg (12,125 lb) |

PERFORMANCE

Max level speed at 1,750 m (5,740 ft): 139 kt (258 km/h; 160 mph)

Econ cruising speed: 100 kt (185 km/h; 115 mph)

Min flying speed: 49 kt (80 km/h; 56 mph)

Landing speed: 46 kt (85 km/h; 53 mph)

Service ceiling: 4,400 m (14,420 ft)

T-O run: hard runway: 150 m (495 ft)

Landing from 15 m (50 ft) hard runway: 427 m (1,405 ft)

Range at 1,000 m (3,280 ft) with 500 kg load: 485 nautical miles

Fuel capacity: 317 gallons wing tanks, 390 auxiliary tank

appendix III

a brief note on mapping the arctic
Miklos Pinther, Chief Cartographer, United Nations

'The Polar Regions, Scene of Hunt for the Unknown' was the title of a huge map spread over two pages of the Sunday edition of the *New York Times* on 11 April 1926. The map was to serve as a guide to the armchair explorers at home about the progress of aerial expeditions. By 1926, the Arctic had become a familiar place to the public. Nansen (1893), Cagni (1899), Peary (1909), MacMillan (1914) and Stefansson (1917) made heroic penetrations into the frozen cap of the earth that had captured the imagination of young and old.

But on that spring day, the *New York Times* heralded a new discovery-adventure: exploration from the skies, which gave scientists and mapmakers new means to diminish that large, white patch on the map of the Arctic labeled 'unexplored'.

While reporters of the *New York Times* were busy making arrangements to take wireless outfits by dog sled to Point Barrow, Alaska, and set up another office at Etah, Greenland, a quiet revolution was taking place in another part of Manhattan, at the headquarters of the American Geographical Society on the Upper West Side. There, on the top floor of the recently completed building, explorers gathered to receive instructions in field surveying and navigation and to map out their routes. It was here that on several occasions Sir Hubert Wilkins met with the staff of the Society in preparations for his flights. And it was also here where he returned with his notes, calculations and aerial photographs for a final analysis of his exploits.

Founded in 1851 by a group of New York businessmen and others interested in exploration and geography, the American Geographical Society (AGS) is the oldest geographical institute in the United States. Its first president, Henry Grinnell, was keenly interested in Arctic explorations, which set the tone of the Society's focus on this region for over half a century. Mapping was a natural extension of the work of AGS. Its journals were filled with maps and diagrams. A growing team of cartographers prepared a large variety of maps from cartograms to wall charts to planning maps for explorers. By the time Sir Hubert Wilkins made his first visit to the Society, there was a fully staffed Cartographic Department and a Map Library that was one of the largest in the Western Hemisphere. In 1923, a School of Surveying was also established. According to one of its pamphlets, the School of Surveying is primarily a place of instruction for those who intend to become professional mapmakers. It also is intended for the use of travelers, explorers, and the like who wish to train themselves to make maps of the regions they visit, as precise as the conditions of travel allow. The school had a comprehensive surveying library and a valuable collection of modern surveying instruments. It also published field notebooks and *Special Azimuth Tables for Use by Navigators in Latitudes above 70°*, no doubt of interest to Sir Hubert.

The principal instructor at the Society's School of Surveying was Osborn Maitland Miller, a young British officer who joined the Society in 1922. Miller had an unconventional, inquisitive mind that eventually led him on a long, brilliant career in mapping. In 1925, there were seven students at the School, among them Lincoln Ellsworth and Hubert Wilkins. Miller instantly understood the new opportunities flying and photography from the air extended to mapping. One can only imagine the long hours of discourse the three of them had in preparation for flying over the Arctic. In 1926, while AGS cartographers were busy making maps and navigational charts of the Arctic Basin, Miller traveled to Switzerland to visit the Wild Instrument Company. There he saw the first Wild stereoscopic plotting instruments in operation, stimulating his imagination so much that he spent an entire weekend in his hotel room trying to figure out the mathematical principles behind them. Upon returning to New York, enriched with ideas, he discussed several plans with Sir Hubert for photographing from the air. The field procedures suggested by Miller were eventually brought to fruition by Wilkins on his subsequent flight over Antarctica.

Following his 1928 flight from Point Barrow, Alaska, to Green Harbor, Spitsbergen, Sir Hubert Wilkins returned to the American Geographical Society for a debriefing with O. M. Miller. His field books, charts and calculations were deposited in the Library. In honor of his flight, Captain Sir Hubert Wilkins was awarded the Society's Samuel Finely Breeze Morse medal. The experience Wilkins gained enabled him to better prepare for his Antarctic flight. Both polar flights were of immense value to cartographers, who with new improved maps set the groundwork for a whole new generation of explorers. The scientific work and observations were recorded in a series of publications by the Society, among them *Problems of Polar Research* (1928), *The Geography of the Polar Regions* (1928), *Brief History of Polar Exploration Since the Introduction of Flying* (1930), and a new physical map of the Arctic (1930) at the scale of 1:20,000,000 with inset maps at larger scales. In 1930, this map represented the most up-to-date compilation of the region.

Meanwhile the mapmakers at AGS, with Miller and Senior Cartographer William Briesemeister in their lead, set a new course in utilizing aerial surveying. The use of maps in aid of air navigation was one of the first to receive scrutiny. AGS by this time was involved in numerous aerial surveys in many parts of the world, as were other institutions. Mapping of archeological sites, sources of remote rivers, and shifting coastlines all benefited from the work of daring pilots. The Society's efforts in assisting pilots resulted in the research and publication in 1932 of an experimental air navigation map using innovative cartographic symbology. Analyzing photographs taken from aircrafts, Miller realized that if photographs were to be made more useful for mapping, ways had to be found not only to eliminate the radial distortion that occurs away from the center of an image, but also the additional scale exaggerations that are caused by tilting. Miller's efforts resulted in new techniques in planetabling from the air and plotting from tilted or oblique aerial photographs. He also devised an instrument for measuring angles on photographs which he called a photogoniometer and another, a single-eyepiece plotter, for plotting from oblique photographs. These new techniques were brilliantly demonstrated in a set of new maps of Northern Labrador, which were based on photography flown in 1932 and 1935 and published by the Society in 1938.

These maps heralded the nascence of modern photogrammetry. In 1945, in recognition of Miller's contributions to reconnaissance mapping and photogrammetry, he was elected as president of the American Society of Photogrammetry.

Almost fifty years after Sir Hubert Wilkins' historic flight, the American Geographical Society published in 1975 a new *Map of the Arctic Region* at the scale of 1:5,000,000. O. M. Miller, who was still active, contributed to the calculation of the map projection and to the preparation of a scale departure diagram for assisting in the measurements of distances. Theodore Shabad, former Moscow bureau chief of the *New York Times*, edited the Siberian portion of the map to correct for the disinformation the Soviet Union published during those years. And Dr Bruce Heezen of the Lamont-Doherty Earth Observatory gave the final word on the depiction of bathymetry. These efforts, once again, made this map the best and most accurate at the time. There was yet another aspect of the map that signaled a major change from the air age ushered in by explorers like Wilkins. For the first time, from a much higher observation platform, newly acquired imagery from satellites were utilized as an aid in mapping the Arctic.

appendix iv

pembroke capital limited

Pembroke Capital was formed in 1993 to take advantage of the rapidly expanding needs of the airline industry. Pembroke's expansion is fueled by finding new ways to source and finance aircraft to meet the high growth in passenger traffic around the world.

There is an ongoing requirement in the airline industry to replace much of the existing world fleet to maximise economic efficiency, while also meeting increasingly stringent noise and emission requirements. The airline industry's capital needs over the next two decades are measured in trillions of dollars. This funding requirement has resulted in the need for a wide variety of innovative means of financing. Today, nearly 30 percent of 'single aisle' jet aircraft are owned by third parties and not by the airlines who operate them, under what is known as an 'aircraft operating lease'.

Pembroke Capital provides services related to modern commercial jet aircraft designed to meet this growing market demand. These services include aircraft marketing for both lease and sale, either as principal for its own jet fleet or on behalf of third parties. They arrange finance for airline and third party purchasers through creative structures, utilising both on- and off-balance sheet tax-efficient techniques. Other services include management of aircraft on behalf of owners from an administrative and technical standpoint, lease monitoring and compliance oversight.

Pembroke also provides technical services from aircraft specification definition through to registration, inspection and condition monitoring. In several areas, Pembroke provides financial services for other large transportation projects. Pembroke's core team of fifteen senior executives and owners brings a wealth of aviation and banking industry experience. Their earlier careers include management positions with industry leaders General Electric, KPMG Peat Marwick, Guinness Peat Aviation (GPA), Rabobank and AIB.

Pembroke's clients include airlines, lessors and aircraft manufacturers, banks and financial institutions. Since its inception five years ago, Pembroke has structured the financing of US $1.5 billion of commercial jet aircraft, managed US$1 billion in value of aircraft, and owns an aircraft fleet valued at US$500 million.

appendix v

Biographical notes

Shane Christopher Lundgren
Born 1961, California. B.A. in History from the University of San Diego. Began flying in 1978 at 17 years of age. At 21 had completed Boeing 737 training, at that time the youngest B737 pilot in the world. Has flown for Air Berlin in Berlin, Germany, since 1982. Became Captain in 1987. Flown 10,000 hours in Boeing 737-200/300/400/800 models.

Began mountaineering in the Alps in 1985, summiting Mt Blanc, the Matterhorn, and the Eiger via the Mittelegi Ridge. Organized climb to Mt Elbrus in Russia in 1986. Team member of Snowbird Everest Expedition 1987. Climbed Mexican volcanoes, Mt Rainier, and on Aconcagua in Argentina.

Sailed extensively with family and friends. Fastnet race on maxi yacht *Nirvana* in 1985 (still holds record time), and 1987. Bermuda race on *Nirvana* in 1986. Sjaelland Rundt, Gotland Rundt, Kings Cup, Long Island races on *Nirvana*. Sailed across Atlantic Ocean with family in 1979; to Spitsbergen, Norway, in 1992; around Cape Horn in 1994; to Antarctica in 1995 and Indian Ocean in 1997. Cruised extensively in the Mediterranean. Planned and led the Arctic Siberian Expedition 1994 with the Antonov An-2 biplane. Also led 1995 Siberian Expedition, as well as 1997-98 North Pole flights.

Developed communications projects linking expeditions to the Internet. Undertook first 'online' expedition with *Wired* magazine on 1994 Siberian flight. Launched Discovery Online with 1995 Siberian flight. Initiated packet radio communications experiment for Explorers Club, 1997 North Pole Expedition.

Joined Explorers Club in 1993 and has carried the Club flag five times, including flag #7, the Wilkins flag, on its final expedition, the 1997 North Pole Expedition. Appeared in National Geographic television special to commemorate the history of flying the Arctic. Member New York Yacht Club, Arlberg ski club and the Royal Geographic Society.

Ronald C. Sheardown

Ron Sheardown began his flying career in Canada in 1953, earning his private pilot's license at 17. His family lived across the street from what is now Toronto/Lester B. Pearson International Airport and he was inspired by spending much of his time around aircraft and experienced aviators as a youth.

Ron began his career as a company pilot for a mining company in British Columbia, and from there worked as a pilot on transport aircraft for the DEW line construction in the High Arctic and Greenland, as well as on charter flights to Europe and the southern United States.

He holds US airline transport, US commercial, and Canadian senior commercial pilot licenses with instrument and helicopter ratings. He is licensed to fly single- and multi-engine land and sea aircraft, including jets and helicopters. He has over 15,000 hours flight time gained in all 50 of the United States, Europe, Mexico and South America, including more than 9,000 hours in the Canadian Arctic, Greenland, Norway, Siberia and Alaska.

He became involved in the North Pole expedition in 1997 and again in the Trans Polar flight in 1998 after facilitating the release of Shane Lundgren's AN-2 biplanes from Providenya, in the Russian Far East, and flying them to America. This was when he learned of Shane's interest in the expedition and the two discussed taking their AN-2s on the expedition.

Ron is a professional miner and CEO of Greatland Exploration Ltd, with interests in Canada, Chile, Mexico, Russia and the US. Besides aviation and world travel, his interests include skiing, photography, camping and fishing.

Ferdinand von Baumbach

Ferdinand von Baumbach, 34, lives in Munich, Germany. He studied Business at Fachhochschule Munich, obtaining his degree in 1996 and worked with a jung Gallerist through December 1997, joining the BMW public relations department in 1998. From childhood he has been interested in technical things like cars and motorcycles and in his free time he works on them, particularly his 1981 Harley Davidson FXB Styrgis — an excellent form of training for an Antonov as there is always something to repair and you always have oily fingers.

Ferdinand met Shane in 1996, skiing with friends in the Austrian Alps. Shane related the story of his first two expeditions through Siberia and Ferdinand and Andrea visited Shane in the summer of 1996 in Oregon, where they looked at photographs from Shane's journeys and Ferdinand's interest was first sparked in joining Shane on an expedition.

They first considered flying from Alaska to Argentina, following the Pan American Highway, but this was soon discounted due to the distance and political risk. However, Shane later phoned and invited Ferdinand to join him on a flight to the North Pole. After a few meetings in Munich, Ferdinand decided to join as a partner on Shane'a An-2 so in November 1996 purchased a half share in Shane's Antonov.

He began his private pilot's license training in Jesenwang, a small airport close to Munich, in February 1997. On 4 April 1997 he received his license. He is now working on his helicopter license as well.

Ferdinand first saw an Antonov in March 1997, while with Shane at an aircraft museum in Munich. He remembers it as a very special day, the Antonov being so much bigger than he had expected. He didn't see his own An-2 until a month later in Anchorage.

Ferdinand assisted Shane in the production of their 1997 promotional brochure in New York in November 1996 and then began the initial fund-raising. He has since purchased a 1950 Cessna 170 A, much smaller but in some ways similar to the An-2. It is fun to fly, but not so much fun to work on as it runs like a Swiss watch. He now has over 200 hours airtime, a good proportion of it in the Arctic accompanied by Shane, Ron or Donny.

Ferdinand is married to Andrea and they have one child, born in 1998, Géza Maximilian.

Trevor Henderson

Trevor Henderson was born in Ireland in 1945. He was educated in Ireland and earned engineering and arts degrees from the University of Dublin, Trinity College, where he graduated in 1967. He worked for fifteen years in a number of countries in the then emerging commercial computer industry in both machine and application related software development and later in marketing roles. He admits to some responsibility for potential millennium bugs.

He moved to the aviation and finance industry in 1983. He enjoyed considerable success in that area and was president of a division of Guinness Peat Aviation which under his direction grew to control and market over one hundred modern Boeing commercial jets including B737s, B757s and B767s. This work involved much travel throughout the world to interesting and unusual places and dealing with many diverse cultures. He was later the Chief Marketing Officer of General Electric Capital Aviation Services based in Shannon, Ireland, which controlled nearly nine hundred aircraft.

He moved in 1995 to help grow an emerging Pembroke Capital, where he is Executive Vice President responsible for marketing to the world's airlines. He prefers the working atmosphere of young and nimble companies. Trevor was key in committing Pembroke Capital to the major part of the sponsorship cost of the Trans Polar Flight. Trevor learned to fly, first in sailplanes (gliders) in 1968, and later gained powered landplane and seaplane licences. His flying experience also includes balloons and microlights. Flying and light aircraft related matters are his chief leisure pastime, along with tennis, cycling, sailing, skiing and boats to improve his chances of keeping his medical certificate current. He was second pilot on Polar Two during the flight from Eureka to Spitsbergen via the Pole, and rates the polar expedition as the most challenging, potentially dangerous, and satisfying flying experience of a lifetime.

Robert Mads Anderson

Robert Anderson graduated from the University of Puget Sound in the US with a degree in Writing and began his advertising career selling mountaineering equipment through direct marketing in the US and Europe. He had begun climbing in his native state of Colorado when he was 15, as a technical rock climber, before moving into the higher mountains with solo ascents of new routes on the Matterhorn, Huascaren in Peru and over 50 first ascents in Norway.

He moved to New Zealand as a writer for Ogilvy & Mather in 1983, spending a year in the Australian office before returning to establish Ogilvy & Mather Direct in Wellington in 1985 as General Manager/Creative Director. In 1986 he founded his own advertising agency in Auckland, New Zealand. Clients included BMW, Bayer Pharmaceutical, Roche Products, Tetra-Pak and Sheraton Hotels. The agency won six national and five international awards for creativity in TV, radio, print and direct marketing. In 1988 he took time out to lead the first and only expedition to successfully ascend Everest's Kangshung Face without oxygen. His advertising agency was sold to international affiliate WCRS in 1990.

In 1991 Anderson started Seven Summits Solo Ltd, a sports marketing company, working with British Airways, Compaq Computer, Kodak, Rolex and SmithKline Beecham. These supported his solo climbs on the Seven Summits, the tallest peaks on each of the world's seven continents. The expeditions were detailed in his two books, *Seven Summits Solo*, a large photographic book published by David Bateman (titled *Summits* in America and co-published by Clarkson Potter, a Random House imprint). His second book, *To Everest via Antarctica*, was published by Penguin. He has published numerous articles in magazines and newspapers in Europe, UK, USA and Australasia on topics ranging from ascending Everest to Asian direct marketing strategy. He currently manages the OgilvyOne office in Seoul, Korea.

Anderson is an International Fellow of The Explorers Club, New York, a Lifetime Member of the New Zealand Outward Bound, a member of the National Ski Patrol, Far East, and a Fellow of the Royal Geographical Society, London.

Werner Maier, lithographic artist

Werner Maier, 42, was born in Munich and attended the Akademie der Bildenden Künste, Munich, graduating in 1987. He specializes only in black and white drawings and prints. His work is shown in the following museums: Albertinum, Vienna; Stadtarchiv, Munich; Graphische Sammlung, Munich; and the Museum of Modern Art, Denver.

The prints of the Antonov An-2 were designed especially for the Trans Arctic Flight Team. The print is made using a rare and historic technique, the Hilogravur.

acknowledgements

Shane Lundgren, Ron Sheardown, Ferdinand von Baumbach, Trevor Henderson and Donald Olson for their invaluable personal contributions and assistance in improving and adding to the manuscript.

Michael Gifkins, my literary agent and editor, for taking on the manuscript, prepared to a timetable matching Wilkins' own, and then adding the finishing touches with his customary skill; Paul Bateman, at David Bateman Ltd, for seeing a story in our adventure even before we took off; and Chris O'Brien for weaving all the elements together into something worthy of the journey.

Penguin Putnam Group and Florence Eichin for assistance with permission to quote from Wilkins' book, *Flying the Arctic*.

The American Geographical Society and Mary Lynn Bird for access and copying of their extensive archives.

Miklos Pinther for the historical and detailed maps depicting our journey.

And to all those who assisted us in our explorations with funding, encouragement and support:

Trevor and Daphne Henderson	Trent Carbaugh
Shane Cooke	Larry Moss
Philip Bolger	Laura Thorpe
Peter Moylan	Martin Cary
Roland Putan	Greg Jones
William Sullivan	Rev. Anderson Bakewell, S.J.
William Sandburg	Father Frank Mueller
Mairead Byrne	Michael Palin

Frasier Barber
Mike Bergt
Ken Epperson
John Spensor
Dr. Fred McLaren
Karen Brush
John Bruno
Eileen Harsch
Dick Wasacase
Nina Moldstad
John Utsi
Mike Kimbrell
Lee Wareham
Aimee Moore
Mark and Susan Lutz
Dr. William Hammel
Elise Hsieh
Richard Wien
Jan Dziedzic
Waldomar Miszkurka
Dr. Marvin Grendahl
Rodney Stayrook
Ted Spenser
Einar and Ingrid Pederson
Christine O'Brien
Don Meyer
Grendal LH
Alan Lathan
David Hamlin
Jim Arnold
Robert Arnold
Laurs Rasmussen
Jess Larsen

Henning Baek
Henrik Miller
Dan Laursen
Lars Uls
John Bay
Nils Lorentsen
Margaret Anderson
Mary Lynn Bird
Stephen Fraser
Dan Bauer
Michael Gifkins
Paul Bateman
Chris O'Brien
Deborah D'arcy
William Fitzhugh
Ted Carpenter
Adelaide de Menil
Peter de Roos
Marc Bryan Brown
William Gasperini
Liesl Clarke
Bill Joy
Thomas Schubert
Yevgeney Otrabannikov
Vladimir Nesterov
Peter Esmonde
Ron Davies
Daniel Gillman
Eric Triesman
Louis Rosetto
Jane Metcalfe
Alexander Lindsay
Erin Porter

Companies and Organizations:

Pembroke Capital
Rolex Watch USA
National Geographic Television
The Explorers Club
The North Face
Petro Star
Signature Aviation
Lufthansa
Boeing
Air Berlin
Thomapyrin
GCI
Kodak Korea Ltd
Olympus Camera
Precision Aircraft
American Geographical Society
Aviation Heritage Museum of Anchorage
Pioneerland Aviation Museum of Fairbanks
Carl Ben Eielson Museum of Hatton North Dakota
Arctic Slope Search and Rescue
Elmendorf AFB
Jeppesen
Wired Magazine
Comsat
Discovery Communications
Smithsonian Arctic Studies Center
California Microwave
Store Norsk Kull Kompani
Kings Bay Kull Kompani
Nord Station